TOO BIG TO JAIL

CHRIS BLACKHURST

TOO BIG TO JAIL

Inside HSBC, the Mexican drug cartels and
the greatest banking scandal of the century

MACMILLAN

First published 2022 by Macmillan
an imprint of Pan Macmillan
The Smithson, 6 Briset Street, London EC1M 5NR
EU representative: Macmillan Publishers Ireland Ltd, 1st Floor,
The Liffey Trust Centre, 117–126 Sheriff Street Upper,
Dublin 1, D01 YC43
Associated companies throughout the world
www.panmacmillan.com

ISBN 978-1-5290-6503-9

1 3 5 7 9 8 6 4 2

A CIP catalogue record for this book is available from the British Library.

Typeset in Minion Pro by Jouve (UK), Milton Keynes
Printed and bound by CPI Group (UK) Ltd, Croydon, CR0 4YY

Visit **www.panmacmillan.com** to read more about all our books
and to buy them. You will also find features, author interviews and
news of any author events, and you can sign up for e-newsletters
so that you're always first to hear about our new releases.

To Rose and Donald Blackhurst

Contents

Preface

The origin of this story lies in a chance remark. In early 2020, I visited HSBC's headquarters at Canary Wharf, in London. The offices were buzzing and crowded, full of people huddled behind their screens, some talking into headsets or on phones, others standing in small groups. Still others were sitting in meeting rooms carrying out the everyday business of one of the world's largest and most profitable banks. There were growing reports of a new virus reaching Europe from China. Shares in London, New York and around the globe had taken a tumble as they always do when uncertainty hits. Banks, mining, energy and industrial companies were especially vulnerable, amid fears of a slowdown in consumer demand. The price of oil was down. But there was no cause for great alarm. Leading the news was the conviction of film mogul Harvey Weinstein for rape and sexual assault. In the US, President Donald Trump was predicting a stock market crash if he failed to win re-election. UK Prime Minister Boris Johnson was letting it be known he would be getting tough with the EU in forthcoming trade talks. In consumer banking, there was talk of free-to-use ATMs disappearing and banks imposing charges on customers accessing their own cash.

It was clear, looking around, that everyone had a sense of purpose. There was a feeling of prosperity, too. This was an energetic, successful place, which was hardly surprising since the bank's most recent annual surplus would later be reported at $15 billion. On the way out, my companion, who used to work there, was running through recent events in the bank's history when he made reference to 'of course, Mexico'. I knew what he was talking about: how the bank had been hit with a fine of $1.9 billon, the biggest in American history, and required to endure a five-year remedial programme for enabling Mexico's leading drugs cartel – and the biggest drug-trafficking organization in the world – to launder cash through the bank's branch network and systems. Thanks to HSBC, from 2003 to 2010, the Sinaloa cartel, one of the most notorious and murderous cartels in the world, was able to turn its ill-gotten money into clean dollars – billions upon billions of them. When this finally came to light in late 2012, American law enforcers proved that at least $881 million found their way from the US into HSBC bank accounts controlled by 'El Chapo', the crime gang's fearsome leader, and his henchmen. The bank admits to allowing its services to be used by the Sinaloa from 2006 to 2010, but the laundering had been going on for much longer. The Americans can point to further, unexplained, currency movements running into billions. What they uncovered was a hugely respectable, seemingly well-run, global business, a corporate colossus, where the systems of checks and procedures were either unfit for purpose or were simply being ignored, where members of staff were complicit and covering up. The question I was left wondering as I left the industrious, serious HSBC offices was, how had this happened? How had a bank, the one that likes to call itself 'the world's local bank', which in its advertising boasts 'we're committed to helping protect the world's financial system on which millions of people depend, by only doing business with customers who meet our high standards of transparency', journeyed down this road to facilitating Mexico's richest drug lord? Chapo was a gang leader, a major mobster, who was number 701 on the *Forbes* 'Rich List', sandwiched between Swiss fuel distribution tycoon Jean Claude Gandur and Campbell Soup heiress Dorrance 'Dodo' Hamilton. *Forbes* also produces a 'World's Most Powerful People' list, and here Chapo was 67th, after Elon Musk – who was at that stage at number 66. The 'Rich List' citation said: 'CEO of the Sinaloa cartel, "El Chapo" is the world's most powerful drug trafficker. The cartel is responsible for an estimated 25 per cent of all illegal drugs that enter the US via Mexico. Drug enforcement experts estimate, conservatively, that the cartel's annual revenues may exceed $3 billion. This February the city of Chicago branded him the first "Public Enemy No. 1" since Al Capone.'

How did a bank that as recently as 2002 had been named 'one of the best-run organizations in the world' become so entwined with such a criminal, with one of the most barbaric groups of gangsters on Earth, how did it help them wash their blood-soaked money?

HSBC is a brand that is respected and trusted the world over, whose chiefs are feted at home and abroad, that has the ear of governments and senior politicians. To give you a sense of the hand-in-glove relationship that the bank has with world leaders, the HSBC chairman once sent an email explaining the bank would not be attending that year's IMF meeting in Washington, DC, because it already 'has access to Finance Ministers and leaders of Financial Institutions around the world without needing the IMF meeting to achieve this, so we decided we would save our shareholders money!' Yet underneath it all, they were receiving the proceeds from street drug dealing and putting the crumpled dollar bills through its systems. The treasured HSBC name was giving legitimacy to a bunch of criminals whose trade is misery and death. To add to the hypocrisy, for the period in question – which covers from 2003 to late 2010 – HSBC was run by Stephen Green. I have met Stephen; I know that as well as being chief executive, then executive chairman, of the bank he is someone of deep religious conviction. He has written books on 'ethical capitalism'; he preaches from the church pulpit on a Sunday morning. And yet, somehow, on his watch, HSBC was opening thousands of accounts and funnelling vast amounts of dollars on behalf of monsters who beheaded, butchered, massacred, slaughtered, without so much as blinking. Thanks to Green's bank, Chapo and his crew were able to enjoy their riches and source even more drugs, more weapons and feed the cycle of violence that has ruined hundreds of thousands of lives in Mexico and beyond.

Today, Stephen Green is now Lord Green, as he went uninterrupted from HSBC to becoming a UK government minister with a seat in the House of Lords. Chapo was not so lucky. He was captured by Mexican marines in early 2016, extradited to the US and received life plus thirty years and was ordered to forfeit $12.6 billion in ill-gotten gains. At the time of writing he is in the US Colorado 'Supermax' prison, ADX Florence, and he will most likely die there. His lawyers maintain there should be a retrial on the grounds that he was kept in solitary confinement prior to, and during, the trial, and that this impaired his mental faculties. They also claim that an article reported that five jurors had consumed news reports and social media commentary about the trial, contrary to the rules. Green, by contrast, remains a pillar of respectability. Along with being a member of the House of Lords he is the recipient of honours and awards, involved with various prestigious bodies. Many of Chapo's associates are similarly incarcerated; meanwhile, the HSBC directors and managers who were employees of the bank while the money washing was going on are able to carry on living their comfortable lives, playing golf, fishing, going to the opera, assisting with charities, attending dinner parties.

For much of my career I've written about business and finance. That has meant tracking the rise of some of the world's biggest enterprises, and spending countless hours with their bosses, listening to their expansive talk, their strategies to grow the business and their claims as to how their organization really is better and different than that of their competitors, and sometimes how, by implication or occasionally explicitly, they are personally better and different than the rest. The narrative of these business success stories usually follows a familiar pattern and entails lauding their ever-larger financial numbers, their profits and returns, and rarely do these financial masters of the universe have reason to stray too far from the script. Occasionally, something goes wrong, and questions are asked. Very occasionally, major scandal will unfold, and their accounts of triumph are challenged.

With HSBC and Mexico there was media coverage of the case, but there was also a collective shrug, almost as if the concept was either too far removed from everyday life, or simply because people thought that because it was Mexico it was to be expected and, unlike the crash of 2008, it did not directly affect most people's lives. The bank was slapped with a fine, which was huge in actual numbers, but barely caused a stir to this juggernaut in profits generation. They admitted what they had done, said they were very sorry and promised to reform their ways. In the UK, there was no official inquiry, no government intervention, no punishment, nothing – this, despite HSBC being headquartered in London. The view seemed to be: what's the big deal? And no one stopped, either, to ask the simple question: how? How was it that HSBC got itself into bed with Chapo and his organization in the first place? How was it that no one from HSBC was ever charged or convicted? It's not only the likes of Chapo and his heavies who can expect to go to jail. Ordinary drug pushers are also sent to the slammer – for life in the US if they're caught three times. Not, seemingly, the bankers who wash their money. In the case of HSBC, the crime appears especially egregious. They confessed to a systemic failure, one that lasted years and enabled the cartel to launder many billions, but a criminal prosecution, let alone conviction, wasn't deemed appropriate. HSBC admitted what it had done and a financial penalty against an institution that trades in finance, that is awash with finance, with a promise to do better, was somehow regarded as a suitable reprimand.

There are stark similarities to the way HSBC was treated and how the bankers who nearly tipped the world into financial catastrophe in 2008 were dealt with. After that disaster, no senior banker was pursued through the criminal courts for almost – it was that close – bringing the world's capital markets to their knees. Then, it was said we could not afford to allow the major banks to collapse, they were said to be too big to fail. But for the interventions of governments across the globe, using their taxpayers' money, it was claimed that meltdown would have occurred. As it was, the bill for the bank bailouts ran into hundreds of billions, economies did slump, governments launched austerity drives to pay for the rescues and untold numbers of jobs were lost. The similarities, as we will see, run deeper than just the ways the banks were let off in 2008 and how HSBC was given a slap on the wrist. Both instances were born out of the bankers displaying appalling greed and reckless abandon – in 2008, from pushing home loans to people who did not have the means to repay them, then rolling up those loans into packages to sell on to unsuspecting investors who believed they were purchasing something that was secure. Or in the case of HSBC in Mexico, seeing a volatile, untapped market and turning a blind eye to events that were being beamed around the world in their pursuit of becoming the largest bank in the world.

In many ways, the case of HSBC and Chapo is even worse than the circumstances that led to the 2008 crash. In Mexico, HSBC were giving safe harbour to the funds of one of the world's most dangerous, murderous criminal enterprises. As we will see, repeated warnings – internal and external – were ignored, as was the graphic evidence of what was occurring on the ground. The war, and it was a war, being fought between the Mexican government aided by the US and the cartels, led by the Sinaloa, and the resulting mounting death toll on both sides, was of little concern to the bank's bosses. Meanwhile,

HSBC presented, and presents itself, as the most honourable of corporations, a body run by a management that genuinely cares about the state of the planet, that in all their publicity tells us how much they want to benefit mankind. Sincerely. Have we reached the stage where the world's largest banks can simply behave as they choose, that they are able, literally, to walk away from the most heinous offences, to turn their backs on the effects of their actions? And what has been done to stop it happening again, since the upside in profits and bonuses far outweighs the punishment of being caught, since even the largest fine in American history equated to little more than one month of HSBC's profits that year?

The more I ponder, I wonder if this isn't a searing, modern example of the peasants' historic inclination to doff their caps and tug their forelocks. To take their punishment and to remain silent. The banks tell us to believe the hype, the spin, to praise their brilliance and sophistication. They're smart because they say they are – and we accept they are because they say they are.

Even after the disaster of 2008, our prevailing attitude is that the bigger you are as a business, the better you are, and the more we applaud you. As a society, we're drawn to worshipping the power of 'big' – big bank, big corporate, big numbers, big salary, big bonus, big house, big car, big boat. Big. And we are blinded by it. The result is that when a bank like HSBC, which likes to pride itself on ethical banking, but is so big and so close to the governmental institutions that are supposed to monitor it, is found to have sinned, or at least when their executives could and perhaps should be interrogated in a court of law, that is not allowed to occur. They have quite literally made themselves too big to manage, but also too big to fail and too big to jail. As the US Attorney General, Eric Holder, explained about the connection between HSBC and Chapo: 'I am concerned that the size of some of these institutions becomes so large that it does become difficult for us to prosecute them when we are hit with indications that if we do prosecute – if we do bring a criminal charge – it will have a negative impact on the national economy, perhaps even the world economy.'

Where does this end? No senior banker was prosecuted over the 2008 financial crisis. Similarly, no HSBC banker was charged for enabling the Sinaloa to flourish, for supplying the drug-trafficking organization with an acceptable veneer and entry to the world's banking network and markets. If bosses cannot face trial for heading a corporation that acts as a laundromat for the most dreadful of criminal organizations, where does that stop, where is the responsibility for feeding this gross heart of darkness? Must giant banks, once their expensive lawyers, entourages and professional boosters have weighed in, literally get away with serving people whose trade is murder? In HSBC, Chapo's cartel found a bank only too able to accommodate their needs. It was a case of scale meeting scale, sophistication meeting sophistication, ambition meeting ambition. The Sinaloa reached the summit by shifting narcotics in huge volumes, often by using methods that seem to belong to fantasy, by building specially designed midget submarines, and long tunnels complete with electric lighting and railway tracks that were breathtaking feats of design and engineering to transport bulky loads across the border. In HSBC, they met a financial organization that displayed identical prowess when it came to selling financial and investment products, and to cleaning and securing their funds.

Picture the scene. The year is 2007. A car pulls up in a town square in rural Mexico. Three men get out and walk casually to the local bank, the HSBC. Two are carrying soft, full pouches, one is looking around nervously. There is a bulky shape under his jacket, suggesting he is armed. They enter the bank, seconds later they emerge, minus the folders. The folders are bespoke, made to exactly squeeze under the tellers' windows. The teller takes the case, puts it to one side, reaches for a credit slip that has already been made out, tears off the stub and gives it to the customer. When the cases are opened, they contain bundles of smoothed-out used dollar bills held together with elastic bands.

Another scene. A pickup truck races to a halt. A man on the back tosses a large bin bag to the ground. The truck roars off. Later, passers-by nervously poke the bag – as if they've seen this happen before and they suspect what is inside. A dark liquid is seeping from the bag, making a trail across the earth. It looks like blood. They rip the plastic open and tip out the contents. It contains a headless torso. They recoil and cover their faces, gagging.

In London, in a packed hall at the Barbican Centre, the crowd wait expectantly for the main event to begin. A group of mostly men in suits file onto the stage and sit behind pieces of card bearing their names. They are the directors of HSBC. On a giant screen behind them, the bank's annual results are displayed. They're impressive. It's been a good year. Turnover is up, profits are up. One of the highlights is that 'Latin America contributed pre-tax profit of US$1.7 billion, with Mexico providing over US$1 billion for the first time.' Looking ahead, the signs are encouraging. Shareholders can expect more of the same. Mention is made of the underlying strength of the bank, its international reach and size.

Questions are taken. All are batted away with ease; none is especially challenging. There are grumblings about executive pay. They're easily dealt with. Votes are taken according to a show of hands, and universally carried. Minutes later, the shareholders' annual general meeting of HSBC is over. The bank chairman and directors and their advisors mingle with the appreciative audience, before filing out for an excellent lunch.

Three incidents. Each is different, one is utterly horrific. All of them are linked. All of them join bank and client, HSBC and Sinaloa, together. The men who make the deposits with the custom-made cases are members of the same cast as those who decapitate the victim in the refuse bag. They answer to Chapo, and they make their living from moving industrial quantities of drugs to the United

States, and instilling terror in those who dare to cross them or investigate them. To enforce the message, they will sometimes post videos of their most gruesome slayings. In many respects, of course, they are separate, the bankers and the Mexican butchers. Certainly, if quizzed, the HSBC hierarchy would always condemn the Sinaloa's practices, of course they would. But these were their customers, which means that at a fundamental, financial level, they are inextricably tied, the one provides valuable services to the other, and nets considerable profits as a result. The bankers can't say they were not told – that many people did not come forward inside and outside their corporation to draw attention to a lackadaisical approach to compliance, to a banking operation that was not being properly policed, to an organization that was only intent on chasing bigger and bigger profits. Eventually, the authorities rumbled what was going on. They understood the pivotal role played by the company that claimed to be a force for good, whose name adorned the walkways of major airports with posters advertising how it assisted entrepreneurs and artists, those with great, world-enhancing genius ideas and creative talents. For the young people's orchestra providing wonderful music, thanks to HSBC; for the criminals who ply a deadly product and think nothing about wiping out entire families of parents, children and elderly relatives, thanks to HSBC.

My interest in Mexico and HSBC, the fueller of evil, because that is what it was, I admit, is partly driven by personal experience. I am a long-time customer of the bank. If I go overdrawn or a transaction does not seem right, they will be on to me immediately. I can't use their ATMs until the problem is resolved. Now and again, I am hit with an extra charge for straying ever so slightly into the red. If I pay in a large amount from an unexplained source, they will quiz me as to where it originated. If I want to borrow money for any reason, they will question what exactly it is for. This was also the same institution that was collecting metric tonnes of dollars from the Sinaloa and its associates. Effectively, they were users and beneficiaries of HSBC, just like me. Yet the rules and standards that have always applied to me do not seem to have applied to them.

As well as paying the fine and admitting their guilt, the bank also entered into a Deferred Prosecution Agreement, admitting the US government claims and giving it five years to clean up its act or charges would result. When I visited the bank's head office it was just recently out of the DPA. My fellow visitor and ex-HSBC staffer talked of them 'recovering from Mexico' in hushed tones, as you would speak admiringly and sympathetically about someone having come out of rehab or painful medical treatment. To apply some context, record-breaking as it was, the penalty amounted to just five weeks' profits. As for the bank reforming its practices, the progress in that regard was never publicly revealed – HSBC fought tooth and nail, drawing on its slick lawyers, to prevent us seeing just how they changed, and to this day, we still don't know. We've no idea either if other banks saw what occurred at HSBC and quietly tightened their own procedures, if they, as we, the little people, are always assured by the high-ups in such situations, 'learnt the lessons.' Process apart, did the bankers, the super-rich titans, look in the mirror and pledge a virtuous reawakening? One author once wrote in praise of the market, saying it was the most powerful engine for development and liberation. He went on to say, but at its worst, 'it is a dangerous moral pollutant that nourishes some very poisonous weeds in us.' The challenge was to strike a balance to preserve dynamism while taming excess. The writer was Stephen Green, former head of HSBC and now Baron Green of Hurstpierpoint, and he managed a bank that for years on his watch was cleaning dirty money for the world's number one drug baron.

ONE

'Scottish banking principles'

HSBC began its life by serving drug dealers. Indeed, one of the mighty bank's first bosses was a leading player in the drugs trade, although you would be hard pressed to find official acknowledgement of this from the bank. Instead, the HSBC website opens with the hardly enticing but typically unabashed lead-in of 'How did a local Hong Kong bank become one of the world's largest financial services organizations?' Read the story of HSBC's birth and international expansion – and how it has been connecting customers to opportunities for more than 150 years. The bank, the website tells us, 'was born from one simple idea – a local bank serving international needs', which is so broad-brush in approach as to be almost meaningless. Nor will you find mention of narcotics in the official corporate history: 'Thomas Sutherland was sailing along the South China coast on the steamer SS *Manila* in 1864 when he read an article on Scottish banking in *Blackwood's Magazine*. He was a Scot himself, and despite never having held a bank account, he resolved to found a bank in Hong Kong based on sound Scottish banking principles. Unlike all other foreign banks in the territory, the new bank was to be locally headquartered and managed, unhindered by overseas directors with little knowledge or interest in the affairs of Hong Kong. Sutherland drew up a prospectus, and the bank's Provisional Committee met in August 1864. Total capital was set at HKD5 million, all the shares allotted to Hong Kong were quickly taken up and the bank was born.'

Thomas Sutherland was born in 1834, in Aberdeen. His father died when Thomas was young and he was brought up by his mother's grandfather, owner of a cooperage and fish-curing business in the north-east of Scotland. The grandparents were strict Calvinists, and the intention was that the young Thomas would go to the local Aberdeen University and study to become a minister. Thomas was not interested, and he dropped out of college and joined P&O, the shipping line, as a clerk. Still in his teens, he went to Bombay for the firm, then to Hong Kong. Before long he was promoted to become the company's 'Hong Kong superintendent', overseeing P&O in the new British colony, and in nearby China and Japan. In 1863, this phenomenally ambitious young man was made chairman of the Hong Kong and Whampoa Dock Company, managing the construction of warehouses and wharves, and all of this before he had turned 30. Although, oddly, he still did not possess a bank account. He was just the sort of driven individual that HSBC would be looking to fill their glass office towers with nearly 150 years later as they went in pursuit of their goal to become the biggest bank in the world.

Sutherland fell in with two brothers in Hong Kong, Thomas and Lancelot Dent. There is no mention of the Dents in the HSBC history, but what we do know of them is that they were fellow travellers, young buccaneers who had originally come from farming stock in Westmorland in the north of England. It was a tough existence, and they left to seek their fortunes, travelling east, to India and China. Thomas and Lancelot subsequently ended up in Hong Kong, where they went on to form Dent & Co, a trading company, one of the original Canton Hongs.

Dent & Co had spun out of another company, Davidson & Co,

which itself grew out of a business set up by George Baring of the Baring banking dynasty. The upright, image-conscious Barings disapproved of the burgeoning traffic in opium, which was being shipped from India to China via Hong Kong and the Chinese port of Canton, or Guangzhou, where it was exchanged for porcelain, tea and silk for sending to Britain and the British Empire. At that time, the narcotic accounted for 70 per cent of all maritime freight from India to China, and by 1833 the East India Company, which enjoyed a monopoly over the opium trade running into China, had grown the business from shipping 4,000 chests of opium a year, each containing 77kg of the drug, to 30,000 cases. While opium had its medicinal uses for easing pain, aiding sleep and alleviating stress, it was also highly addictive. By the late 1830s, there were burgeoning numbers of addicts in China, and so dependent was the country becoming on the narcotic that China's balance of trade was in danger of being heavily skewed. Americans, in the shape of the ancestors of Franklin D. Roosevelt and Senator John Kerry, also wanted in on the action, routing opium from Turkey into China, all of which acted as the precursor to the First Opium War of 1839. In Britain, the concerned Barings ordered their operatives to cease, at which point William Davidson took over, naming the business Davidson & Co. He was joined by Thomas and Lancelot Dent – hence, when Davidson and the Dents also went their separate ways, the rebranding to Dent & Co.

Thomas had no concern about the forthcoming hostilities, and instead of pulling out of trading opium he aggressively started to undercut its rivals, even reneging on a deal they'd struck at a meeting with the other heads of the firms to fix the price of opium. Dent & Co flourished, so much so that when the Chinese authorities moved to crack down on the socially destructive and economically wrecking drug pouring into their country they issued a warrant for the arrest of Lancelot Dent. The Chinese were also keen to target the *compradores* – local Chinese agents who could bridge the language and local custom barrier, and who feature in the official history of HSBC, although not in relation to opium. Instead, they cited how compradores employed by the bank were able to arrange and negotiate short-term 'chop' loans in China, to help fund the trading – without saying what that trading actually comprised. The Dents were specialists in this field, in acting as financial fixers and money men for the drug pedlars, and it was the move against Lancelot at Dent & Co that sparked the First Opium War, which lasted from 1839 to 1842, and witnessed the bombarding of the Chinese port district of Dinghai and several violent naval encounters, as Britain's government ordered the Royal Navy to rush to the rescue of the British drug traffickers as they sought to shore up their trade and influence in the area. Superior British firepower saw the Chinese succumb easily, and the subsequent 'unequal' Treaty of Nanjing saw China cede Hong Kong Island and the neighbouring smaller islands, set up treaty ports and make a settlement payment from China to Britain. It was after the Second Opium War (1856–60) between China and Britain and France that Thomas Sutherland, still in his thirties but now fabulously wealthy and a major player in the Far East, dreamed up the idea for the bank that would become HSBC, when he heard about the plans to create a Bank of China, to be floated on the stock market in India. The fledgling HSBC was, therefore, only formed at all because of the dramatic intervention of the British government. As an official British military account puts it: 'British forces fought a war in China that benefitted drug smugglers. Their subsequent victory in the conflict opened up the lucrative Chinese trade to British merchants.'

Sutherland was offered shares and he thought about it, until he happened upon the article in a copy of *Blackwood's* on how Scots made good bankers. This encouraged him to go one better: rather than let the new Bank of China clean up, Sutherland, a Scot, would start his own bank, operating out of Hong Kong. The idea was further developed at a dinner party with friends. Sutherland would form a bank, but rather than have his name on the launch prospectus it was signed by the local well-known firm of Dent & Co. With China and the lucrative opium trade in his sights, and determined to head off the Bank of China, Sutherland hired compradores to lubricate the dealings with the Chinese. At the same time, to maintain its standing with the British government back home, he made Francis Chomley, Dent's senior partner in China, chairman of the new Hongkong and Shanghai Banking Corporation. Within a month of launch, the start-up bank had opened a branch in Shanghai. Three months later, it had an office in London. In 1866, disaster struck Hong Kong banking. Runs on six of the territory's eleven foreign banks caused them to collapse. HSBC survived, and here the official story does purr, boasting the fledgling bank 'earned a reputation for resilience', so much so that the Chinese population of Hong Kong began to give HSBC another name, based on its Chinese letters, of 'Wayfoong' which means 'abundance of remittances' or 'focus of wealth'. Sutherland anchored his enigmatic 'abundance of remittances' and 'focus of wealth' on 'sound Scottish banking principles', and as HSBC's version of the story goes, this allowed Thomas Sutherland to focus his vision for the bank on a simple idea: to be 'owned and managed locally, which would support international trade.' From financing drug runners and opium traders and maximizing the chaos in China after the Opium Wars, Sutherland went on to become a pillar of the British Imperial establishment, a member of Hong Kong's Legislative Council, and then managing director of P&O. In 1884, he was elected an MP in Britain's Parliament. He was made a 'Sir' and died in 1922, in London, and was greatly mourned. In Hong Kong, he received the accolade of having a main street named after him.

Sutherland and his senior colleagues had been aided in their endeavours by the actions of the British government. History, as we shall see, has a funny way of repeating itself.

HSBC did indeed adhere to a Scottish Presbyterian, strictly moral code, which leaned heavily on tight, military, colonial discipline for its running and expected its employees to adhere to their rigid rules.

'A mix of paternalism and authoritarianism' is how the widow of one late HSBC Asian manager wryly described it.

As the bank grew through the twentieth century it came to be dominated by International Officers, or 'IOs' as they were referred to internally. Later, they were called International Managers or 'IMs'. Typically, they were white, male, keen on rugby, ex-minor British fee-paying school but not university graduates. There was an understanding among the new recruits and the management itself that joining the bank was akin to being commissioned into the British Army and being sent to a comfortable post overseas, and they received a lifetime's employment for going out 'east' and for giving up control of their working and often their social lives. The moral code of the bank stretched well into the employees' private lives: holiday was known, as in the army, as 'leave', junior male employees were 'junior officers', and they were not allowed to marry unless they'd worked for the bank for at least ten years. Even this period of singledom was known as being 'on ice', and as though to remind them of just where they fitted into the scheme of the bank, the bachelors were forced to reside in a 'chummery', a name adopted from the British Raj for shared quarters for male single staff, fostering an atmosphere similar to that of an army officers' mess. The bank was, in other words, a perfect mirror of the Victorian Empire that it had been born into, and maintained these traditions long after that imperial might itself started to erode. To listen to a former bank staffer recall how, in the 1960s, he needed to take unpaid leave from Hong Kong to visit his ill father, who it was thought might not survive much longer, might make you think that bank struggled to find a new identity in the modern world. His boss told him he couldn't go – 'I'm afraid it's the exigencies of service'. And as recently as 1989, some still sought the permission of the chairman to marry. This disciplinarian tradition earned HSBC a nickname: 'Heart and Soul Breaking Corporation.'

The directors saw it differently, of course, and part of what made the bank unique – what made it stand out from the competition.

Analysts at the investment firm Williams de Broe were once asked to examine HSBC's 'enduring and competitive advantages'. Top of their list came 'a management culture and discipline that permeates the organization'. This 'HSBC way' was exemplified by a complaint from one senior bank executive that he'd noticed a 'lack of urgency and activity' among head office staff, that there were 'liberty takers' who 'were not at their desks by 9 a.m. or were seen to be entering the building with shopping during normal working hours.' The International Officers were the keepers of the organizational DNA, the conveyors of orders from the centre, the people who ensured some semblance of homogeneity. They were expected to impose, enforce and uphold the HSBC 'culture', those 'sound Scottish banking principles', all of which was achievable when the bank was relatively small but more difficult when it grew to serve 40 million customers across sixty-four nations and territories as it would become on entering the twenty-first century.

For most of its history, the bank expanded in fits and starts. Then, in just six dramatic years in this century, HSBC embarked on a headlong charge. From 2001 to the end of 2007, the bank's staff count nearly doubled, from 171,000 to 330,000. The number of subsidiary businesses that form part of the same HSBC group or, as they like to call themselves, 'family', that all need managing and supervising, rose from 417 in 1999 to a colossal 2,277 by 2009, which made it a very real challenge to remain 'one of the best-run organisations in the world', as described by *The Banker* magazine in 2002 when HSBC was named 'Global Bank of the Year'. What was the root cause of this furious rush? And, more importantly, how was HSBC going to ensure that it was going to adhere to the same solid, if unadventurous, principles that had seen it through nearly a century of banking? The answer to the first question is greed. The answer to the second is that it self-evidently couldn't. Put simply, being that superb, being Global Bank of the Year, was not enough. The bank's shareholders, senior management, wanted more, but in wanting more, they turned their backs on the one thing that their reputation depended on: integrity.

In August 2002, the bank produced half-year profits of $5.5 billion. Nevertheless, critics in the investment community, like those at the US firm Merrill Lynch, were sniffy: 'A resilient performance but, as has been the case for some time, the growth profile remains more uncertain.' Investors craved an even bigger bank, yielding even greater profits and even larger returns. So did the senior management, who were only too happy to meet their wish. However, there was nobody saying they could deliver that, but at a price – that the organization would be so huge management could not keep a handle on what it was doing, what was occurring in every nook and cranny, in all its lands. Shareholders were not concerned; it was not their responsibility. That was down to those in charge, and for a while they were right. In 2008, HSBC was the most profitable bank on the planet, with profits of $19.13 billion, and was lauded by *The Economist* as 'the largest banking group in the world' and the 'world's most valuable financial brand' by *The Banker*. At the heart of this race to the top of the pile was Stephen Green, the chief executive, then executive chairman.

STEPHEN GREEN JOINED HSBC from McKinsey, the management consultants, in 1982 as a group strategist, and was appointed to the board in 1998, having gained steady, sure progress through the company, adhering to all the principles that had made HSBC so dependable. Five years later, Green became chief executive, then three years after that he secured the top job. Growing the bank, satisfying the owners and his fellow managers, making it even bigger, was his responsibility. In 2006 I met Green at HSBC's steel-and-glass main headquarters in London's Canary Wharf as he was beginning his reign as executive chairman. I was ushered into his office and was immediately struck by the floor-to-ceiling windows and the spectacular vista from his forty-first-floor corner room. Down below was the River Thames, with its winding, glistening bends, and in the distance the landmarks of the City and West End. These high-rise financial buildings across London's skyline were not new, but the jaw-dropping view still took some getting used to and it achieved its intended purpose of conveying a powerful statement of might and status. At the time, almost 9,000 group colleagues were working on the floors beneath Green's in HSBC's sky-hugging tower. He was clearly master of everything, boss of the bank – but not just any old bank, the second-biggest, and destined to be the biggest, bank in the world. Green, though, was not like other tycoons and liked to make sure you knew that. His office was small, the furniture functional, the chairs simple black leather, the desk neat and compact. The message was that this was a workstation, not some grand, senior executive play station. Green did not go in for self-aggrandisement. There was no show-off memorabilia, no framed black-and-white pictures of Green meeting world leaders and celebrities. There were some photos of his wife, Janian, their two grown-up daughters and other family members, and that was all.

Aged fifty-seven, Green was taking over from Sir John Bond, who in his eight years in charge had proved a charismatic leader: high-profile, good with clients and juniors in equal measure, an urbane schmoozer of the rich and powerful in Asia, the Middle East, Europe and the US. He had also been with the bank forty-odd years, one of a cadre of senior HSBC men, ex-IOs, who had spent all their work-ing lives at what is still referred to in the financial industry as 'Honkers and Shankers'. The little-known Green, by contrast, was regarded as a newcomer, despite having been with the bank for nearly a quarter of a century. 'I'm a new boy because I didn't join straight from school or university – but I've been here twenty-three years, so I'm not exactly a new boy,' he volunteered, managing to combine a certain peevishness with admiration that his organization puts such store by longevity of service. His dress is blend-in corporate executive, rather than power-dressing, global wheeler-dealer. No loud pinstripe, no red braces, no luxury watch for him, but a two-piece suit, white shirt, plain tie, black polished shoes. His taut face, lean physique and don't-look-at-me clothes made him seem somewhat austere. Green was always going to be a curiosity of a bank chief: he isn't a sports nut (he plays golf 'badly'), a rugger bugger, but an arts-loving aesthete, and a publicly out Christian. In that respect, he is more than just a believer, he is full-on, an activist, an ordained Anglican priest who preaches from the pulpit on Sunday mornings. His colleagues maintained he wrote sermons while on business flights. He'd also written a book: *Serving God? Serving Mammon? Christians and the Financial Market*. Similarly, whereas many wealthy bankers conspicuously consume, and love to own and to parade expensive items and the latest must-have gadgetry, Green likes to go hill-walking, listen to a favourite piece of opera or read a classic novel – if it is foreign, preferably not the translation but the original-language version. He speaks French and German fluently and tells me how he wants to learn Italian and Russian – Italian because it is a beautiful language, and Russian 'because I want to read Pushkin, and you can't really read poetry in translation'. He only ever speaks about himself extremely reluctantly. He is the son of a solicitor from Brighton and went to nearby fee-charging Lancing College as a boarder, which was about as much of his childhood as he was willing to share. 'I got through school, I just got through it,' he said hurriedly, wanting to talk about the bank and the business. He was being modest. 'Getting through school' meant him winning a place at Oxford to study modern languages. No sooner did he arrive than he switched to philosophy, politics and economics because it 'provided a terrific grounding for the modern world'. After Oxford, Green had a gap year before heading to the British civil service. He spent seven years at the Overseas Development Administration, two of them on a Harkness Fellowship to study in the US at MIT (for an MSc in political science). Then he quit, for strategists McKinsey, and it was immediately clear that they were a perfect fit: thinker and thinkers, planner and planners. 'McKinsey is unique. It gives you experience of trying to solve significant business problems and of interacting with very senior management and boards,' he enthused. Green was based in the consultancy's banking practice, and after five years had risen to one level below partner, as a 'senior engagement manager'. A headhunter contacted him and said they were working for a 'dynamic Far East financial institution' – was he interested? The job was in HSBC's business planning and strategy department. Green's contract was for two years and he mentally allocated four years to the bank before again moving on, but for once his carefully calibrated schedule unravelled and he stayed for longer.

Green was never going to be a roll-your-sleeves-up money man. He'd arrived from McKinsey into a senior backroom role and he was prickly whenever his lack of personal frontline banking know-how was raised. 'I set up treasury for the bank – that was running a business, meeting clients, being responsible for a profit and loss account. What's that if it isn't coalface?' The cerebral, quiet type who'd never served behind a counter, never put together a funding package for a client, never earned a commission, never gained his spurs in banking terms, in 2003 he nevertheless beat the better-known Douglas Flint, the bank's long-time finance supremo, and Bill Dalton, its retail head, to the CEO's job. He also succeeded Sir Keith Whitson, another respected HSBC veteran.

Green's elevation was a shock to everyone who was not in the know, but what Bond spotted in Green was somebody who was able to think, to plan, and to grow the bank. Green had also proved himself capable of taking tough, unpopular decisions. On joining the board, Green was put in charge of the investment banking division; when several of the staff missed their targets, his response was swift: he scrapped their bonuses. He did and still does not like discussing himself, but where Green is visibly more relaxed is in referencing the bank's tradition and history, or as he put it repeatedly, 'continuity'. The bank, he said, would 'evolve and change, but it will remain anchored to the same fundamental continuities', which he didn't see me wince at, but it is just the kind of corporate management-speak that has the shareholders purring, even though its actual meaning is deeply opaque. Bond espied in Green someone who would make a big bank even bigger. Most of that enlargement, it would transpire, would come from targeting the untapped, emerging markets, in Asia and Latin America, countries that play to HSBC's imperial, far-flung roots, away from the established, heavily exploited financial centres in Western Europe and the US. One board paper from the time that Green took over set the direction and tone of HSBC by saying that the bank sees 'emerging markets growing faster than developed countries.' The aim that Green set the bank on taking office was that 60 per cent of group profits would soon originate from these under-achieving, primed for take-off lands. His HSBC was to be expansionist and all-conquering, aiming for global leadership. But what had set HSBC apart from the rest before 2002 was that they had generally eschewed this kind of big talk, preferring to focus on resilience and cautious growth instead. Now, though, they were trying to become number one. What was so jarring was that the vehicle for this ambition was being driven by an otherwise mild-mannered, thoughtful Anglican priest. Gordon Gekko he was not.

Whenever I am in the company of top businessmen, and invariably they are men, listening to their boastful, alpha talk of taking over this, or making a play for that, of moving into a new country and using it as a springboard for somewhere else, I am reminded of the popular board game of military strategy I used to play in my youth with my male friends. It was called Risk and entailed moving armies around the globe and obliterating your enemies. If you rolled the dice and got the numbers and then the moves right, you could sweep all before you and the world would be yours. Get it wrong, and you were swallowed up. We were mad about Risk, playing for hours, plotting to take over entire continents and, eventually, the whole planet. Any one of us trying to follow a cautious, safety-first route would be met with ridicule. To be a true Alexander the Great or Genghis Khan or Napoleon Bonaparte you had to be daring and bold, even if it ended up in complete failure.

In their real-life game of Risk, after 2002 Green and his fellow top bankers at HSBC raised their sights. They didn't want to be comparing their corporation to smaller, Asia-centric concerns such as Standard Chartered, or to British banks like Barclays; they saw HSBC as playing with, and defeating, the multi-national industry behemoths of Bank of America, JP Morgan Chase, Citibank. After 2002 their single focus was on becoming the biggest bank in the world, whatever it took. Getting bigger pleases investors, and for them and the senior management it would bring yet greater rewards. From 2002 the banks that HSBC increasingly came to measure themselves up against were American, and it is perhaps no coincidence that from the late 1980s onwards the global banking sector had become infected by the annual performance bonus, a phenomenon that began in the US but has spread worldwide. Those who manage and grow HSBC are well rewarded, some of them enormously so, but for HSBC this bonus was a recent development and not something the bank liked to crow about, since they preferred people regarded them as not a high payer, in keeping with HSBC tradition. Sure enough, there came the bank's annual meeting in 2008 where shareholders were asked to approve a remuneration scheme, which, if all the contributory factors fell into place, would net the top six executives £120 million over three years. There was the disclosure, too, that HSBC had set aside, in just one year, £6 billion in staff pay and bonuses and that the bank was paying more than £1 million each to 235 individuals, of whom eighty-nine worked in London.

By the time Stephen Green was set to take over, HSBC was enormous, far beyond anything conceived in Thomas Sutherland's day. Still, I asked him, how big would he grow HSBC? He nodded. 'It's a question we ask ourselves each time we think about an acquisition.

We ask, does the "management stretch" become a bridge too far?' If the answer is yes, the deal is a non-starter. So far, he said, despite the bank's size, it remained, 'entirely manageable. It's huge, but other companies, like IBM, employ bigger numbers. Now, *ab initio*, there must be a point where you hit a wall, where to get any bigger, that would be counter-productive.' His face broke into a smile. 'But financial services are a long way from being consolidated.' In other words, there was much to aim for, plenty of deals to be had and opportunities to exploit, and tons of money to be made.

Green demanded high standards of the bank's staff. He liked to tell university graduates they would have to work hard and stay on their toes, reminding them of the old Chinese proverb: 'Today's rooster is tomorrow's feather duster'. With me, he referenced the bank's claim to possess a culture different from other banks. He stressed, though, that 'everything within HSBC lives and dies by the P and L [profit and loss account].' So don't be fooled, we may make these claims, but always it comes down to the numbers. I asked him how he squared his religious conviction with the quest for profits? He looked down and stared awkwardly at his plain watch. 'This will be a 30-second answer. First of all, I'm not concerned whatever about people's different faiths. There is, though, a great deal of commonality that runs through everyone who works here –which is that they subscribe to the same professional standards and have the same integrity and morality and the same desire to meet customers' needs.' He glanced at his watch again – 30 seconds. But he wished to talk a bit more about his credo. Only by behaving properly do businesses acquire sustainability; the role of the banks is to improve people's lives, not to hinder them and 'society can't run without well-functioning banks as the core of the economic system.' Surely, I asked, there are occasions when Green questions what he is doing? Another flick of the eyes to the watch. 'I look in the mirror and, if I'm honest, I'm not always perfect. But that's true, if they're also honest, of anybody in any walk of human life.' Later, in 2009, Green followed up his earlier religious treatise with *Good Value: Reflections on Money, Morality and an Uncertain World.* In an interview to promote that book he said HSBC is 'an organization that does think carefully about its own values and culture, which we inherit from our predecessors over decades' and to the *Church Times,* he said HSBC is 'a bank that genuinely seeks to be an ethical bank, though it's a business not a charity, to be sure.'

GREEN, THE GLOBAL bank chief, disagreed with the conclusion of the free-market guru, Milton Friedman: 'There is one and only one social responsibility of business – to use its resources and engage in activities designed to increase its profits so long as it stays within the rules of the game, which is to say, engages in open and free competition without deception or fraud.'

Friedman, argued Green, is 'dangerously simplistic'. Businesses, the banker wrote, 'must consider value from the perspective, not just of investors, but of customers, employees, suppliers, communities and – increasingly – the environment, too.' The banking supremo admitted to mixed feelings about free-market capitalism: 'At its best, as we have seen, there is no more powerful engine for development and liberation than the market. At its worst, it is a dangerous moral pollutant that nourishes some very poisonous weeds in us.' He quoted Paul: 'The love of money is the root of all evil'. Money, declared Green, has become 'the modern Mephistopheles', the spirit of the Devil, the tempter of Faust. That was some statement, coming from the head of one of the biggest money-making and money-handling machines on Earth, but it was the kind of rhetoric that Sir John Bond was no doubt looking for – he wanted the next boss of HSBC to be hugely ambitious, but know himself to be accountable, to take responsibility of growing with integrity; all of which Green spoke to publicly as he explained his approach to HSBC's long-term plans. 'The underlying question will be whether world leaders can construct a shared vision of a global economic order that preserves the dynamism of market forces while taming their excesses (in both risk-taking and reward).' He hoped that 'ethical capitalism' would prevail, and free-market capitalism would recede. Overall, he said, 'My interpretive prism is Christian.' He invoked Paul again: 'There is no longer Jew or Greek, there is no longer slave or free, there is no longer male or female, for all of you are one in Christ Jesus.' Green added: 'The ideal, and the hope, stand the test of time.' No one could be left in any doubt as to Green's inner struggle. It was difficult, though, to imagine his banking peers ever sharing his torment and coming out in sympathy. Ethics or not, Green did make a curious point of saying that large banks are difficult to rein in, that in his view they're not the same as other businesses, because they can't just be allowed to fail. If other enterprises go down, the damage is confined to their owners, suppliers and employees, and their customers can usually switch elsewhere, but major banks, they have tentacles every-where, they're embedded in so many things. The benefit of hindsight suggests that Green knew the pitfalls of the growing spree that he was about to embark on, but perhaps he was just covering his bases for the future? It was hard to tell. What was clear, though, even in those early days in charge, was that Green believed that neither banks nor the markets could just be left to their own devices – regulators have to be allowed to intervene. 'Exactly how the taming will be done remains to be seen.'

Green's long-time number two was Michael Geoghegan. In due course, if HSBC pursued its usual pattern, Geoghegan would take over from Green in the top job. Other large companies searched far and wide externally for their chairmen; HSBC looked internally. 'They do things their own way at HSBC,' was one newspaper judge-ment. 'A tradition of appointing the chairman from within was never going to be derailed by the Johnny-come-latelies of the corporate governance movement.' The contrast with Green was marked: Geoghegan was a classic HSBC banking lifer, a well-travelled IO; Green had never been one. Geoghegan joined the bank in 1973, aged just nineteen. He went to school in Windsor and in Ireland, and was offered a place at University College, Dublin, but eschewed studying for a degree for a job as an IO with HSBC, instead. He spent the next three decades working across North and South America, Asia and the Middle East, much of it at the sharp consumer retail end. Naturally bullish, Geoghegan is one of life's bruisers. An internal HSBC report euphemistically testified to his 'driving leadership style'. One HSBC staffer put it differently, describing Geoghegan as 'hard cop' to Green's 'soft cop'. In the City he was hailed as 'a banker's banker' – a description that would never be afforded to Green. Geoghegan liked to micro-manage and he loved the power play of the new brand of HSBC. One HSBC Group Board minute said that 'each member of the Group Management Board should submit their expenses claims to M. Geoghegan for approval', which meant that the second-most senior person in the bank, while running day-to-day an enormously complex concern spanning entire continents, markets and industries, was spending huge amounts of his time going through senior colleagues' restaurant bills and taxi receipts with a microscope.

Geoghegan's own solution to trying to get to grips with the monster that HSBC was becoming was injecting the staff with the management's much-favoured C-word: culture. While other banks preached the same ideal, he made good on his word and made a commitment to getting around the group's global offices and personally meeting as many of them as possible. 'Nothing beats hearing things from the coalface.' In the time he worked with Green, Geoghegan would spend a whopping 70 per cent of his year journeying around the bank's operations. He would regularly embark on whistle-stop tours of the HSBC network. On one of the occasions I met him, in the early days of his tenure and HSBC's surging empire-building, he was heading off to South America, to Buenos Aires, then Sao Paulo, followed by Mexico City. Then came Vancouver and New York. In all, he was going to sixteen countries, finishing up with the UK and presentations in Birmingham and at London's Leicester Square

Odeon cinema. In some places, he was addressing as many as 7,000 employees at a time. 'Sometimes, it's true, I don't know where I am,' he said, laughing. During one other global tour, Geoghegan emailed a former colleague while in transit: 'We started in Buenos Aires eleven days ago, and we have travelled across America, Europe, the Middle East and now we are in the remaining countries of Asia. In a few hours' time I do Hong Kong and then on to Shanghai and we close it in Beijing tomorrow morning. This physical and administrative challenge will have taken us to nineteen countries in twelve days, flying just over eighty-four hours and covering approx. 86,000 kilometres – but even then, we will only have been to 25 per cent of the countries where HSBC is represented. This is one big group! I do the challenge in this format because I want to hear what people are saying and thinking. The theme of Joining Up the Company is where the shareholder value will in future be recognised – I hope – if I get it right.' For the most part, the crowd of staffers lapped up the Mike Geoghegan Show. 'I left the event,' Ana Dhoraisingam in Singapore told *HSBC World*, 'thinking that the only firm in the world that can rival and beat Citibank globally is HSBC.'

In Geoghegan's London office he showed me a large, flat touchscreen on the wall. It was covered in flashing electronic coloured charts and numbers. He swept his hand across it and instantly, up came the latest piece of data from the bank from any corner of the world. It was a compelling piece of kit, doubtless useful but seeming like an enormous video-game console. Through this one screen he could drill down and down, through layers of HSBC, from region to country to areas within the country to individual branches. Seemingly, all he ever needed to properly oversee the world of HSBC was right here, at his fingertips. But what was also striking from seeing this extraordinary piece of technology at work was how mind-boggling the sheer volume of data available was, and I came away wondering whether he would ever bore down far enough and wide enough to get to the heart of specific issues. No matter, though, for the shareholders, because the combination of the contemplative Green and the micro-managing Geoghegan were determined to become the biggest and best. And this technology, the ability to drill down into the detail of any corner of the bank, anywhere in the world, gave them what the table-thumping Geoghegan, like any testosterone-fuelled Risk devotee, termed an 'awesome advantage' over the competition.

TWO

Waterless urinals

O n 23 March 1994, Luis Donaldo Colosio was feeling good. He was forty-four years old and he had been born into a political family – his father, Luis, was a senator for the long-time ruling party, the Institutional Revolutionary Party, or PRI. Colosio himself was standing for election for the most important post in his native Mexico and the polls had him well in the lead as he arrived in Tijuana, in Baja California, for a day's campaigning.

Colosio had studied economics at ITESM in Mexico and had done his postgrad at the University of Pennsylvania, along with research in applied systems analysis in Austria. He had worked in the Ministry of Budget and Planning, was elected to Congress in 1985, joined the PRI's executive before successfully running the election for President Carlos Salinas, and had then followed his father into the Senate. He entered the Cabinet as Social Development Secretary. In November 1993, Colosio was declared the PRI's presidential candidate. He was seen as modern and progressive and his speeches attracted large, enthusiastic crowds. Colosio's popularity was sealed with an address he gave that March in front of the Monument to the

Mexican Revolution in Mexico City, in which he spoke of the country's deep-rooted social problems. What grabbed the popular attention was that he did not stop there but, unusually, he went on to blame his own PRI ruling party for corruption and failing to prosecute well-connected offenders. 'I see a Mexico that is hungry and with a thirst for justice, a Mexico of mistreated people . . . women and men afflicted by abuses of the authorities or by the arrogance of government offices people . . . I declare that I want to be the president of Mexico to lead a new stage of change in Mexico,' proclaimed Colosio. It was a barnstorming, JFK-style performance that sealed his appeal with the voters, who had long suffered from corruption at every level of government, and the speech saw him lay down a direct challenge to Salinas and the PRI. Here was Colosio, a party man, accusing the president and his people, and promising a new, different PRI and a new, different Mexico.

However, while Colosio earned plaudits there was immediate speculation the party would not stand for his impudence, and that he would be replaced as the PRI candidate. The nation held its breath to see what the response would be. Then, seventeen days after his landmark speech, at 5 p.m., an hour after he began addressing a rally in the poor Tijuana neighbourhood of Lomas Taurinas, two shots rang out. Colosio had been hit in the head and stomach and he was rushed to Tijuana hospital where he died hours later. Mario Aburto Martinez, a twenty-two-year-old factory worker, was arrested at the scene and was hastily charged with murder and subsequently convicted and jailed for forty-two years. Aburto Martinez was a Jehovah's Witness and it was claimed that by shooting Colosio he was seeking to publicize his pacifist views, which seems somewhat contradictory. The police were said to have found a notebook of Aburto Martinez's containing sketches showing his spirt entering Colosio's body.

Colosio's assassination raised plenty of questions: his final address had not been in his diary and it was an impromptu decision, which meant that only those close to him would have known his intentions.

Added to which, since it was unscheduled, that meant that his personal security was lighter than usual. Most strikingly of all, the man who had been seized at the shooting was scruffy and unshaven, whereas the Aburto Martinez who appeared in court was more smartly dressed and shaven and, to top it off, the bullets seemed to have struck Colosio from different directions. It smelled of a classic cover-up. Aburto Martinez confessed and maintained he acted alone, but Mexicans were unconvinced: they thought the man in the dock was not the man who pulled the trigger, or at the very least that he had an accomplice. The man who went to jail was real enough, he really was Mario Aburto Martinez, but the feeling persisted that he was innocent, or his guilt was shared, that the actual killer or fellow killers had escaped.

In the intervening years, doubts have never receded about who really killed or ordered the killing of Colosio. Since the assassination five special prosecutors have looked at the case and multiple other suspects have been questioned, including an ex-police officer and an intelligence agent for the since disbanded Center for Investigation and National Security (CISEN), but only Aburto Martinez has ever been convicted, and suspicion about whether his confession was made under duress continues, even today. Nine police officers came forward as witnesses, then it turned out seven of them had not been present when Colosio was shot. Aburto Martinez's girlfriend said he discussed having a gun, then said he hadn't. His relatives said they knew he was planning the murder, then it transpired they were intimidated into saying so. Many theories were considered by the federal Attorney General's office, but after each enquiry, the government returned to the line that the Aburto Martinez in prison was solely responsible. Regardless, one widespread belief, voiced by Colosio's father Luis until he died in 2010, was that those linked to Colosio's own PRI were behind his shooting.

After the shooting the PRI selected a replacement, Ernesto Zedillo, Colosio's campaign manager, who duly won the election and was president until 2000. Critics of the PRI said the PRI had chosen a patsy, someone who would not dare to undermine the legacy of Salinas or the party in the manner in which Colosio threatened he would. What is certainly true is that the ramifications of Colosio's death extended far and wide. Crucially, it was a key factor in the decision by foreign investors to dump Mexico. Prior to his death, Mexico seemed to be on the up. Foreign capital was coming in, attracted by the recently signed North American Free Trade Agreement and the promise from the PRI of large-scale investment. Combined with Colosio's candidature, Mexico looked like it was offering citizens and foreign investors real hope of reform for a nation that had been ravaged by corruption and crime. Colosio was seen as the face of a new optimism for the country, thus his slaying afforded confirmation that Mexico was not progressing, that its future was lawless and bleak, and so it proved. In the years after Colosio's death Mexico was plunged into instability and catastrophe and, as a result, the country attracted a higher international investment risk rating, which effectively warned off foreign investors, a disastrous outcome for a country trying to pull itself together economically. The government tried to keep the currency, the peso, pegged to the US dollar and issued dollar-denominated debt, but the markets believed the peso was overvalued and took fright. The government stepped in again, buying up its own securities, which in turn hit the central bank reserves, and before long the country was in a downward spiral. A move to devalue the peso in December 1994 led to an even higher risk rating and the economy went into freefall, one of the consequences of which was the collapse of Mexico's banks and their nationalization. The message was clear to foreign banks – investing in Mexico was to be avoided at all costs. In 1995, a US-led $50 billion bailout, promoted by President Bill Clinton and arranged by the IMF, working with the G7 nations and Bank for International Settlements, eventually brought a breathing space, but it was too little, too late. The economy was already hurtling into deep recession and the death knell came in 1995 when interest rates reached almost 100 per cent, meaning that people were having to pay back virtually double what they borrowed from the bank. Borrowers showed that they had had enough and simply stopped paying on their debts.

Until Colosio's murder and the ensuing Peso or Tequila Crisis, as it became known, Mexico was firmly on HSBC's radar. In 1994, it had a population of 90 million and most of the population did not use a bank because they were so poor and preferred to keep their savings with them, just in case. However, before the assassination, investors also saw in Mexico a country that was oil-producing, had a growing tourist industry, fast-paced technology and service sectors, high productivity and a developing infrastructure. In short, it was a place where HSBC wanted to be and they had made no secret of coveting that part of the world. 'Willie Purves was very much more aware than anybody else about Latin America,' said Geoghegan of the HSBC Holdings' chairman from 1990 until 1998, adding: 'He even went on honeymoon in the region', as though this gave an extremely wealthy European banker a unique insight into how 90 million Mexicans, many of whom were impoverished, spent their money and their time. Another HSBC heavyweight erred on the side of caution about investing in Mexico in the nineties. 'We knew that we wanted to expand in Latin America,' said Keith Whitson. But he explained, 'it isn't just a question of going out and buying something. You really have to wait until a suitable opportunity arises.' The upshot was that Mexico was very much on HSBC's shopping list and in 1993, the bank was running the sums over taking stakes in local Mexican banks.

In 1994, the Group executive committee had fixed on Mexico. 'Consideration will be given to expanding the current Group presence in Mexico in recognition of the importance of Mexico's economy, which represents 40 per cent of the Latin American market and is growing.' That changed with the Colosio assassination, devaluation and crisis. Although, no sooner was the peso devalued than

HSBC dabbled with investing in Mexico, in the country's third-biggest bank, Serfin. It had been rescued by the Mexican government and HSBC was told they would welcome the foreign bank stepping in and taking a stake. During the ensuing talks, Purves let slip that he wondered if HSBC had 'the necessary Mexican expertise.' It was an intriguing remark, a sign perhaps of nervousness on high within HSBC of Mexico's potential to blow up. At the very least it showed an early recognition that Mexico would require special handling and that it was not at all the same as other countries on the Risk all-conquering global map that HSBC had in their sights. Eight years would pass before HSBC returned to Mexico, while they waited for the economy to recover, but that did not slow down HSBC's ambitions, as the bank made land grabs in Argentina, Brazil, Malta, France and Turkey, amongst others. By the time they revisited Mexico the banks that had been rescued by the Mexican government had since been privatized and sold to foreign banks, amongst them Citigroup, BBVA and Santander, which had snapped up Mexico's three largest banks. The HSBC directors knew that if there was one thing that shareholders disliked nearly as much as losing money, it was missing an opportunity. Anxious not to be left without, or left further behind by their rivals, HSBC jumped. In 2002 it targeted Grupo Financiero Bital, or Bital for short, the country's fifth-largest bank, which was majority owned by the Berrondo family. HSBC was in a hurry: the bank was also 30 per cent owned by rival Santander of Spain and HSBC was fearful, lest Santander added Bital to its existing Mexican banks, Mexicano and Serfin. To ensure everyone knew that the deal had to happen, HSBC's leadership deliberately raised the temperature. They gave the project to buy Bital the straight-out-of Risk, *Boy's Own* codename of 'High Noon'. In the rush not to get left behind, any anxieties about the state of Mexico, its corruption and crime, any fears that HSBC lacked specialist knowledge of the country – all of which had been raised as issues only eight years earlier – were abandoned. The men at HSBC had convinced themselves that this deal wasn't only about a country in Latin America, but about something much more important. Those doing the deal were implored by senior management: 'Our credibility with our board and our international credibility as a winner will be on the line if we are out-bid by Santander in a competitive situation.' For those at the top of a company that had once preached the gospel of resilience and steady growth, they were about to go all-in with a country that had only recently been written off by people in the same bank, all for the sake of their reputation amongst their banking peers.

In the pursuit of global domination, on becoming as big as possible, safety first had been thrown to the wind, and the macho-titled 'High Noon' wasn't even for Mexico's biggest or even second-biggest bank, but the country's fifth-largest bank. It was bizarre, nonsensical and out of all proportion. The bank's bosses liked to view the world in gladiatorial terms and theirs was a must-win approach. Yet, outwardly, this was the same HSBC that prided itself on a tradition of care and hesitancy. 'Our safe culture is a huge strength,' said one manager during an internal survey at the time. Another commented in the same period, 'we are cautious and methodical, which does serve us well.' Except, it seems, when it came to High Noon, where it appears that all the safeguards were abandoned in pursuit of victory.

For all its attraction on paper, in reality Bital was a mess. It was the last Mexican bank that had yet to clean up its balance sheet as a result of the 1995 crisis and locals said the bank still required an injection of $450 million to meet Mexico's tightened capital reserves regulations. Bital was also operating at a cost-income ratio above 70 per cent, which compared poorly with HSBC's average of 52 to 55 per cent. The Mexican bank was deficient in another, vital respect. At the time of the acquisition, David Bagley, the HSBC group director of compliance in London, sent a memo to John Root, a senior compliance office who worked under him. It was a summary of a meeting between Bagley and Sandy Flockhart, the HSBC executive who was put in charge of integrating Bital into the HSBC 'family'. Reported

Bagley: 'Sandy acknowledges the importance of a robust compliance and money laundering function, which at present is virtually non-existent.' He continued: 'There is no recognizable compliance or money laundering function in Bital at present . . . Sandy thinks it is important to look both at issues affecting Mexico City, but also closer to the border where there appears to be substantial cross-border flows of monies, including USD in cash.' And it was not only Bagley who had grave concerns. Keith Whitson, the wise veteran who previously warned against just 'going out and buying something' and who remembered the 'sound Scottish banking principles', the strict moral staff code and the culture of caution that the success of HSBC had been built on, was also not impressed by what even the cursory Bital due diligence had thrown up. 'Shortfalls of $700 million, poor controls, 5–6 years of economic loss has put a different perspective on the proposal. If one adds to this the prospect of further Latin American woes and the general world economic climate, I think we could be well advised to stand aside.' However, the warnings were not heeded, nor did the bank err on the side of Green's 'ethical capitalism', and so Whitson's colleagues continued with their pursuit of pulling off High Noon. Barely little more than a month after Bagley sent his flashing red-light email – and before any detailed examination could be made of the gaping holes in Bital's procedures and proper thought given as to how to correct them – in late 2002 HSBC went public with its agreement to pay $1.14 billion for Bital, and HSBC's journey into the heartlands of the drug cartels had begun. The acquisition – for $1.20 a share, 20 per cent above Bital's share price – was top-spun by HSBC's cheerleaders as a vote of confidence by the bank in Mexico, and the securing of a major footing in Latin America, the seizure of a bridge between North America and South America. The corporate boosterism flogged the positives. 'It will enable us to become one of the few banks that can facilitate trade seamlessly among the three NAFTA countries [Canada, US, Mexico],' declared Flockhart.

In acquiring Bital HSBC bought a bank with 6 million depositors and 1,400 branches, which made it HSBC's second-largest branch network. Although most of Bital's customers were small depositors, according to the new owner, it was already earmarking them for an expanded range of loans and financial products it aimed to introduce. Flockhart spoke excitedly about widening Bital's business to include middle-market commercial banking, institutional banking and private banking. This was also how the industry in Mexico saw it, as they swallowed the HSBC line and rubbed their hands in eager anticipation at the arrival of the foreign banks. Analysts said they expected that consumer lending will loosen up as the newcomers look to boost their returns. 'Mexico is really going to see a lot more competition in the coming years,' said Bruno Pereira gleefully, Latin America banking analyst for UBS Warburg in Rio de Janeiro. That's what all the chatter in Mexico City was about: looking forward to a banking boom. All that was needed to spur lending were new laws making it easier for lenders to collect collateral in a default, said Yolanda Courtines, Latin America banking analyst for JP Morgan Securities. Starting the following year, she added, payments on mortgages would be tax deductible, which would stimulate demand, she summarized optimistically. It was unremittingly heady stuff. HSBC's approach, as laid down in a group management note for those executives responsible for integrating Bital, was about: respecting Mexican culture but adhering to HSBC world-wide values; establishing close relations with the financial authorities; drawing on the group's experience and resources; building a broad team of supportive executives; not rushing to rebrand; and being as visible as possible. Flockhart was instructed from the top of the bank that 'a few "early wins" for employees [17,000 of them] would be highly desirable to show how life with HSBC will be better.' So much as well for saying it would not rush to rebrand: within twelve months of the Bital purchase being concluded, the bank was renamed HSBC Mexico – and it was claimed this is what the local staff desired, they wished to be part of the wider HSBC 'family'.

The advertising blitz that accompanied the name change was unheard of for a bank in Mexico. 'Overnight, the Bital name just disappeared. They threw a lot of money at marketing. HSBC was not a name in Mexico, but they spent a lot of money developing a strong brand. Everywhere you went there were adverts. At the airport, flying out, coming in – the HSBC name was everywhere. All the luggage carts were HSBC. "It's not Bital, it's HSBC". All the way down the streets to and from the airport there were signs, everywhere, on all the main streets in the city, on the radio. They did a great marketing job,' says a Mexico bank regulator. 'They changed the name real quick.' He paused for effect, so I could take this next bit in and get the significance of what he was saying: 'They didn't change other things anywhere near fast enough.'

Any fears that HSBC might have chosen the wrong time to be splurging over $1 billion on a bank in Mexico were soon displaced, because just at the moment the Bital name was being removed and replaced by HSBC, the world's investment community piled in to make the most of the potential of the emerging markets, with the seal of approval coming from the doyen of investment banks, Goldman Sachs. In October 2003, its chief economist, Jim O'Neill, and his team produced a paper, 'Dreaming with BRICs: The Path to 2050'. They estimated that within decades the size of the four BRIC economies combined – Brazil, Russia, India, China – would be larger than that of the established G6 nations. It was a ground-breaking report, and the City, Wall Street, anywhere there were investors, lapped it up. As ever whenever these reports are published, some eager speculators moved ahead of the pack, and began searching for the next batch of BRICs. O'Neill and Co followed with the 'Next Eleven', or as they are known, N-11: Bangladesh, Egypt, Indonesia, Iran, Korea, Mexico, Nigeria, Pakistan, Philippines, Turkey and Vietnam. The HSBC investor relations and PR machines were ecstatic at this apparent seal of approval for their strategy and shifted into overdrive. The line they pumped out was that HSBC was poised beautifully to cash-in, and at a meeting in Chicago, Green told management colleagues that 'we have a good emerging markets story, but it's only 20 per cent of the total by assets and profits.' He went on to share with the *Wall Street Journal* the bank planned to use its consumer-finance business to pull ahead in these markets, and investors were informed that from then on the emphasis would be heavily on the developing nations.

Back in London, Geoghegan announced: 'We are at the foothills of what we can do in emerging markets.' With the ink barely dry on the completion of High Noon, the HSBC leadership was already thinking big picture, and of using Bital as a springboard for further expansion in the region, for grabbing neighbouring countries. In other words, it was a classic move straight out of the Risk handbook. The ecstatic reception to the deal within HSBC meant that Bagley's memo, Whitson's warning and all the other doubters seemed far away. The HSBC strategic plan covering Mexico argued strongly for more acquisitions, more flag-waving. Central America, it said, was 'an attractive collection of markets with a decade of stability, favourable demographics, and trade and growth potential.' Against this gushing positivity, the $1.1 billion paid for a Mexican bank with so many customers and branches looked like clever, savvy business and, true to their word, HSBC and its consumer salesforce threw everything at the new acquisition. Within the year, HSBC Mexico quickly became a leader in innovation, with its branches opening for longer hours, the first bank in Mexico to introduce fixed-rate mortgages aimed at lower-income customers, the first to make personal loans via ATMs, and the first to use computer modelling to site the cash machines according to their usage and the return generated for the bank. HSBC Mexico was first in the entire HSBC 'family' to set up a system allowing people to make charitable donations at an ATM – an idea that was taken up and replicated elsewhere. The speed of advancement was furious – Mexico had never seen anything like it. What HSBC needed to go with all this activity, it was decided, was a new prestige local headquarters, one that would befit such a get-ahead operation, one that everyone associated with the whirlwind of HSBC Mexico could be proud of. And so in 2002, with the ink barely dry on the signatures of the Bital purchase agreement, HSBC bought the Torre Angel building on the Paseo de la Reforma, Mexico City's main arterial thoroughfare.

'The Reforma' is Fifth Avenue, Champs-Élysées and Trafalgar Square blended into one. It's a cavernous road, with tree-lined pavements beneath tall, imposing buildings, concrete, glass and steel statements of serious commercial achievement and intent, standing all the way along. Walking along the Reforma is like being at the bottom of a long, wide river valley, with vertical, forbidding sides, while at road level there are shops, souvenir sellers and restaurants, crowds of people and, this being Mexico City, queues of cars. The avenue is the pulsating centre of a great global city, a source of patriotic pride, of commemoration, celebration and of protest, and of power, both business and political. Anything that kicks off in Mexico City kicks off here; anything worth going crazy about, like the supporters of Cruz Azul glorying in their football team winning the Clausura tournament in May 2021 or protestors marching against a new government measure, does so here. Up above, the offices are quiet, aloof, immune from the mayhem. Worldwide, the new HSBC Torre in Mexico City joined no less than fifteen other iconic structures in the HSBC pantheon, in other cities all bearing the muscle-flexing address HSBC Tower, HSBC Building, HSBC Plaza, HSBC Centre, HSBC Center or HSBC Arena. In Mexico, this was HSBC sticking its four-letter brand right in the commercial beating heart of Mexico City, in the epicentre of Latin America, and the message the bank's management wanted to communicate to the locals as well as shareholders and competitors was that HSBC owned BRICs, possessed the Next Eleven, and that the emerging markets, with all their potential of great riches, belonged to HSBC. The striking edifice, in front of the Reforma's revered national Angel of Independence monument, had to be more than that, however, as a symbol of the new Mexico, a new Latin America, a new state-of-the-art method of banking, one that had HSBC at its very heart.

Back in London, head office took a keen interest in the flag-raising. Gisca, a major Mexican developer, was appointed to redesign the facade and public spaces, and HOK, the industry-heading US architects and engineers, were asked to design the interiors. Said HOK: 'This project served as a pilot for HSBC, as its Corporate Real Estate group began to rethink the company's global workplace stand-ards. HOK helped HSBC to study ways to increase the density of its Mexican headquarters building. Strategies developed for a 100-person pilot group include implementing alternative ways of working such as telecommuting, hoteling and space-sharing.' The reconfigura-tion was on a scale that Mexico had never witnessed before. The tower was to be 446 feet tall, covering thirty-six floors, reached by eighteen lifts and housing 2,800 people.

Global banks and towering buildings are not new, and what they have in common is that each one has got to be more lavish and grand than the last, than that of their rivals; they must be the final word in detail and thought and, these days, ultimately eco-friendly. The early 2000s were a golden period in this giant bank phallus erecting, and it's no coincidence that at exactly the same time HSBC was deciding just how jaw-dropping it should make its new Mexican head office, in Edinburgh another banker was planning the same for his head-quarters. Sir Fred Goodwin also inherited a bank based on 'sound Scottish banking principles' in the Royal Bank of Scotland and around the time that HSBC was making public its global mission statement, Goodwin declared: 'I want us to be bigger than JP Morgan.' To make good on his ambitions, Goodwin set about devis-ing a prestige building on land outside Edinburgh. It was to have a fountain complete with 'a large external reflection pool with a 40-metre long overspilling weir edge' framing the main entrance, 'providing a crisp reflection of the architectural form.' The exterior was to be cast in dark glass and sandstone. The place would have its own road bridge, complete with giant 'RBS' logo and a 'scallop kitchen' so that Goodwin and his staff could enjoy their favourite scallops and other perfectly prepared local seafood. When she opened this new temple to capitalism, the Queen said: 'For many years, Scotland has had an enviable reputation for efficient financial management in a highly competitive international market. This building is a fine tribute to the many generations of "canny" Scottish bankers, who have made – and are still making – such a valuable contribution to the national economy.' Three years later, RBS collapsed and had to be bailed out by the UK taxpayer.

To RBS's lavishness could be added other banks. Over the next few years there were numerous banks, certainly those with global aspirations, that splashed out on new, grand offices. They did so in the same way that billionaires buy ever longer and more expensive superyachts, trying to outdo their rivals in largesse. There's even a website devoted to the banks' willy-waving. 'The Architecture of Money – The World's Most Spectacular Bank Buildings' is compiled by Emporis, the building data provider. 'Occupying smart offices with sheer endless views over the skyline,' gushes Emporis, 'banks do not just speculate high, but even work in palaces above the clouds. Leading banks administer our money from impressive headquarters that fulfil the latest standards in sustainability, design and functionality.' On those criteria, HSBC's new Mexico City Torre did not disappoint. It was the first in Latin America, declared its champions at HSBC, to be awarded LEED (Leadership in Energy and Environmental Design) Gold status from the US Green Building Council, in recognition of its eco-friendly, sustainable features. These included: 'Using the best available technology to minimize water and electricity consumption, including low consumption bathroom furniture and waterless urinals; collecting rainwater on the 4,000-square-foot green roof; filtering pollutants and CO_2 out of the air; ensuring daylight was accessible to as many building occupants as possible through an efficient open office plan; limiting the "urban heat island" effect; and selecting low-VOC carpeting and using GreenGuard certified furniture from Knoll, Herman Miller and Haworth'. At the time of its opening, HSBC declared triumphantly that the building would use 55 per cent less water and 40 per cent less energy than comparable structures. 'We hope this project serves as an example for greening the community and encouraging the Mexican government to offer more incentives for creating environmentally friendly buildings,' said HOK Project Manager Javier Presas. 'The project already has created more interest among developers, clients and architects in Mexico.' Everything about HSBC's plans for Mexico suggested that this investment was only just part of their sweep towards world domination.

The Torre HSBC took four years to complete, at a cost of $150 million and the opening, on 5 April 2006, was a super-smart affair, attended by the President of Mexico, Vicente Fox Quesada, his wife, Marta Sahagún, Secretary of Finance Francisco Gil Díaz, central bank governor Guillermo Ortiz Martínez, assorted guests, and HSBC executives Flockhart, Green and Bond. For all the up-to-the-minute use of design, materials and technology, the Torre HSBC contains an older addition that sits completely at odds with the gleaming new futuristic building. Outside, by the entrance, are two gold lions, which are replicas of the statues that stood out front at the bank's old Hong Kong headquarters and can be found at all HSBC head office buildings around the world. Based on the Greek lions that were added to the entrance to the Venetian Arsenal in the late seventeenth century, the first pair were commissioned for the Shanghai office on the Bund in 1923. Tradition dictates that staff and passers-by stroke the lions in the belief that power and money will rub off on them, and over time they have become known as Stephen and Stitt, named after Alexander Stephen, the former Shanghai manager and in 1923 chief manager of HSBC; and Gordon Stitt, the then Shanghai manager. Stephen's mouth is wide open, and he looks to be roaring,

Stitt is quiet; supposedly the different expressions represent the characteristics of the two bankers, and when combined, the strength and calm of the ideal HSBC banker, but they are not to everyone's taste. 'Not the f****ng lions,' says one former HSBC banker when I mention them to him, shaking his head. 'God, they used to go on and on about them.'

The lions were not the only pieces of art in the Torre building. At the opening, Flockhart and President Vicente Fox unveiled a breathtakingly large fresco in the reception called *Credit Transforms Mexico*, by the Mexican painter and architect Juan O'Gorman. The work was originally commissioned by Bital and is in the local mural style – part historical narrative, part conveying a serious message. Its colours are earthy and native, the characters and the landscape are simply and non-fussily presented, symbolizing the world at that time, scenes and the ages folding into each other. While the painting had been covered up for years in the Bital offices, HSBC managers had the mural minutely, lovingly and expensively restored, and in the new office, since it measured a whopping 3 metres by 21 metres, it was impossible to miss, even for those who were merely passing the building, and that was entirely the point. At the opening, HSBC proclaimed that in its new home, the mural would have 'a more stable structure, a climate-control system that would keep the microclimate ideal for conservation of the work, and protective glass to shield it from UV rays.' It seems that at HSBC even the artwork was not immune from Risk-speak as the bank went out of their way to declare their own faith in High Noon, labouring the point somewhat with metaphors. 'Corporate personality is the most important competitive advantage a company can have because it means the firm is aware of, understands and can learn from its past to be better in the future.'

In hammering home the line about the perfect marriage between HSBC and Mexico they said that O'Gorman was an appropriate choice of artist because he was 'a mix of his father's strict British spirit and the passionate Mexican blood of his mother's side.' *Credit Transforms Mexico*, burbled HSBC, 'is a fascinating, majestic testimony that should remind the current generation at HSBC that we are in debt to the past and must meet our obligations of the future.' The theme of the mural, for those who care to take a closer look, is Mexico before and after the introduction of financial services. On the left-hand side is a wild, untamed Mexico; on the right is a nation transformed by factories, highways, bridges, dams and irrigation systems. Four groups of people stare out across the different scenes: peasants, labourers, O'Gorman himself and those closest to him. The suggestion is of the positive change wrought by banks, such as HSBC, although on closer examination, O'Gorman's work is laden with subtle irony and humour, which may also explain why Bital did not put it on display. O'Gorman may have been part-British, part-Mexican, as HSBC says, but he was very much a local 'red', a socialist who only late in his life suddenly joined the PRI and even then he stressed, 'I belong to the left of the PRI, which is perfectly commendable.' For the majority of the time, though, he was an avowed leftist. In one scene in the mural O'Gorman depicts himself lying on the ground sleeping and apparently dreaming and he is holding a red book in his left hand, Karl Marx's *Das Kapital,* while wearing a hat, alluding to the defence of peasants. Behind him there is a stack of more books and a globe turned to the Americas. On the right there is a hotel with a sign on its roof, 'CUCU-LAND', and on a billboard there is a poster advertising beer and next to it a watermelon marked with a peso sign – the fruit of the land has a price. Next to a domed building, there are three initials, which appear to be 'PRI', but on closer inspection they're 'RRI': the first 'R' is faded – so a way of saying 'Not PRI' – and below them the word 'MARKET' appears horizontally on a sign and immediately below it, vertically 'AFTER' – suggesting a distinct lack of enthusiasm for money-making. All of these subversive, anti-capitalist messages were picked up by O'Gorman's Mexican followers and art experts after the piece went on show at HSBC properly for the first time. One local report carried the headline: 'Experts intrigued by signs bearing messages that the painter introduced into his work.' The article quoted Walther Boelsterly, director of Mexico's National Center for Conservation and Registry of Real Estate Art Heritage, as saying he believed O'Gorman wished 'to laugh a little'. HSBC's view on this when they found out is not recorded.

Every five years, whoever is in charge of HSBC presents a strategic plan to the board, and in 2003, it was Stephen Green's turn; he titled his paper 'Managing for Growth'. 'The sheer scale of the Group has significantly increased management complexities and posed challenges for us,' he wrote, and he advocated four positive actions to achieving their global ambitions:

- Grow our revenues by building a world-class, ethical sales and marketing culture.
- Increase our focus on meeting customers' needs.
- Be a low-cost producer by increasing productivity and managing costs strategically.
- Ensure line of sight to TSR [total shareholder return] so that everybody knows what is expected of them.

The Green five-year plan majored on sales. 'Selling will drive our thinking and actions', it stated in relation to pushing financial products to personal clients, and in public Green told *HSBC World* that the bank's 'biggest weakness' was that 'we need to do a better job of developing a sales and marketing-oriented culture, so that we approach the challenge of revenue growth with as much creativity and energy as possible.' In other words, Green, the ex-McKinsey strategist, was going to make that carefully nurtured culture much more sales-driven. As part of the plan, staff were to be awarded points for selling a product to an individual customer, and those points were totalled up to help calculate their bonus award. The results would be immediate and one branch employee, interviewed in *Team Talk*, the bank's UK in-house journal, boasted that he had racked up 138,000 points in a single year. 'There's no secret,' he said, 'it's actually all about listening to your customers, not just to what they are saying, but also to what they are not telling you! Just because people come in for a credit card doesn't mean they won't want to discuss their mortgage.' But not everyone was so enamoured by this shift to a rewards-based sales culture, since while HSBC maintained it would still behave responsibly, 'undoubtedly a cultural shift did take place during these years,' wrote Richard Roberts and David Kynaston in *The Lion Wakes – a Modern History of HSBC*, and outside the HSBC family the protests in this new direction were more sharply vocalized. In the UK, the trade unions complained, and one of the union leaders publicly stated that 'The anger and the disaffection of the employees were tangible. The whole emphasis is on sell, sell, sell.' The response to these complaints from Green's emissary, Geoghegan, was to tell a group of retired HSBC managers that he saw his mission as to 'convince staff and unions that sales is not a dirty word', and because investors wanted bigger profits and returns, the PR patter was also determinedly on message. Meanwhile, the financial community and the media, which has always had a habit of focusing on larger and larger profits without questioning how they've been achieved, often until it is too late, believed the management, led by Green and Geoghegan, when they said they would deliver. Doubts they might lose their moral bearings were assuaged by the company's 2003 Annual Report, which introduced the new Managing for Growth strategy:

'HSBC's core values are integral to its strategy, and communicating them to customers, shareholders and employees is intrinsic to the plan. These values comprise an emphasis on long-term, ethical client relationships . . . HSBC has always aspired to the highest standards of conduct, recognizes its wider obligations to society and believes there is a strong link between [Corporate Social Responsibility] and long-term success. Moreover, the pressures to comply with public expectations across a wide spectrum of social, ethical and environmental issues are growing rapidly. The strategy therefore calls for a renewed emphasis on CSR . . .'

With High Noon complete, and the Mexico branch of HSBC now up and running by the end of 2003, everything emanating from the bank and its bosses was financially bullish while seeking to assure the few doubters who remained that the bank would continue to be 'ethical' and would be 'aspiring to the highest standards of conduct', since HSBC recognized its 'wider obligations to society'. At the end of the next accounting period, in 2003, HSBC announced that they were making a staggering $12.8 billion profit a year, up from $6.5 billion five years previously, and as promised, almost half of this figure was coming from individual, as opposed to corporate, customers. In the British press, HSBC was saluted for its 'astute management and the benefits of globalization.' Everything was set fair and there were pats on backs all round and hefty bonuses paid out in record numbers. It was clear for everyone to see that winning the game of Risk was in the bag.

THREE

The Blood Alliance

Joaquín Archivaldo Guzmán did not entertain strategy papers with titles like 'Managing for Growth' or five-year management plans. Neither had he been to university, nor did he attend business school and he certainly never worked at McKinsey. He is unlikely, ever, to have been invited to attend the opera with the likes of Stephen Green, but there's no doubting his commercial and strategic abilities, and it is clear that he would be brilliant at Risk.

Guzmán is just as expansionist as any ambitious corporate or bank chief and has always been a firm believer, just like Green and his peers, in the essence of big. Just as HSBC have nicknames so does Guzmán, and the one that sticks most often is 'Chapo' or 'Shorty', in relation to his 5-foot 6-inch height and stocky build, although others include 'Old Man' and 'Uncle' out of deference and the tightness of family, and 'Boss' and 'Rapido'. Chapo more than makes up for his lack of physicality with cunning and guile, with ruthlessness, and a sharp eye for opportunity and total attention to planning and detail. Some of his methods are barbaric and callous – pure evil – but there is no denying, Chapo knows how to grow a business and take it into new markets. He also does his version of 'sell, sell, sell' – albeit without the assistance of a strategy paper entitled 'Managing for Growth'. Chapo's reputation as a ruthless drugs lord, his reach, the claims that swirl around him regarding his links to senior politicians, his entrenched base, his position in Mexican folklore, were already well known when HSBC arrived in Mexico to complete High Noon and acquire Bital. As Chapo once said himself, 'I may not be the president of Mexico, but in Mexico I am the boss.'

Chapo ran the Sinaloa drug cartel and for a generation of Mexicans he was long the face of the corrupt, crime-riddled country that people like Colosio were trying to put behind them. In his position of power he cajoled, manipulated, controlled and drove his cartel to become the mightiest drug-supplying organization in the world, and in the process he earned for himself the title of the world's most famous drug lord. Chapo represented everything that HSBC should have known they were going to have to face up to at some stage when they put down roots in Mexico and started to ingratiate themselves with the Mexican government and locals.

In Sinaloa, in the Sierra Madre mountains of north-western Mexico, where Guzmán was born in 1957, they call the sticky substance the opium poppy produces gum, and it is easily refined to make morphine and, from that, heroin. The people who farm the opium resin and scrape it from the buds are called gummers or *gomeros* and so ingrained is this way of life in Mexico that, for a period, the local baseball team was known as the Gomeros or Gummers. The opium plant, *Papaver somniferum*, is not indigenous to Mexico and arrived thanks to the Chinese labourers who were smoking opium imported from India, courtesy of the likes of Sutherland, Dent and their bank, HSBC. In the 1860s, railroads and mines were built in the hills, as industrialization came to Mexico, and American and British companies imported cheap labour, 'coolies', from China to work the railroads. They brought with them opium poppies, seed and gum, and they set up their smoking dens just like back home, and in time, to their delight, they discovered that the Asian poppy was suited to the Sierra Madre soil and climate. The first official recognition that the opium poppy was part of the Sinaloa flora came in a Mexican government study in 1886. It's common currency in Mexico, however, that the opium trade didn't take off until the Second World War when the US government placed an order for poppies to make industrial quantities of morphine for its returning wounded troops. In his book on the history of the Mexican trade, *El Narco*, Ioan Grillo says this theory was dismissed by Harry Anslinger, the first director of the US Federal Bureau of Narcotics. Nonetheless, points out Grillo, hanging on the wall of the headquarters of the Mexican Defense Department in Mexico City is an official history describing the deal to supply opium to the US, and by the time Guzmán was growing up in La Tuna, high in the Sierra Madre, opium was a well-established crop.

In many ways La Tuna is representative of the rural poverty that defines much of the country that HSBC were hoping to turn into their new customers. For generations the town's main economic activities have been cattle ranching, forestry and growing tomatoes, oranges and opium, and most of the houses remain shacks of two rooms, the exception being the large finca that Chapo had built for his mother. Even today it is difficult to believe that many of the inhabitants have a bank account. The Chapo who was born here was a *campesino*, a peasant, but he was clever and articulate, and spoke in a high-pitched, nasally, sing-song voice. Even as a child he had a good turn of phrase, liking to slip into a personal, home-schooled philosophy. 'I remember from the time I was six until now, my parents, a very humble family, very poor. I remember how my mom made bread to support the family. I would sell it, I sold oranges, I sold soft drinks, I sold candy. My mom, she was a hard worker, she worked a lot. We grew corn, beans. I took care of my grandmother's cattle and chopped wood.' His father was a *gomero* and looked after cattle and grew opium, but he also used to hit the young Chapo and eventually the boy went to live with his grandfather. 'From the time I was fifteen and after, where I come from, which is the municipality of Badira-guato, I was raised in a ranch named La Tuna, in that area, up until today, there are no job opportunities. The only way to have money to buy food, to survive, is to grow poppy, marijuana, and at that age, I began to grow it, to cultivate it and to sell it. That is what I can tell you.' Thenceforth, he was guided by a simple life principle: he never took anything or anyone for granted. 'You should never feel better than others. Even the rain that comes from the top, ends falling always at our feet.'

From La Tuna, the opium gum is sold to those higher up the drugs chain in the Sinaloa capital of Culiacán and while Chapo was growing up, thanks to the US deal or not, the opium trade was lucra-tive. Then along came the Sixties and demand from the US for psychedelic narcotics, for opium, heroin and marijuana, soared – and with it, too, Chapo's fortunes. The Guzmán family had a connection with a Culiacán drugs boss, Pedro Avilés Pérez, who has a special place in narco folklore since he was the first narco to use small air-planes to smuggle the drugs into the US, and Pérez took the youthful Chapo under his wing and the youngster soon proved to be an excel-lent organizer, transporting drugs from Sinaloa to the border. Over the coming years, as the opium trade between Mexico and the US boomed, Chapo's reputation grew and through his fierce ambition and direct approach to dealing with those who let him down – he interrogated and killed them personally – he got noticed by Miguel Angel Félix Gallardo, also known as El Padrino, 'the Godfather' of Sinaloa drug trafficking. Any qualms Chapo may have had about what he was getting into were quickly dispelled. 'It's a reality that drugs destroy. Unfortunately, where I grew up, there's no other way to survive.'

Like Aviles Pérez, Félix Gallardo was special. Ten years older than Chapo, and 6 foot 2 inches tall, he was raised in Culiacán and tow-ered over Chapo. While in his twenties he joined the police as a motorcycle cop, but he also worked as the family bodyguard of the Governor of Sinaloa and from enforcing the law, like several of the leading drugs players of the period, Gallardo segued neatly into breaking it when he partnered up with a Honduras drug dealer called Juan Ramón Matta-Ballesteros. Together, they trafficked opium and cannabis from Mexico to the US. Using Matta's Central America connections, they linked up with Colombians to diversify and add a third item to their range: cocaine. They brought in the white powder from Colombia to Mexico for onward shipment to the US. Their Guadalajara organization – they relocated from Culiacán after attempts by the Mexican authorities to close down Sinaloa drug trafficking – constituted the first Mexican cocaine cartel and were following quickly in the footsteps of the Colombian Medellin's first cartel boss, Pablo Escobar. From the earliest days of his reign, Escobar was politically minded, building a housing project for the homeless and being elected to Colombia's parliament at one stage, and his Medellin cartel was a blueprint for others, because what Escobar showed was that if he was popular with the poor, he could hide his murderous violence behind them from the government and the police. So when heavy rains wrecked the crops in the hills, Chapo gave tens of thousands of dollars to the gomeros. Another time, one Christmas, the locals received the gift of 100 all-terrain vehicles. Neither Escobar or Chapo forgot where they had come from, even when their names started appearing on the *Forbes* rich lists, and this continued long after Chapo had been imprisoned. During the Covid-19 pandemic, the Mexican cartels organized food banks and deliveries to the shielding and vulnerable, and Chapo's daughter, Alejandrina, packed boxes with toilet rolls, masks and groceries and distributed them in Guadalajara. They were branded 'El Chapo 701', with a stencilled image of her father, after his placing on the *Forbes* 'Rich List' as the 701st richest person in the world.

Gallardo, who held a business degree, was another visionary of the drug-trafficking industry, and not only did he and Matta diversify the drugs they were trafficking, but they also cut out the middleman by owning their own cannabis farms before realizing true economies of scale by making the farms industrial-sized. In one raid, recorded Grillo, 'the bust set a world record for marijuana farms that hasn't been beaten since. Crops spread out across miles of desert and were dried in more than twenty-five sheds, most bigger than football pitches.' It was the perfect environment for Chapo to learn his trade, and he was a keen student: 'In most cases the best advice that can be given is just listening.' By the mid-1970s, Chapo was married with a young family to provide for and Gallardo acted as Chapo's mentor, giving him the job of running logistics for their trafficking business which meant that he was in charge of coordinating the planes, boats and trucks to shift the drugs across Mexico, often from the south from Colombia, and into the US. Another Gallardo innovation was that he understood rival gangs fighting for territory would only lead to bloodshed, division and weakness. So, like a scene in *The God-father*, the head honchos were summoned to a meeting in a villa that had been previously rented by the Shah of Iran overlooking Acapulco Bay. Over a week-long 'management offsite' they agreed to carve up Mexico and the southern United States into 'plazas'. For each boss, or *capo*, the plaza was their territory in which to grow, parcel, store and transport narcotics. If another capo's activity encroached on their turf, they had to pay a fee. The trusted Chapo and his close friend, Ismael 'El Mayo' Zambada, were rewarded with the Sinaloa franchise. Chapo was now a made man.

For all his genius, however, Gallardo was still human and suscep-tible to hubris. In 1989, after the Guadalajara cartel became complacent and overplayed its hand, he was captured and jailed in the US for the kidnap in Guadalajara, torture and brutal murder of the US drug enforcement agent Enrique 'Kiki' Camarena in 1985, which prompted a fierce reaction across Mexico. 'When we are good, nobody remembers us. When we are bad, nobody forgets us,' Chapo said later. Kiki's horrible end, together with the alarming number of deaths of US sports stars from cocaine overdoses and the advent in the nation's cities of highly addictive crack cocaine, encouraged US president Ronald Reagan to ramp up the 'war on drugs', and Gallardo was sentenced to thirty-seven years in prison. Matta, too, fled to Honduras and was subsequently arrested and extradited to the US. In the early nineties, back in Sinaloa, Chapo was left in sole command of the Sinaloa cartel, which was sometimes known by its other name of the Blood Alliance.

If Gallardo was good, Chapo was even better. 'Planning, organization, negotiation and looking to the future' were the new head's strengths, according to the Mexican Attorney General's LinkedIn-style endorsement of the drug lord's skills. From the moment he took over, cocaine was Chapo's product of choice, each shipment netting more in profit than equivalent cargoes of cannabis or heroin. He opened smuggling corridors from Colombia and Bolivia to Mexico, to Sinaloa, and then over the border via Arizona and on to the wider US.

All along the shipping routes, from South America to Mexico and into the US, he employed lieutenants to execute his orders and ensure deliveries got through and arrived on time. It was a formidably sophisticated operation fuelled by the twin motivations of money and fear: step out of line or even just be suspected of having stepped out of line or about to step out of line, and the consequences were severe. Chapo was always acutely alert to what may lie around the corner, and he trusted no one. 'Loyalty, honour and respect are words that forget ordinary people,' said Chapo. 'Envy and betrayal do not sleep, they are two things that always go hand in hand.' To make it absolutely clear what was expected of those who worked for him, Chapo ran a brand marketing campaign, of sorts, although rather than using press releases or lunches with journalists, or TV adverts with actors, he employed *sicarios,* or killers, to commit gruesome executions that were filmed and posted as warnings to others. Chapo put his philosophy simply: 'You take care of me, I take care of you. You betray me, I kill you,' and like any good businessman he liked to

keep meticulous records, storing all receipts and logging all his transactions, however small, in accounting books. It was in his nature. 'It's
rude to talk with an empty head' was his take.

He and his people also made use of the latest technology as the
power of the cartel grew, and they communicated via secure walkie-
talkies and every member of the Sinaloa was given a mobile phone
and a personal identification code. By the turn of the century, when
email was just taking off, Chapo, the ultimate capo, was never without his laptop, issuing orders to kill from secure chat rooms. By the
time that the net was closing in on Chapo, one intercept by drug
enforcement investigators showed just how sophisticated the cartel
had become and highlighted just one example of the level of micro-
managing that Chapo employed to stay on top of his enterprise. He
sent a Sinaloan called Jesus Herrera Esperanza, who went by the
name of 'Hondo', to Vancouver. He was twenty-two years old and said
that he was enrolled on a business course at Columbia College in the
city, although the real purpose of his moving to Vancouver was to be
Chapo's representative in Canada because Hondo was supposed to
arrange for the distribution of drugs and collect the takings. Unfortunately for Chapo, Hondo was also careless and drew attention to
himself and his association with the Sinaloa leader. US agents managed to hack into Hondo's Facebook account and found he'd changed
his status to Puro#701. They puzzled over what this meant until they
realized it was 701, Chapo's *Forbes* 'Rich List' ranking.

Hondo was slow with his collection rounds and, in frustration,
Chapo sent him a direct order: 'I want a report every night at seven,
sharp. How much you've sold and how much money you're sitting on.
Break it down by city.' Each night, Hondo did as he'd been told to.
Vancouver: $560,000 and 95 kilos of coke. Winnipeg: $275,000 and
48 kilos. Toronto: $2 million and 150 kilos. In just one day, US inves-
tigators picked up a request for a senior henchman for payment of his
fortnightly expenses of $10,000; authorization for payments to mili-
tary commanders of $40,000 each; a discussion about using heavy

machinery to make an airstrip in a jungle clearing; the granting of permission to spend $200,000 on the transport to move 20 tonnes of marijuana up to the US border; a change of plan about holding a family barbecue in Culiacán because they may be observed and switching to a Chinese restaurant instead; an instruction to a gofer to collect some drugs-packing equipment from a ranch; a request to his accountant for his cash balance and to pay 4,190 pesos to repair a car; a message to his son that he will meet him tomorrow; a breakdown of drugs flights made from one of his airstrips; telling his lawyer to hurry up with the deeds for nine properties; plans to buy a *casa de cambio* – money exchange bureau – that was going out of business; an update on a legal hearing about the seizure of a ship; the sending of flowers and a local five-piece band to a girl in his neighbourhood to serenade her on her birthday. Each morning Chapo received reports from his trusted senior team, and the detail was microscopic. One message read: 'Four *sapos* [toads, a reference to the green uniforms worn by Mexican troops] will be conducting patrols in the Canadas, Las Quintas, Loma Linda and Villa Ordaz neighbourhoods today.' And 'Federal Police will be leaving the airport this morning and there will be movements from Mazatlán to Los Mochis . . .'. This attention to detail, and the need he had to know everything that was going on across his growing empire, was indicative of Chapo's ability to stay one step ahead of the authorities and shows just how plugged in he was to their efforts to seize and defeat him.

Chapo didn't have it all his own way, though, and his main rivals for the market trafficking cocaine into the US were the Arellano Félix brothers, who ran the Tijuana cartel, and Amado Carrillo Fuentes, who claimed Juarez. Some of the time the capos got along and partnered and shared consignments together; on occasion they didn't, violence ensued, and the body count soared. Then relations calmed down, until the next blow-up. In 1993, things took a damaging, very public turn. The Arellano Félix brothers and Chapo were fighting over selling drugs into highly profitable California. On 24 May 1993, a white Mercury Grand Marquis sedan pulled up in the car park at Guadalajara airport. Abruptly, there were rapid bursts of gunshots, and a Wild West-style firefight erupted, during which an AK-47 pumped thirty bullets into the vehicle, and the person in the passenger seat, the driver and five others were killed. The passenger was Cardinal Juan Jesús Posadas Ocampo, the Archbishop of Guadalajara, and fourteen gunshots punctured his body. Soon, word got round: the much-loved Catholic leader and the others were victims of a mistaken identity, of a narco hit gone wrong, and the intended target had been Chapo, who had been in the airport car park, but not in his usual white car; instead he had been using a green Buick and in the chaos that ensued he managed to slip away by taxi. In their search of the car park, police confiscated grenades and high-powered automatic weapons, and in the space of one bloody afternoon what had been a shadowy, largely unseen and little-noticed world, contained within the 'narco on narco' violence in the shadows of the country, exploded onto the national and international front pages and TV news bulletins.

Until that afternoon, in Mexico, the activities of Chapo and his kind had provoked resigned weariness and uncaring shrugs. While people had enjoyed the tales about new-fangled techniques for hiding drugs, they cringed at the stories of the gaudy, flash lifestyles of some of the capos and their families; and now and again, they gaped, then turned away from evidence of an especially theatrical piece of savagery, but generally they were little bothered. Drug trafficking and the flashes of carnage belonged to pockets of the country, usually in the border regions of the north and north-west, and normally involved groups of criminals. Cardinal Posadas's death changed all that; suddenly, all Mexico knew that they had a major problem. Overnight, Chapo acquired national and global notoriety. Sketches of his fleshy face adorned newspapers and TV screens, and everyone came to know and have an opinion on 'Shorty', his riches, drug trafficking and disregard for human life, his devotion to his mother, his love and admiration for the opposite sex. 'Women can be quiet, heartfelt or angry, but you will never see them defeated,' he once said. After the cardinal's shooting, sensing it was when, not if, the Mexican authorities snared him, Chapo made a run for sanctuary. He paid senior cronies to look after his family and left the country using a false passport, accompanied by a girlfriend and bodyguards, and crossed the southern border into Guatemala. His evasion was short-lived and on 9 June 1993, little more than two weeks after the cardinal was shot, Chapo was traced to a hotel near the Mexican border and arrested.

Shortly afterwards, Chapo was flown back to Mexico and taken to Altiplano high-security jail, all in the full glare of national and international publicity. The Mexican government milked his seizure for all it was worth, exhibiting to a watching world their determination to defeat the cartels. This was the very point when HSBC was contemplating moving into Mexico. At first glance, what unfolded was reassuring. But if they had stopped and considered, they might have been less persuaded. Cardinal Posadas bore no resemblance to Chapo. He was tall; the latter was short. He was wearing a dog collar, not the garb you'd normally associate with a gun-toting drug baron. He was in a white car, Chapo's was green. Arrests were made in connection with the shootout, but no one was convicted directly of the cleric's death – they never have been. The Tijuana cartel was blamed, but they were said to have recruited members of a gang from California and several of the latter were convicted, but not of the cardinal's actual murder. Far from being a planned clinical assassination of Chapo, there were several people from rival factions in the car park armed to the hilt and what transpired was more a Wild West, every-man-for-himself shootout, all of which was covered by a feverish press, eager to fill their pages with increasingly gory stories of Mexico's bad lands. Then it was alleged that the cardinal had been warned his life was in danger, that he knew too much, linking members of the Mexican ruling political elite with the narcos, with drugs and prostitution. And next came the claims of police obstruction and key evidence going missing, which led many Mexicans, including politicians and senior figures in the Catholic Church, to believe the cardinal's death was politically motivated and that he was, in fact, deliberately targeted. No sooner had the cardinal's death occurred and been pored over than along came Colosio and the promise of a cleaner, less corrupt Mexico. With Colosio running for president and leading in the polls, and Chapo, the drugs kingpin, behind bars and awaiting trial, optimism appeared well-founded. The killing of Colosio put paid to that. As with the previous murder of Posadas, the name of Chapo quickly surfaced in connection with Colosio's assassination. Several theories suggested that Chapo was secretly funding the politician's election effort, that he saw the country's would-be president – or 'the leader', as Chapo was said to call Colosio – as getting him closer to political power and impunity, that his underworld rivals knew this and therefore Colosio must be stopped. Or, because Chapo was backing him, members of the already furious PRI concluded he had the financial wherewithal to mount a successful campaign and there was only one way to prevent him becoming president. What was certainly the case was that Chapo was in jail when Colosio was murdered. Twice he was asked about his involvement, and his answer was simple: he knew nothing.

On 22 November 1995, Chapo was convicted of possession of firearms and drug trafficking and sentenced to twenty years, then was quickly moved from the prison in Altiplano to a secure jail in Guadalajara where he proceeded to lead a life of luxury. Prison officials were bribed to allow him conjugal visits from his wife, girlfriends and prostitutes and he had access to alcohol and was made special meals. He arranged for a female prisoner in another jail to be transferred to his jail, where she became another of his girlfriends, and all the while from his cell he continued to run the cartel, diversifying its product range from cocaine, marijuana and heroin to take in the manufacture and smuggling of methamphetamine. It was while he was in prison that Chapo even managed to arrange for the precursor chemicals needed to make 'crystal meth' to be imported from Africa, China and India. But it wasn't all plain-sailing – a dark cloud was looming. In 1995, Chapo was charged in the US with racketeering and conspiracy to import cocaine. A subsequent Mexican court ruling made extradition easier and would mean transfer to the US and the less amenable US legal system was a real possibility.

To be isolated from his friends and family, from his network, in an undoubtedly maximum-security US federal jail was the last thing he wanted and so, on 19 January 2001, the day after the extradition ruling moved into law, he slipped out of the prison and made a run for it. For a while he'd been assiduously courting and paying officials and police and had even funded the medical operation of the son of one of the guards. When the time came to call in the favours, he hid in a laundry sack and was driven out of the gates in the back of the laundry truck. Chapo's exit had cost him $2.5 million in bribes. 'It doesn't matter how many times you feel trapped. There is always a way out. Don't give up,' was his attitude. The escape was sensational news, and the government of Vicente Fox was so mortified that it threw everything at trying to find him. The army was drafted in to launch a manhunt, press and poster adverts requested anyone with information to call a hotline. Chapo, despite his thuggish cruelty, despite his deadly trade, had captured the public imagination. The hotline received plenty of calls, but from people roaring with laughter. As for the man himself, he hosted a party for his sidekicks in the cartel boss's native Sierra Madre hideaway.

He may have vanished but Chapo was unavoidable throughout Mexico. Part-expression of sympathy at the plight of the poor, part-protest at the corruption of the government and police, the popular *narcocorrido* ballads salute those who live and die by trafficking drugs. In all, Chapo has at least ten songs written about him. One is '50 Mil Rosas Rojas', 50,000 Red Roses, on the shooting dead of Chapo's twenty-two-year-old university student son Edgar by sicarios working for another drugs boss. A grieving Chapo bought 50,000 red roses – all the stock in north-west Mexico – for his grave. Another is 'El Primer Ministro', the Prime Minister. On 'El Encuentro', the Encounter, the singer sings from the point of view of Chapo and refers to army soldiers as being 'no match' for the drug baron. There's also 'El Papá de los Pollitos', the Father of all Chickens, which portrays Chapo's lifestyle, and 'El Señor de la Montaña', the Mountain Man, which describes the protection Chapo enjoys from high-ranking officials. After his escape, two more songs were being raucously sung across the country: 'Las Voces del Rancho' portrayed Culiacán in festive mood. Another was 'El Regreso del Chapo', the Return of Chapo 'the brave', one of 'the greats'.

The *narcocorridos* have been likened to the current rap and drill. To a point, in that they also glory in crime and violence, in gangs attacking each other and defeating the police, garnering riches. But the more recent genres do not reach the wider population and the older-age demographic, and the same is true of the Mexican songs. Folk who have no connection with the cartels, with drug trafficking, will merrily sing along, because they're seen as defiantly going against a government and authority that is historically linked to corruption and trampling over ordinary people – the same people so vividly portrayed by the famous local artist Juan O'Gorman in his epic mural in HSBC's Mexico City palace, *Credit Transforms Mexico*. Given the *narcocorridos'* popularity, if you were HSBC, you might have thought twice about plunging into a country where such behaviour was venerated; you might have wondered whether it was wise to be buying a bank with an extensive branch network in the cartels' regional heartlands, and you may have had your doubts about the effectiveness of the president and government where law and order was concerned. There again, you may have assumed, as HSBC did, that Fox and his government would get on top of the gangsters and that the narcos were confined to one small area, that it's a localized Mexican issue, of no lasting importance, that it would soon go away.

This lofty view by a giant bank, the focus on global matters, on higher topics, the disinterest in the little folk, has a familiar ring. I recall asking a friend who worked at a US bank in London in a senior capacity on the eve of a general election ballot in Britain whether he was excited about the contest, who did his bosses want to win? He was nonplussed and replied that his employers really were not bothered – the bank was more interested in the bigger picture, in events internationally, and that right now, for instance, they were more concerned about the development of privatization programmes in the Tiger economies in Asia. On another occasion, I was having lunch with a senior banker at Goldman Sachs in London, ahead of the Scottish referendum vote. Britain was convulsing, the battle was close-fought, passions were riding high on both sides and there was a very real likelihood that Scotland would gain its independence and the centuries-old union would disintegrate. Again, the banking chief was disinterested. Strategy, and making big plays and bold strokes, were what he did. Like the players of Risk seeking new territories to invade and conquer, the two international bankers ranged globally, in the stratosphere. Their lives were ones of private jets and business first, criss-crossing the planet in search for more deals, profits and bonuses. What was occurring below, to ordinary people, did not bother them.

For their part, Mexicans had zero faith in Fox's ability to crush the cartels and a large proportion went further and believed their president was in league with the crime bosses, which was how Chapo's absconding and non-capture were widely seen. The recurring theory was that Fox and his colleagues must have been in league with Guzmán and his Blood Alliance for him to be able to escape and hide in the way he did. Most people suspected that it suited the government to have one drug lord as the undisputed number one because by doing so the country became easier to manage, and that with Chapo free the divide between the administration and the country's other ruling elite, the wealthy criminals, would be cleaner, or at least the government would know who it was dealing with. In other words, it was far better to work closely with one boss to bring the cartels into line, and with them the nation, rather than risk the alternative chaos that might ensue in a free-for-all over the drugs trade. It's a theme that is repeated constantly in Mexico – the marriage between elected and unelected power – to a degree that doesn't exist in many other countries.

Unfortunately, there is no evidence connecting Chapo with Fox. More probable was that the Sinaloa chief was too good, too smart and was able to run rings around the authorities. That, too, should perhaps have made HSBC tread cautiously. Fox, in any case, was keen to play down the significance of Chapo's disappearance. 'It is an important case. But it is not the hallmark of my government. One swallow does not make a summer . . .' That was not how it felt out in the countryside, where the army and police were moving heaven and earth to find and recapture Chapo. But with every month that passed and he still had not been recaptured, his legendary status grew. He was popularly described as 'another Osama bin Laden', a public enemy number one who was beyond the reach of the law. Sightings were reported, but by the time the police got there, he'd departed – if he was ever there at all. He was rumoured to be moving around his native Sierra Madre from one safe house to another, or else he was living on one of the ranches he owned, or he had undergone plastic surgery and now looked totally different. There were reports of Chapo's men turning up at restaurants and demanding everyone's mobile phones, then the door would open again, and in would walk Chapo with his bodyguards. They would proceed to the back, where they would consume plates of meat, squid and shrimp washed down with bottles of cold beer and when the other diners were told they could leave, their phones were returned, and they were informed 'the Boss' would cover their bills.

While on the run Chapo became attracted to a teenage beauty queen called Emma Aispuro and a dance was held in her honour. On the day of the festivities, the roads into her rural village were sealed off by men on motorcycles wearing balaclavas and carrying weapons. A small plane landed at a nearby airstrip bearing one of Chapo's favourite music groups and then a second aircraft landed. From the steps of one of them disembarked Chapo, dressed in jeans, sweatshirt and trainers and holding an AK-47. Chapo and Emma enjoyed themselves, dancing until late. A few weeks afterwards, Chapo was married for the fourth time, to Emma. Photos appeared of the newlyweds dancing and smiling together. 'The most beautiful woman is the one who is never divulging, she knows what she is, what everything else is worth to her,' Chapo once mused on how to buy a woman's silence. Meanwhile, troops and police scoured the hills, towns and villages for him, to no avail. They attempted other tactics that involved female intelligence officers being sent in to seduce senior narcos. On one roadside, two military intelligent agents who had been working undercover, pretending to be campesinos growing marijuana, were found dead. A note was left by their bodies: 'You'll never get Chapo.' Wherever Chapo was, he was able to still manage the Sinaloa cartel and steer it on an explosive growth path and defeat rival cartels – coincidentally, at exactly the same time the HSBC bank was embarking on its own upward expansion curve and taking a fresh look at Mexico. The fact he was a fugitive did not affect Chapo's business because he always operated in the dark recesses – it was not like he'd been managing a chain of retail stores; he'd not exactly been front of house, even in previous times.

His world was secret well before he climbed into a laundry sack and disappeared. So long as he had his close protection and he could count on those nearest to him to be absolutely loyal and silent as to his whereabouts, and provided he was vigilant, he would function effectively. He had everything he required. In a description that could easily apply to a bank intent on becoming the biggest in the world, the Attorney General's office said of Chapo that his aim was 'to attain an omnipotent status that will allow him to form international alliances.' In the US, the DEA was alive to Chapo's expansionism: 'The spread of the Sinaloa cartel is a direct threat to the safety and security of law-abiding citizens everywhere,' said the agency's chief Michele M. Leonhart. What was especially concerning was the thought of Chapo's organization joining with gangs in the US, to flood the nation with drugs. The idea of the Sinaloa teaming up with the heavily armed gangs in cities like New York, Chicago and Los Angeles was frightening. Medina Mora, the Mexican Attorney General, hailed this vision, 'the sleeping monster in the US basement.' But it wasn't just the gangs that they were concerned about. The former US DEA chief of operations, Michael Braun, said he was haunted by global tie-ups between Chapo's people and terrorists. 'They're staying in the same shady bars, sharing the same prostitutes, and developing relationships today that will soon evolve from personal to strategic.' It was conceivable that shortly, 'corporate al-Qaeda will be able to pick up the phone and call corporate Sinaloa . . . it's going to bite us in the ass.' The comparison with Osama bin Laden was not so far-fetched after all.

FOUR

HSBC's new clients

In *Breaking Bad*, the TV drama's central character, Walter White, is asked whether he is 'in the meth business or the money business?' Replies White: 'I'm in the empire business.' Jesus Zambada, a Chapo senior lieutenant and the Sinaloa's 'chief accountant', would later, in 2018, describe his criminal organization in the sort of management terminology that could just as easily apply to any ordinary, legitimate enterprise: 'The object of the business is to control the market and prices of the product that the cartel manages, and also expenses for the services that are necessary to make the product arrive at the customer.' Jesus detailed: a shipment to Los Angeles would sell at a street value of $20,000 a kilo, with transport costs of $7,000, so that a delivery for which the Sinaloa were 'in' for 15,000 kilos would reap $13,000 a kilo – a total of $195 million to the cartel. For Chicago, the transport cost rose to $9,000 a kilo, but the street price was higher – $25,000 a kilo – so that 'the profits would be $16,000 per kilo', netting $240 million. New York was the prize market, with costs still at $9,000 but a street price of $35,000. 'That would produce a profit of $26,000 per kilo,' said Jesus, making $390 million in total from a single articulated truck. When pressed on the overall numbers he was seeing in an average year, Jesus, the chief accountant, replied, 'billions'. Most of it came 'back to Mexico' to be 'invested in other shipments'.

AS SIMPLE AS it sounded, in 2003 Chapo had a major headache, because as adept as the Sinaloa were at smuggling narcotics, arranging for their sale, and covering all the bases in-between for their own protection – from bunging bribes to officials and police to butchering anyone perceived to be a risk – theirs was a cash-only business and everyone along the chain dealt in used US dollar bills. Handling cash worked well for the cartel, up to a point, because it avoided leaving a trail and allowed them to evade the authorities, but as they grew bigger and increasingly engaged with the legal, visible, above-ground world, the Sinaloa had a problem. The trucks, ships, aircraft and trains they required, the machinery they needed for the airstrips, train lines, the fuel all required payment by bank credit card, cheque or wire transfer. As did the gaudy mansions they built and bought, including the two private zoos Chapo owned where guests could take a little train and gawp at crocodiles and panthers, a yacht called Chapito and a $10-million beach house at Acapulco, plus ranches in Guadalajara with tennis courts and swimming pools, the flash cars they craved to drive, the powerboats, the jewellery and watches, their wives' and mistresses' designer clothes, their children's smart education. These were not the sort of things you could pay for with bundles of used dollar bills. As the cartel business grew, so Chapo and his crew came to realize that they would need to launder the money, clean the cash, by paying it into a bona-fide bank, into accounts with names and numbers. The additional challenge they faced was that Chapo couldn't keep the drugs proceeds in the US, where it was virtually impossible for anyone to turn up at a bank branch carrying a holdall bursting with cash since, by law, any cash deposit of $10,000 or more has to be reported. The regulations were made tighter still after the terrorist attacks in 2001. To start with, the Sinaloa cartel tried to get around the rule by hiring an army of people to make small deposits, a technique with the technical name of 'structuring', but this kind of money laundering is time-consuming to organize, entailing the use of numerous people, and many of them end up getting rumbled.

What Chapo increasingly realized was that they needed access to a suitable banking operation in Mexico that would allow them to clean billions of used dollar bills with minimal scrutiny. And so, in 2003, while the HSBC senior executives were enjoying planning the 'greenest tower' in Mexico City, poring over the design of waterless urinals, approving advertising posters for the blanketing of Mexico and discussing bringing HSBC-branded, sophisticated financial products into the country, from his hideaway Chapo decided to probe and test the new arrival, and to his delight, the Sinaloa boss discovered that his lieutenants could pay enormous sums in cash into HSBC branches, with few, if any, questions asked. As the years passed the sums being paid in grew exponentially, but their record was $933,000 paid in, all in one go, from one customer at one branch handed over by a courier who stood in the bank paying in eighteen bundles of $50,000, plus remaining notes.

However, depositing huge amounts of dollars regularly at bank branches is also not without its risk, even in Mexico, and even for Chapo and his henchmen – who worked hard at maintaining their reputation for savagery and instilling terror in the community. The deposits they were making were many and constant and dollar bills in that quantity are heavy and cumbersome – $1 million in $100 bills weighs 22 pounds; in $5 bills, 440 pounds. The deliveries required protection because there was always the chance the couriers themselves could fall victim to an armed robbery and Chapo soon grasped it was obvious to anyone outside a branch watching someone entering a bank with a large bag and leaving minutes later with it empty, what was going on. So Chapo came up with one of his creative, leftfield solutions, and having arranged for someone to take the measurements of the slot under the window inside HSBC through which the money is deposited to the bank teller, he made his own secure, low-key, business-like, ease-of-use cases. These cases were custom-made to fit exactly the size of the gap under the teller windows and could be attached to the wrist of the carrier so someone couldn't grab them and make off with them. 'A guy goes in,' said a former Mexico banking supervisor. 'He's carrying a portfolio or pouch that is thick and long, he pushes the portfolio under the window. In some cases, the teller takes it and puts it on the floor and reaches for a cashier's cheque which is already written out. They give it to the guy, who leaves. The whole transaction takes five seconds. Or they wait while the money is discreetly counted, a cheque is written out. It still does not take long. It happens again and again.' Chapo and the Sinaloa were thrilled with this new system of depositing their cash for laundering, because it was much more secure and discreet than the previous system, which involved suitcases and carrier bags bursting with notes. Every time one of his crew arrived at the bank they looked like an ordinary customer and could be mistaken for any other business client handing over what seemed like a large envelope.

As the business grew, so too did the demand for greater capacity to deposit money, but a flaw was discovered with the specially designed holders because the cases could only ever be as large as the slot under the teller's window. To be able to deposit more money in one go they would need to use bigger cases, and the only way to do that would be to change the size of the window in the banks to enable them to accommodate larger cases. In the subsequent case brought against HSBC for enabling Chapo to launder money, it was claimed that at some branches of HSBC that were the most heavily used by the Sinaloa, particularly in its home turf of Sinaloa state and capital Culiacán, the windows were actually widened on request so they could take larger boxes. This might appear relatively trivial, but it is not: the windows used specially reinforced bullet-proof glass, and along with the glass the frames would have needed to be replaced as well, which is the sort of thing that requires regional bank management approval. And to place it in context: this happens nowhere else in the world, not ever. Understandably, no one at HSBC has ever admitted it, and there is no hard evidence for this assumption, but a senior US Attorney insisted to me it was true. No one wanted to admit it, he said, because this was 'a step beyond', as it involved altering the very fabric of the bank's buildings. 'The branch staff knew what was going on, the manager knew, the reporting line above the manager knew, the regional manager knew, the builder knew, the glazier who cut the new window knew. You can't do this without everybody knowing.' All of them, he said, knew this was being done to assist the Sinaloa in legitimizing the profits of their murderous trade, and none of them want to talk.

The money itself, once safely handed over at the local branch of HSBC, was deposited into accounts that were not held in the names of known cartel members or their families – they were never that stupid, and the real ownership of the accounts was obscured, buried under ordinary-looking front companies and people acting as stooges. The Sinaloa heartland and border territories housed thousands of small businesses that ticked all the boxes and appeared perfectly respectable on paper, but closer scrutiny by the bank should have revealed there was not much behind them – they were acting as conduits for drugs money. Individuals, too, held bank accounts, and money flowed freely in and out of them even though the nature of the owners' day jobs suggested they could not possibly be handling such sums. Often, the cartel moved money around between HSBC and two firms that have branches in Mexico and the US: Casa de Cambio Puebla, a currency exchange, and Sigue, a business specializing in transmitting money from the US around the world. One woman opened an account at a HSBC branch in Mexico near the border. As it happened, she used to be an employee of

HSBC, but she claimed her job was now running a small business growing vines, melons and asparagus. In just three months, cash deposits totalling $162,000, which were always of less than $10,000 to avoid close scrutiny, were paid into the account of her backyard business. The money remained in her account only for a very short time before being transferred five ways, via accounts at Casa de Cambio Puebla. One of the recipients was an account belonging to a company buying airplanes via Insured Aircraft Title Service Inc, an aviation brokerage in Oklahoma City in the US – which seemed an odd connection for someone harvesting a few vines, melons and asparagus in up-country Mexico. Following the money, it was clear that this woman was sending it to a company funded by two people, Jorge Barraza and Jorge Medina, who were buying the aircrafts. Through this single chain of transfers and accounts, which was one of thousands used by Chapo's crew, they bought thirteen airplanes, including a DC-9, Falcon 20 and Super King 200, all of which ferried drugs for Chapo from South America to Mexico. The total figure discovered to have been channelled through accounts like this as payment to Barraza and Medina alone came to $13 million – and they were all held by HSBC.

Under Chapo's command, Sigue Corporation arranged for the electronic transfer of dollars to Mexico and other countries in Central and Latin America through a network of more than 7,500 agents across the US. The firm was targeted by US undercover agents in their hunt for Chapo and they found that 'tens of millions of dollars' from drug deals were being sent to Mexico. In one exercise, the agents arranged for $500,000 in cash to be paid into Sigue offices and then wired to Mexico where the money was deposited in small stashes – 'structured' so as to avoid the disclosure requirement. In all, they visited fifty-nine Sigue offices across twenty-two states, and they made no secret of where the cash came from – they openly told the Sigue staffers that they were transmitting illegal drug proceeds, and they were doing it this way to avoid being caught. The Sigue staff went ahead and sent the money anyway. Cheques disclosed that in one year alone, Sigue sent 159 wire transfers for $485 million, all to HSBC accounts in Mexico where HSBC employees were roped in – either as willing accomplices, or under coercion. One network, involving eighty-one clients of the bank, all of them Sinaloa, relied upon the connivance of at least four HSBC workers based in border branches. In cartel-speak they were made the offer of 'silver or lead' – take a bribe or be shot.

The scale of the operation that Chapo was running through HSBC, and the audacity with which he flouted his power in the Mexican countryside, meant that it was not long before word got back to HSBC management as to the vulnerability of some of their staff to corruption. One HSBC senior executive, Paul Thurston, who was based in Mexico City, ventured out to visit the branches and was horrified. 'Bank employees faced very real risks of being targeted for bribery, extortion and kidnapping . . . this was not HSBC as I knew it.' It became clear that staff had been told in no uncertain terms by Chapo's operatives that they 'know where their family lives'. It transpired that they would arrive at the bank with a photo of a relative of the bank worker and flash it to them – to get their attention and their cooperation – then they would deposit their ill-gotten cash and no questions would dare be asked. In other instances they would request and receive a quick loan, handing over wads of used dollars as security. Separating those who acted willingly or those who were forced was not easy, particularly when a system developed that functioned like clockwork. The Sinaloa would deposit their cash, the bank teller would accept it, sometimes with a chit already waiting, and on the money would go into the national and international banking systems. The sums involved were colossal. In 2002, at the time of its purchase, Bital held deposits of $647 million. Under HSBC, that total soon escalated. In one three-month period alone, HSBC Mexico took in nearly $742 million, in cash. For one year, more than $3 billion in cash, in dollar bills, was paid into HSBC Mexico and in another year, the figure was $4 billion. These were totals far ahead of any comparable large Mexican bank and any other HSBC country operation. Chapo quickly came to adore this 'world's local bank'.

For their part, from the very first day HSBC management were more than satisfied with their purchase. The Bital rebranding, the 'sell, sell, sell' instruction, the advertising campaign, the new, brilliant headquarters – they all combined nicely to produce thumping results. Soon, HSBC Mexico broke through the $1-billion profits barrier for the first time, making it the fourth-largest country contributor in the whole of HSBC. Its profits were far in excess of its Latin America siblings – twice those of Brazil and comfortably four times ahead of Argentina's. What was the reason given for this triumph? An internal HSBC management paper said it was due to a strongly performing economy, underpinned partly by oil-related revenues and partly by 'remittances from the USA'. The reference to 'remittances' invoked the historic 'Wayfoong' Chinese moniker for HSBC, meaning 'abundance of remittances', at a time when the payments also partly came from financing the trade in opium. Quite what sort of remittances these were, and where they came from, exactly, the management paper didn't specify, nor did it give any further detail of the provenance of what Bagley called 'substantial flows of cross-border monies'.

Soon enough, their origin would become dreadfully apparent, but for the time being Chapo had nothing to fear – not from HSBC, at any rate. For while Mexico was the darling of Latin America for HSBC, the heads of the bank's bosses were turned firmly elsewhere in their pursuit of the ultimate goal of becoming the biggest bank in the world. The sad reality was that as bold and iconic as the new Mexico City building was, for all the care taken over its design and artwork, and despite the proclamations about the country's significance, day-to-day Mexico was not high on the list of the senior bankers' priorities, not back in group HQ in London. High on the forty-first floor of HSBC in Canary Wharf, the directors were focused on big and bigger, on expanding still further their already mighty corporation. For the bank's top leadership, Mexico, from the moment the HSBC flag was unfurled and the territory seized, had attained a 'been there, done that' aspect to it. The country was simply one more box to be ticked. High Noon was accomplished; in the real-life game of Risk there were new lands to conquer, new markets to attack.

As if to underline this point, shortly after HSBC bought Bital for $1.1 billion, the bank paid $14.2 billion for Household International in the US. How the two came to be together could be straight from a schmaltzy romantic novel – a couple are on opposite sides of a fight, they put their differences behind them, they fall in love and marry. In February 1999, while the bank was busy rebranding, which meant that all parts of the business were going to be herded under the HSBC initials – including Midland, its bank in the UK – they received a writ from the City solicitors, Simmons & Simmons. The law firm claimed there was a danger in HSBC customers believing the bank was linked to their client, HFC, the consumer loan business. When they checked, a stunned HSBC management found that it wasn't a joke and that HFC's bosses in the US, at its Household International parent, really did claim there was a risk of sowing confusion, and as ludicrous as the allegation was nutty, it had to be taken seriously. A court case duly followed, which HSBC, not unexpectedly, won. HFC, undeterred, posted an appeal, and faced with the likelihood of years of protracted legal actions and mounting bills, not to mention a loss of time, two senior HSBC executives flew to Household HQ at Prospect Heights, near Chicago. When they departed for home, in order to save on costs and time, they'd agreed to pay the Americans £20 million to drop the suit, which Household were delighted with.

One of the unexpected consequences of the lawsuit was that the directors at HSBC came away from the agreement impressed with the staff and the operation that they had seen at Household, a company that via HFC and others made loans for pretty much anything to pretty much anyone. HSBC wasn't really in that line of business, so they could complement each other, or that was how it appeared on the surface at least. The fact was that, aside from some consumer finance in Hong Kong and a few other places, HSBC had for most of its life resolutely stayed away from the lower end of the financial market. Historically, most banks, including HSBC, generally like to see themselves as catering for the better off, and they prefer their customers to be affluent, professional types. If they extended personal loans, they were offered to this 'prime' clientele, whereas Household made loans to virtually everyone, right down to the 'subprime' market. Household had begun life flogging payday loans – personal short-term loans for small amounts to tide the borrower over. Then they moved into monthly payment plans that enabled those on lower wages to buy big-ticket items. For HSBC this was anathema. It was not what they did, not where they'd ever wish to be. Or rather they hadn't until they had become emboldened and anxious to do what-ever it took to be the biggest bank in the world.

Bill Dalton, who was head of HSBC UK at the time, is a Canadian who, his colleagues noted approvingly, got his first car loan from Household, which provided about as much strategic insight into any potential deal as Geoghegan's comment that Willie Purves 'knew' Latin America because he had been on honeymoon there. Still, when the globally ambitious bankers got down to crunching the numbers on their downmarket, new 'street' love interest, they liked what they saw. In 2001, North America accounted for 19 per cent of HSBC assets; add Household and it would increase to 29 per cent. House-hold's performance was good; with HSBC and cheaper funding, it could be even better. Like HSBC, Household was another big beast. A Fortune 500 company, at the time HSBC started sizing it up, it had $98 billion of assets, a workforce of 31,000 and 53 million cus-tomers. It sold them loans from 1,400 branches across forty-six states in the US and their customers bought mortgages, took out credit cards, unsecured loans and car loans. The firm held credit finance contracts with 10,500 auto dealers and the credit cards alone had $20 billion sitting on their books, and on acquiring Household HSBC would become, at a stroke, a World Top Ten credit cards operator. This would take HSBC to another level. For the players of Risk, the ultimate prize had never looked so near. By acquiring Household HSBC would be moving, too, into data harvesting and data analytics, since over the previous thirteen years, Household had assembled, according to a Harvard Business School case study, a database that meant it could profile the risk of every adult in the US – all 260 million of them. Household could run sinister-sounding 'neural networks' – described as 'computer programs that can assimilate, adapt and learn from past patterns of consumer behaviour – in order to isolate the personality traits and patterns shared by both safe and unsafe credit risks.' In other words, your data tells Household what you've spent and where, and what you are likely to spend and where. Household may have had its roots in small-town offices and down-home agents dotted across America, but this was a company employing 150 PhDs as data analysts, in its 250-employee 'Data House', at the same time as processing 2 billion transactions a year, or 1,000 per second. Even for HSBC, used to handling large figures, this was head-spinning stuff. As if that was not enough, what whet their appetites even more was the ability to push consumer finance to the entire HSBC 'family' across the world. As Roberts and Kynaston detail in their modern history of the bank, an internal bank report concluded that, 'Household's target customer is not dissimilar from many of our emerging market customer bases', and HSBC saw an opportunity to use Household's expertise and experience to lend to consumers in those new territories it was grabbing, like Brazil and Mexico. The potential was huge, the rewards could be vast. The Risk-players were hooked.

When the engagement between HSBC and Household was announced, HSBC's spinning shifted into hyper-drive and markets and media were told of the 'obvious synergy' – how Household's 'best in class' technology and marketing would combine with HSBC's 'wider geographical markets'. There was much repeating of 'strategic opportunity' and 'unlocking' of strength. To say that Household was 'a subprime' lender was 'unfair', insisted the PRs, as this was but one part of its business. Even so, as with 'Project High Noon', the deal was not well received in some quarters, internally and externally. For some it was viewed as 'un-HSBC', to get down and dirty in what is perceived as the seedier side of finance, in consumer lending. Meanwhile, in Canary Wharf, the bank's leaders were not bothered and they could barely conceal their glee. They told William Aldinger III, Household's chairman, that buying his company was 'the most exciting development in HSBC's recent history', seemingly forgetting that they had spoken in very similar terms about the recent launch of HSBC Mexico. One group of investment analysts pointedly picked up on this and begged to differ, rewording it 'the riskiest move in HSBC's modern history.' The commentator Neil Collins, writing in the *Daily Telegraph*, pointed out that 'changing the culture of a business this big and that far away is quite a challenge and investors are right to be nervous.' Jesse Eisinger in the *Wall Street Journal* was even more trenchant: 'HSBC just went from prudent bank to cowboy.'

The gun-slinger likeness was exacerbated by Aldinger's personal reward of $20 million for getting the deal across the line and a further $37.5 million for staying with the new, combined group for three years. Not everyone was best pleased with Aldinger's good fortune and in the UK, the National Association of Pension Funds did not hold back, saying 'the moral case for the payment is tenuous' – a charge levelled at a bank where Green, the great moralist, promoter of ethical capitalism, writer of sermons on business trips, was the new CEO. At the shareholders' annual meeting, in May 2003, Aldinger's rewards package was raised and the most poignant, contrasting moment was when Abdul Durrant, a night cleaner at HSBC's head office, described the difficulty of raising his family on £5 an hour. Writing in the *Financial Times*, John Plender, too, was unimpressed.

Aldinger's remuneration jars with a bank, 'where the culture remains famously Scottish and penny-pinching.' In *The Times*, Graham Searjeant questioned why Aldinger was so vital, when HSBC 'has operated on regimental lines with an endless supply of trained officers to choose from. That is why, until now, it has stayed successful.' There was a strong sense that since HSBC first took on Mexico and now the US markets in a fashion that was wholly uncharacteristic for a bank like HSBC, the bank was straying not just into dangerous waters, but was also taking itself further away from the very principles on which HSBC had been built. The bank's top tier, however, were undeterred, focusing rather on the fact that now HSBC was gaining national coverage of the US, it would be extending credit, not to the corporation of Coca-Cola, but to the 50 million drinkers of Coca-Cola. The potential for growth was almost overwhelming. The bank would now be taking on the Americans in their own backyard, while edging ever closer to overhauling Citi. It was, in other words, just right for Green's 'Managing for Growth' strategy paper and the new sales-driven culture.

Absorbing a business of Household's size, nevertheless, was a Herculean task. No fewer than thirty-six senior management groups were set up to oversee different aspects of the merger, and for Green, the chief executive, and his team, getting to know the new partner and making the combination work was a full-time operation, and it is not difficult to see how localized issues thousands of miles away, such as Mexico, paled in comparison. But all the hard work paid off and, to the excitement of the HSBC masters in London, the money flowed in almost immediately. The Group Executive Committee was told in July 2003 that 'cost savings might exceed expectations'. In the first year, Household contributed $2.2 billion to HSBC profits; in the second, 2004, $3.6 billion; in 2005, $5.2 billion, and yet, not everyone was so enamoured. One HSBC international manager, who had been sent to New York to help fold Household into the bank, told his wife: 'This doesn't look, feel or smell like Hongkong Bank in any manner, shape or form.' Household's management shared the same desire for bigness and from 2003 to 2006, they doubled the consumer lender's assets from $98 billion to $183 billion. They took the mortgage book from $17 billion to $46 billion and for good measure, they added another credit card operation. An HSBC management paper of July 2004 said that the intention for Household's consumer lending business was to become 'the dominant player in the retail subprime and near-prime markets in our core products, real estate and non-real estate.' The Group CEO, Green, wanted to see all things Household rolled out across the world, telling the Group Management Board that the Group had 'much to learn from the techniques and culture of the US consumer finance operations, with the key to success being [market] segmentation.' The image of the abstemious, hairshirted preacher, expounding on ethical capitalism and agonizing between God and Mammon, now seemed far removed from the reality. In 2005, the drive to export Household's techniques across HSBC World began in earnest, and in less than two years, HSBC in Mexico made consumer loans of $2 billion. 'The emerging market opportunity is even greater than we thought and moving very fast,' reported a Group Management paper.

Even though he was now on the run, at the same time as Green and co. were delighting in their new acquisition and getting to grips with Household's size and scale, and realizing its global profits-generating potential, in Mexico Chapo was getting on building his business empire and between hideouts he plotted a spectacular take-over of his own. In 2003, Chapo ordered a strategy meeting of the Sinaloa leadership and the subject for discussion, just like HSBC, was expansion, getting bigger. Chapo, who attended in person even though he was one of the world's Most Wanted, told those present that their cartel dominated the US-Mexico border from Juarez to the Pacific, but that was not enough. He desired more. Next in their sights, he said, was the region further along the border, the northeast of Mexico into East Texas. Gain control of that and the entire boundary, and all the smuggling routes funnelling up – into the broad land mass of the United States – would be theirs. Their target was Nuevo Laredo, a city of 370,000 inhabitants, sited right on the Rio Grande, where over the water lies the Interstate 35 to San Antonio and the right turn for Houston, or straight ahead for Austin. It was the perfect trafficking gateway into the US. The difficulty for Chapo was that there was already a cartel operating out of the district and it wasn't just any DTO either, but a drug-trafficking organization with a fearsome reputation for especially bloodthirsty sadism called Los Zetas. Theirs is not an outfit that does negotiation, and any move that Chapo made would come with retaliation and, for once, Chapo mis-calculated by sub-contracting the penetration of Nuevo Laredo to another group, the Mara Salvatrucha from El Salvador and Hondu-ras. They were not up to tackling Los Zetas and their dead bodies were identified by the letters 'MS' tattooed on them. That, too, was all police had to go on, as in one gruesome show of strength, the Los Zetas deposited five tortured corpses in one house, each bearing the 'MS' insignia, which was about the only recognizable feature on them. Next to them was a note addressed to Chapo: 'Send more *pen-dejos* for us to kill'. In Mexican slang, *pendejos* means pubic hair. It was grim, and for Chapo, startling and time-consuming.

The Zetas were no pushover; it was as if they'd taken instruction from the master himself, from Chapo, and decided to go the extra distance. As well as bodies, the Zetas hung recruitment banners from bridges. One said: 'We offer you a good salary, food, and attention for your family. Don't suffer abuse and hunger anymore.' Another carried echoes of HSBC, the bank selling its financial products across Mexico with the *Credit Transforms Mexico* mural, promising 'bene-fits, life insurance, a house for your family and children. Stop living in the slums and riding the bus. A new car or truck, your choice.' Chapo had to raise his game to combat Los Zetas and from 2004 the rivalry between the cartels spilled over into a level of grisly blood-letting that left Mexico reeling. One evening five human heads were casually rolled onto a disco dance floor; another day the heads of two policemen were left outside the Acapulco town hall. In response the Sinaloa drew down on their reserves of cash and sourced heavier weaponry and became more military in appearance, kitting out their most elite narcos in combat greens. In one raid on the Sinaloa, in one house, the police recovered twenty automatic rifles, twelve M4 grenade launchers, ten pistols and body armour. The killing got so bad that the Mexican newspapers went so far as to print daily 'execution meters' in a vain attempt to keep up with the rising body count, and while comparisons were made with the dark days after Colosio's murder, this civil war between the rival cartels was worse than anything that Mexico had seen in its long and bloody history of the drugs wars.

While the growing slaughter was making waves in Mexico, thousands of miles away, in the relative peace and calm of HSBC group headquarters, the flashing screen in Geoghegan's office and the reports and strategy papers on Green's desk concerned other priorities. Despite the bloodshed, HSBC Mexico was doing well, and was starting to make a significant contribution to group profits, climbing at pace. As part of HSBC's growth strategy, the senior executives identified another area that, if they got right, could bring in the size, the earnings and returns they sought. The HSBC chiefs had alighted on commercial banking, providing businesses from start-ups to middle market and higher with all the banking services they require. It sounds boring and compared to targeting and taking over an entire country, commercial banking is, but the HSBC leadership was still enthused, not least because it was one of the key components of Green's Managing for Growth. The idea was to hit small, expanding businesses with the bank's full range of products: trade finance, foreign exchange, insurance, hedging, internet-banking, loans, payroll and cash management. Business customers were to receive their own branches, with comfy chairs and meeting areas and dedicated staff, and the atmosphere they wanted to convey was more akin to lawyers' and accountants' offices than a bank. Heady boosterism swept through the bank, from the top down, and the focus on helping small businesses was hailed as 'an incubator for growth, referrals and sales,' by one senior executive. Soon, HSBC was proclaiming 2.5 million business customers generating a 22 per cent slug of overall group profits – several billions' worth, in other words. They gave the strategy a name, the sort they adore: Leading International Business Bank, or LIB for short. While 2.5 million was deemed a success, staff were reminded that there were 9.5 million existing global business customers to go after in total. Country bosses were told to aim to become 'Best Bank for Small Businesses'.

Geoghegan trumpeted it as part of his 'Joining up the Company' policy and the specialist commercial branches were unveiled in Hong Kong and the UK and opened in forty-six countries, and they had their own marketing. 'One of the reasons we're running an advertising campaign reinforcing HSBC's standing as the best and biggest SME bank is because we can,' boasted a top HSBC manager. 'This campaign is designed to help others realise what we already know, namely when it comes to commercial banking no other bank can offer either the reach or the expertise that we do.' As the same manager said, it is about emphasizing 'positive images' and sounding a 'celebratory tone'. From Hong Kong to London, the success of the mood to support small business started to seep through HSBC in Mexico where banking colleagues were either colluding voluntarily or actively assisting the country's most feared drugs cartel and the bank was seeing billions of dollars in used notes come through their branches. In the north of Mexico, coincidentally home to Chapo and the Sinaloa, small businesses galore started opening accounts. While parts of Mexico were being ravaged by the drug wars, the HSBC part of it was booming. The instruction from London came down the pipeline to Mexico to try harder, and to take the 'sell, sell, sell' philosophy that they had so successfully applied to individual customers and extend it to commercial clients, to show them everything the bank could be doing for them and to persuade them to buy, buy, buy. This Mexico did with great aplomb, so much so that in 2005, the Economy Ministry awarded HSBC 'best supporter of SMEs'. And the figures did not lie – thousands of small to medium enterprises across Mexico started using, and being assisted by, HSBC. The bank's Mexico City managers were delighted at collecting such an accolade; the bank's leaders in London were similarly pleased – they were targeting bigger fronts, but Mexico had done everything they'd asked of it and more. The fact that many of those SMEs were fronts for Chapo and his cartel was ignored and only much later did US State Department officials calculate that during this period, from 2003 to 2008, 'as much as US $22 billion may have been repatriated to Mexico from the United States by drug trafficking organizations.' Later, they revised that estimate and said the drug cartels were using Mexican and US financial institutions to launder as much as $39 billion each year: 'According to US authorities, drug trafficking organizations send between $19 billion and $39 billion annually to Mexico from the United States.' The country was awash with drugs and laundered money through a banking structure that facilitated the movement of huge amounts of cash between the US and Mexican borders. But while Chapo remained on the run the set-up of the banking system at least allowed authorities to trace the movement of the money across the borders as they built their case against Chapo in anticipation of finally seizing him again. That was all about to change with HSBC's promotion of the 'Cayman Islands branch', which would allow Chapo's financial movement to go dark on the watching US authorities.

FIVE

The Cayman connection

Despite the bodies piling up, the 'execution meters' in newspapers, the TV newscasts displaying yet more horror; despite all the reports saying that American streets were awash with Mexican drugs and that US dollars were flooding back to Mexico; and despite knowing that Mexico was prone to corrupt and ineffectual law enforcement, from 2002 to 2009 HSBC gave the country its lowest risk rating for money laundering. It gets worse. Under HSBC's own rules, unless there were exceptional reasons why not, a country's customers had the same rating as the country, which meant that the Mexican customers, including all those depositors of the neatly bundled used dollar bills, were categorized as 'low risk' for the purposes of filling out documentation and ID for bank accounts. But it gets worse still, since in the pursuit of ever greater profit, HSBC afforded a system of banking that suited the Chapo's cartel needs perfectly.

The former UK business secretary Vince Cable called secret offshore havens 'sunny places for shady people.' In his book *Treasure Islands: Tax Havens and the Men who Stole the World*, Nicholas Shaxson, a consultant at Britain's Tax Justice Network, said this:

'Offshore connects the criminal underworld with the financial elite, the diplomatic and intelligence establishments with multinational corporations. Offshore drives conflict, shapes our perceptions, creates financial instability and delivers staggering rewards to *les grands* – to the people who matter. Offshore is how the world of power now works.' The former head of the United Nations Office on Drugs and Crime, Antonio Maria Costa, posited that the four pillars of the international banking system are: drug-money laundering, sanctions busting, tax evasion and arms trafficking. Putting a figure on how much they hide is impossible. But the most recurring statistic, used by the various watchdogs, is north of $20 trillion. One estimate reckons the total is $32 trillion, and one of the most well-known centres of offshore banking is the tiny Cayman Islands in the Western Caribbean, south of Cuba, northeast of Honduras, 520 miles from Mexico's Yucatan Peninsula.

The capital city is George Town on Grand Cayman, the most populous of the three islands. The islands were discovered by Christopher Columbus when his ship was blown off course in 1503, says the official history. Later, 'a map was drawn showing all three islands in the area with the name "Lagartos", meaning alligators or large lizards.' By 1530, the trio was called the 'Caimanas' – derived from the native word for the crocodiles that used to dwell there. 'It was our ample supply of turtle that made Cayman a popular port for ships in need of meat for their crews. However, the earliest settlers arrived in the islands around 1658 as deserters from the British Army in Jamaica. The first colonists were named Bodden and Watler – with fishermen, slaves, sailors and refugees from the Spanish Inquisition soon to follow.' Cayman is also a major offshore haven, no less than the fifth-biggest financial centre in the world is a regular assessment. In 2017, Cayman (population 64,000) came higher in the Global Financial Centres Index ranking for international financial clout than Paris. The official guide says the locals like to fish or look after tourists, and make rope and indulge in pastimes like racing catboats. That may be so, but the main business is financial services, enabling people from across the globe, for whatever reason, to conceal their wealth. It could be because they shouldn't have the money; it doesn't belong to them; they got it illegally; or they may not want others to know they have it – prying relatives, employers, business associates, the tax inspectors. Whatever, they require it sheltered, hidden in accounts in ever-so-happy-to-oblige Cayman. The importance of the trade is obvious in George Town, and the flash glass buildings set back from the shops on the seafront selling flip-flops, hats and sun creams aren't hotels, but offices filled with accountants, lawyers and 'wealth management' advisors.

When Barack Obama chose to have a pop at those locations that specialize in helping people and corporations keep their financial affairs well away from the reach of the authorities in countries like his own, the US president singled out Cayman. He alighted on just one office block in George Town: Ugland House, which he said housed 12,000 corporations. 'Now, that's either the biggest building or the biggest tax scam on record.' For the record there are now 20,000 companies registered in Ugland House, and 100,000 companies in Cayman as a whole. However, there is no sign of the companies' physical presence because they don't exist in Cayman anywhere except on paper or in electronic folders where they live as shell companies. Nevertheless, these shell companies crop up right across the world, as the owners of apartments in New York and London and elsewhere, as the names behind villas and yachts and, yes, cocaine-carrying aircraft. The payer of the school fees? A company in Cayman. The purchaser of the coveted painting? A company in Cayman. The brand-new Lambo? A company in Cayman. The island has a small domestic economy but Cayman attracts more external wealth than countries such as Japan and Canada – despite them having economies several hundred times larger. Companies registered there do not need to file a tax return so it's unknown, except to them, how much they make, and hedge funds choose to register in

Cayman because there are no direct taxes, because the legal system follows good old English common law, and because it affords total secrecy. It's true: Cayman levies no income tax on individuals and no corporate tax of any kind. Two-thirds of the world's hedge funds are located there, accounting for $1.3 trillion, and making Cayman the largest holder of US securities in the world. When Hurricane Ivan hurtled towards the Cayman Islands in 2004, a fleet of light aircraft took off from Cayman for Miami. They were carrying computer hard disks, storing details of a large slice of the world's money. As soon as Ivan blew its way through, the aircraft flew them all straight back again, because Cayman is 'home' to 10,000 investment funds and holds one-fifteenth of the world's estimated $30 trillion of banking assets. A sunny place for shady people, indeed.

Obama's speech ruffled a fair number of feathers in George Town, not least those of law firm Maples, the sole tenant at Ugland House. The lawyers huffed and puffed that 'companies registered at Ugland House are described as "shells", owned by individuals to evade tax and take advantage of secrecy laws. This is not the case and mischaracterizes the true purpose of setting up Cayman companies.' The lawyers continued: 'Cayman Islands strongly adheres to international anti-money laundering and anti-terrorist financing standards . . . Offshore vehicles, such as those registered at Ugland House . . . make a lasting and necessary contribution to economies and jobs onshore and play a crucial role in the worldwide economic recovery and growth as a whole. This is a well-known understanding of the nature of institutional financial work by those within the industry but is often misunderstood by the wider public.' The message was carefully worded, as you might expect from lawyers, and this rationale of creating jobs onshore is often repeated by those who use such places. Sir Philip Green was fond of making the same claim to me, whenever he justified relocating the home of his UK retail empire to Monaco and putting it in his wife Tina's name. The billionaire would argue that he had a workforce of 60,000 in the UK who all paid UK income tax, ignoring the fact that they had no choice, unlike him and Tina, who could choose how Arcadia's profits were taxed since the workers' dues were deducted automatically at source from their pay slips. Kurt Tibbetts, the then Cayman Islands political leader, wrote to Obama: 'The Cayman Islands operates a financial services sector that, by any measure against global standards, is regulated, transparent and cooperative.' And he wasn't the only one to take umbrage with Obama. One Caribbean critic of Obama said: 'I was surprised, you know, for a Harvard-educated lawyer not to know how the financial services sector works. There's no money in Cayman; that money is in London, that money is in New York, that money is in the big centres of the world. Cayman is not a big money centre, it is a facility.' That's quite a word, facility. A laundromat is 'a facility'.

Banks like HSBC serve ordinary people, and when they are not looking to grow through scale, as with a deal like Household, they reap the higher profits from looking after individuals with plenty of money. For this privileged echelon banks like HSBC provide 'special services', making available to them a smorgasbord of financial products, advice and schemes, using their networks of offices and ultra-discreet staff, all for a fee. As the former US Senate investigator Jack Blum said, however: 'If you have clients who are interested in "specialty services" – that's the euphemism for the bad stuff – you can charge 'em whatever you want. The margin on laundered money for years has been roughly 20 per cent.'

In Mexico, Chapo had another problem to do with washing the money through bank accounts, because by Mexican law those accounts must be held in pesos rather than dollars. The peso has always been notoriously volatile and weak, which means in both legitimate and illegitimate business the international currency of choice is the mighty US dollar, and what Chapo needed was to be able to open accounts in Mexico in US dollars, which was a facility that HSBC were able to offer through their Cayman branch. Along the seafront from Ugland House, past the Lobster Pot restaurant and towards Bacaro, another favourite of the well-heeled business crowd, as opposed to the native rope-makers and catboat racers, is 68 West Bay Road. This is HSBC House and the low-slung building with the HSBC sign outside looks for all the world like the bank's branch in Cayman. Modern, blue-coloured and designed by an architect from Florida – although for once without the lions guarding the entrance – it is part of the HSBC network all right, and it provides HSBC banking services. However, this is not the section of the bank that looked after the Sinaloa money, which came to be looked after by the 'Cayman Islands branch of HSBC Mexico', which confusingly is not in Cayman at all. It's no use trying to find the 'Cayman Islands branch of HSBC Mexico' on the map or on a George Town street in bricks and mortar. It doesn't physically exist and it never has. The 'Cayman Islands branch of HSBC Mexico' that allowed Chapo to keep his dollars in Mexico and away from the eyes of the US authorities was controlled electronically from the HSBC Torre in downtown Mexico City, 1157 miles away from George Town. It possessed no staff or customers in the Cayman Islands and was totally made-up. It existed, but it is not real in the way bank branches normally are, with proper premises, with branded signs, a solid front door, banking hall, counters and ATMs; instead the 'Cayman Islands branch of HSBC Mexico' existed in the Mexico headquarters and in branches across Mexico, and only in the minds of HSBC staff and their clients, on paper and on computer screens. And yet, by clicking their mouses, by making a few keystrokes, HSBC employees in the branches across Mexico could access it instantly, create accounts there and transfer money there. The people 'staffing' the 'Cayman Islands branch of HSBC Mexico' never went to Cayman and they did not know George Town from anywhere else in the world. And that is really the point: it could have been anywhere in the world and it gave those who availed themselves of its services access to anywhere in the world. As such, US investigators confirmed it 'operated in that jurisdiction solely as a shell entity. It was maintained by [HSBC Mexico] personnel in Mexico. Any branch across Mexico had the authority to open a Cayman account for a client.' HSBC inherited the Cayman 'branch' when it purchased Bital who, twenty years previously, had received a licence from Cayman Islands regulators to offer Cayman US dollar accounts to their customers, but Bital hardly made use of it. After High Noon and the acquisition the Cayman branch of Bital was renamed 'HSBC Mexico' and continued to operate under what's known as a Cayman 'Class B banking license, restricting the branch to operating only "offshore" and open accounts exclusively for non-Cayman residents.' In other words, it's a licence that allows a bank to call itself a 'Cayman bank' but it can only operate offshore – that is, not in Cayman – and it can only serve non-Cayman residents – that is, people not in Cayman – and these financial services come with an entire network of specialists eager to help, like one of the leading law firms in Cayman, Francis Grey. In their publicity they say 'We're a specialist Cayman Islands law firm providing advice on corporate and commercial law for everyone, from large financial service providers to emerging managers and private investors with big aspirations. We offer focused, bespoke legal service. The work that we undertake is cross border, multi-jurisdictional and intricate; requiring senior advisors who are able to give advice with authority.' Who are Francis Grey's clients, the sort of people who are drawn to Cayman? 'Our clients are dynamic, sophisticated and ambitious and we embrace their requirement to challenge conventional hours and ways of working. We consider it a privilege to serve as our clients' trusted advisor and aim to build strong personal connections to our clients and their businesses. We continue to look for ways to improve our service and to provide innovative solutions.' Why set up a bank there? 'The Cayman Islands is a leading international financial centre and is a desirable and favoured jurisdiction for the establishment of banking operations on account of its fine reputation, tax neutrality, reliable legal system, balanced regulatory regime and stable political and economic environment.' Except, says Francis Grey, you're not really setting up a bank there at all. The Category B licence, 'enables the holder to carry on unrestricted banking business anywhere in the world from Cayman, except that it may not service clients within the Cayman Islands itself, subject to limited exceptions. Thus, the licensee is not permitted to:

'take deposits from any person resident in Cayman, other than another licensee or an exempted or ordinary non-resident company which is not carrying on business in Cayman;

invest in any asset which represents a claim on any person resident in Cayman, other than a claim resulting from (a) a loan to an exempted or ordinary non-resident company which is not carrying on business in Cayman, (b) a mortgage loan to one of the licensee's employees for the purchase or construction of an owner-occupied residence in Cayman, (c) a transaction with another licensee, or (d) the purchase of bonds or securities issued by the Cayman Government; or

carry on any business which is outside the express scope of the Category "B" licence without written approval from CIMA.'

At the last count there were 147 banks with a Cayman banking licence – eleven with Class As and 136 with Class Bs, and there is growing interest today in Class As and Class Bs from China, where there are lots of organizations that want to obtain Cayman Class B banking licences. For the record, the practice, and indeed the Cayman Islands as a whole, are condoned and protected by Britain.

For a brief period, under Bital's new owner, HSBC, the Cayman Class B licence wasn't used much and the 'Cayman branch' had just 1,500 accounts, but within three years, as per the Managing for Growth strategy, 'sell, sell, sell' and the furious pursuit of all things big took hold and that figure exploded, to more than 60,000 accounts for nearly 50,000 customers, with total assets approaching $2.1 billion by 2006. The accounts allowed HSBC in Mexico to by-pass local regulations forbidding Mexican residents from holding US-dollar accounts. The fictitious 'Cayman Islands branch of HSBC Mexico' allowed Chapo and the cartel to use their dollars to smoothly enter the world's financial system, to buy whatever they were able to afford wherever they wanted – always with the imprimatur of having the ultra-respectable HSBC behind them – and away from the prying eyes of the authorities. Nobody doing business with them would ever know that there was no actual branch, that the mobsters' front organizations were dealing with the same branch in Culiacán or some other place in Mexico who received and banked their piles of dirty dollar bills, and it is through this system that the Sinaloa were able to buy, for example, some of their aircraft – three airplanes used to ferry drugs were purchased by a company in Miami with dollars sent from the 'Cayman Islands branch of HSBC Mexico'. What is more, this wasn't like a branch, either, where you have to complete lots of forms and show ID – the helpful HSBC Mexico staff did it all for you. The 'Cayman Islands branch of HSBC Mexico' assisted clients in forming Cayman Islands shell companies if they wished, while all that time the branch itself was a shell. As for the petty bureaucratic bit, supplying the security details, that wasn't a problem, either. At least 15 per cent of the accounts, according to internal HSBC findings that came out years later, contained no detail at all that could be checked regarding the account holder. Later, under scrutiny, one HSBC compliance officer admitted that the accounts were being 'misused by organized crime', but at the time it was happening, HSBC did not stop to check the accounts to see what money was going in and out. In more than 50 per cent of cases, nobody from HSBC ever met the supposed account holder; it was not clear what nationalities they were – foreigners were incorrectly described as Mexican nationals; and 7,500 accounts had no files at all. 'How do you locate clients when you have no file?' noted one senior bank executive. But no one was bothered. 'No actions had appeared to be taken to instruct RMs [Relationship Managers] to complete a client's file again.'

As for the rest of HSBC, it did not know what was going on – HSBC in the US, for example, had no idea that the accounts in the

Cayman were so dodgy. As far as they were concerned, they were dollar accounts, same as any dollar account anywhere else in the bank. Management, though, was able to look at their screens and see more than 60,000 accounts, all of them coming out of Mexico, together holding more than $2.2 billion. Instead, under the new, aggressive, push for growth, the culture that was encouraged was to explain that how much the staff in Mexico would be paid was based on how many investment products they could sell. An HSBC internal audit report compiled at the time when the number of new account holders at the 'Cayman Islands branch of HSBC Mexico' was rapidly increasing, said that HSBC Mexico 'offers their clients the option to open USD current and investment accounts in Grand Cayman so that clients profit [from] the advantages of that country, such as tax-free investments, under confidentiality terms.' An HSBC email from around the same time noted, in relation to these Cayman accounts, the extra money-making opportunities they brought: 'Because Mexico's tax scheme is relatively penal (worldwide income) there is a high demand for offshore products.' In Mexico, but not in Mexico; in dollars not in pesos; secret and tax free – HSBC was doing everything that Obama so railed against, and then contrast this treatment afforded by HSBC to its cash-rich clients, those it encouraged to open accounts 'in Cayman', with the ordinary Mexican customer who must put up with long lines and lengthy waits on the phone should they decide to call, hang-ups and transfers, while the Sinaloa had ways of getting to the front of the queue, of ensuring 'special' treatment. One consumer complaint provides a flavour: 'When the news arrived of his mother taking ill, Carlos returned from Mexico City to his hometown in the state of Guerrero in order to take care of her. Due to her worsening condition, a stay that was supposed to last a few weeks turned into several months. When Carlos returned to the capital, he went to take out money only to find that his balance had been slashed. Suspecting robbery or fraud, he made a visit to his branch, only to find that the cause of the missing funds was entirely different: while he was gone, HSBC had raised the monthly minimum balance requirement in his account from $4,000 to $4,500 pesos (US$175 to $200) and, because his balance was beneath the new limit, had been deducting $300 pesos a month (US$13.50) from his account. 'It's a poor tax,' said Carlos. 'If I'd had more money in the account, this never would have happened.' As for the accounts themselves, it seemed that there was nothing that was not subject to a charge or commission, including, but not limited to, making more than three movements per month, checking one's balance, requesting an additional account statement, requesting an account statement for previous periods, requesting the 'unfounded' investigation of a charge, making a transfer, writing a cheque and withdrawing money from a teller. 'Credit cards are openly extortionate, with annual interest rates of anywhere from 25 per cent to 75 per cent; factoring in other commissions such as annual and late fees, total annual costs can easily exceed 100 per cent. Mortgage interest rates, for their part, are three to four times higher than in the United States. In addition, customers often find themselves signed up for insurance policies and other services they have to fight to get out of.'

HSBC also made money out of Mexico by another route. After the peso crisis, the government privatized the pension system, which handed the administration $185-billion worth of individual retirement accounts, known as AFORES, on a plate to the largest banks, HSBC, of course, included. It was a common complaint in Mexico that fees on those accounts rose faster than the funds themselves and, ironically, the banks were accused of operating something called a 'cartel' around managing the pension accounts.

Meanwhile, in London, Green and the senior team had much to pre-occupy them. Even though 60,000 accounts were being opened in tiny Cayman from one country and all at one branch, the 'Cayman Islands branch of HSBC Mexico', the warning signs were not yet flashing. Their focus, as ever, was on growing their monster bank, making it even bigger. They were absorbing Household, imploring the staff to push consumer lending using Household's techniques, selling commercial banking to their business customers worldwide, all including Mexico. By 2003, profits were up 21 per cent and *The Banker* again declared HSBC its Global Bank of the Year, all of which was good, but not enough, and HSBC had to broaden out further, taking the bank deeper into unchartered waters. The view from London was that serving individuals and supplying them with loans, assisting small to medium businesses and selling them financial products, running an international network and adding countries – these were all terrific, but there was room for extra, and Green and his colleagues desired it, badly.

In the City and on Wall Street another one of those embarrassing plays on the initials HSBC was doing the rounds: 'Haven't Seen a Banking Client – in ages'. This was a poke at HSBC for not being a serious player in investment banking and not putting together the mega deals for the very biggest corporations and governments that earn the huge commissions. The idea that HSBC was being laughed at for not being a major force in large corporate advisory, not being top of booming hedge fund and private equity call lists, not counting in the elite 'bulge bracket' hurt badly, since the company that HSBC wanted to be keeping – Morgan Stanley, Goldman, JP Morgan, Deutsche, Bank of America, Credit Suisse – were all in this lucrative, money-pouring-in group. As, of course, was Citi, their ultimate nemesis. Green reacted to this slight by co-authoring with a colleague a management paper, declaring: 'We remain weak in corporate finance.' The *Financial Times* said it another way: 'To many, the failure of the world's second-largest banking group to build one of the largest investment banking businesses ranks among the greatest missed opportunities of modern finance.' This was the sort of criticism that stung the HSBC bankers the most, particularly when the view in-house was that Mexico and Household were success stories that they should have been lauded for, not belittled. Their response provided a unique insight into the mindset of the bank at the time.

The bank's management decided to do something about it. Instead of going out and buying an investment bank, which they could do, they decided to grow their own. Green said they do not want the 'real headache' of trying to integrate an investment bank. They had an investment banking operation of sorts; now, they were going to get serious.

In mid-2003 they recruited John Studzinski, the deputy chairman of Morgan Stanley in Europe. 'Studs' is a well-known, colourful personality, hugely well-connected, a master deal architect and major philanthropist. Superb as he is, Studs is only one person and if HSBC was going to compete with the big boys in investment banking, it would need a lot more. Seven hundred more, to be precise, which is how many staff they recruited in the first year, at a rate of roughly two a day. Some 120 of them were experienced, well-regarded bankers from rivals, lured by generous two-year, guaranteed-bonus contracts. Not only was this expensive and time-consuming – every single one had to undergo a formal recruitment and interviewing process – but it also ran counter to the traditional HSBC culture. As with the purchase of Household and the cash heaped upon Aldinger, the US consumer finance firm's boss, it was contrary to pretty much everything that had gone before. The industry was agog. *Institutional Investor* magazine reported that HSBC's spending spree raised pay levels across investment banks by 30 per cent. Green later admitted it was over the top, although he didn't put it quite like that; instead he said in that understated, reasoned way of his: 'I think we probably tried harder than we should have done to get the business up to critical mass.' Still, the bulk hiring reaped an instant dividend. In 2004, HSBC took part in the Hong Kong government's $2.6-billion global bond issue, something that simply would not have occurred previously. 'HSBC would not have been the first name to spring to mind,' acknowledged *The Banker*. Internally, though, there was dissension. The traditional HSBC bankers resented their highly paid new colleagues, especially as they were on guaranteed, thick bonuses. The newbies also came from banks with very different mindsets and practices to HSBC; they joined from the super-muscular bulge brackets and were seen as mercenaries, guns for hire with no loyalty towards their new employer and no grounding in the company's increasingly receding heritage. The new arrivals were also meant to cross-sell to clients, to convince the client's chairman and CEO, who they were meeting, about a piece of M&A or an IPO, to buy other HSBC services, but since the new people knew next to nothing about the broader HSBC picture, they weren't interested in selling the HSBC 'family', and it just didn't happen.

Having taken the step of building its own investment bank to rival the likes of Goldman Sachs and Morgan Stanley – as far-fetched as that appeared to outsiders – the HSBC leadership found themselves having to devote an inordinate amount of effort to the task. And this was all going on while they were integrating Household and introducing the rest of HSBC to consumer lending, and they were hard-selling to small to medium businesses as well as looking for new territories where they could stamp the HSBC brand. All because they wanted to be the biggest. The price of aiming so big, however, was that Mexico, and Chapo, were effectively left alone.

SIX

World-beater

In Mexico, Ricardo Rodríguez liked to go by the title of Head of the Institute to Return Stolen Goods to the People, or as it is known for short, Indep. What a job spec: 'boss of returning stolen goods to the people'. Sadly, this latter-day Robin Hood, Marxist superhero, had another, more mundane, job description: director-general of the government's property disposal and administration service. Basically, his brief was to get the best possible price for items confiscated from the nation's criminals. Clearly, as the biggest earners and biggest spenders, that usually meant the senior figures in the drug cartels. One Sunday, he held a sale that included an armoured Cadillac Escalade and a luxury BMW hybrid. 'People didn't put down their bidding paddles. We sold around 70 per cent of the goods and there was great enthusiasm,' he said. His yard sales – all the wares laid out, roll up, roll up, make your bid – were major draws. On average, at that auction he managed to raise 56 per cent more than the estimated list price. Jewellery did not shift so well – possibly it didn't appeal to local tastes, as much of it looked to be of Asian origin. So, the bling was up only 27 per cent, whereas aircraft, yes aircraft, fetched 2,500 per cent more than their opening bids. A house in the swish Mexican beach resort of Cancun went for $718,500 and another in Jalisco sold for $191,600. Rodriguez said the money raised would go to the Economic Culture Fund, to be invested in the printing of 2 million copies of twenty-one 'very interesting, very nice, very entertaining' books. Another time, the proceeds paid for scholarships for 544 Mexican athletes. This was from the 2019 sale of a house in the upmarket Mexico City neighbourhood of Las Lomas de Chapultepec. To call it a house was a misnomer. Rock-god mansion or porn-star fun palace might be more appropriate.

Las Lomas de Chapultepec means Chapultepec Heights in English and it's Mexico City's smartest district, green, wooded and hilly on the western edge of the city centre. Las Lomas was created in the 1920s when investors formed the Chapultepec Heights Company to purchase a parcel of land in the hills of the Anahuac Valley. They laid the area out as a 'garden suburb', with large, architect-designed houses on gaping lots, plenty of space, wide tree-lined avenues, manicured lawns and shrubs, and occasional rows of smart shops. Over the years, more grand houses and discreet commercial buildings were added, but not too many. Today, Las Lomas de Chapultepec is home to Mexico City's richest inhabitants, including Carlos Slim, for many years the wealthiest person in the world, but now 'only' the fifth with $68.9 billion; politicians, pop stars and celebrities, including Angélica Rivera, the model, singer and soap actress and, as the wife of Mexico's ex-president Enrique Peña Nieto, the country's former First Lady. There is a bevy of private schools, among them 'Eton School' (no relation to that one – Mexico City's Eton is co-ed and was founded in 1990). And the Mexico headquarters of Google. And crime bosses.

One house that Rodriguez had for sale in 2019, to borrow from the brochure, was a pink, Mediterranean-style, colonnaded, four-storey residence with ten bedrooms, fourteen bathrooms, three Jacuzzis, glass-enclosed swimming pool, sauna, wine cellar, bar and a lift. 'It was a very special event because it was the most valuable piece of real estate that we have dealt with,' said Rodriguez. It sold for $5.2 million. The buyer was the Butaca Enlace Foundation, which helps young people participate in sports events. It was a far cry from the previous owner, Zhenli Ye Gon, also known as 'Charlie Ye' or 'Mr Ye' or 'Chino', a long-time customer of Bital and then HSBC and whose arrest in the US for drug trafficking set the first major alarm bells ringing within HSBC as to what the bank had got itself into in Mexico. He lived at the house, 515 Sierra Madre Street, with his wife, Tomoiyi Marx Yu, the daughter of a Chinese restaurant owner in central Mexico City. He was apprehended at PJ Rice Bistro, a southern Chinese restaurant next to a JC Penny and a Ruby Tuesday in a mall in Wheaton, Maryland, in the US. He and a female companion had just ordered a meal of codfish and carrots when they were surrounded by DEA agents. 'The police came to the table and asked him to go pretty fast,' a bistro employee recalled. 'They didn't stay in the restaurant too long.' The police were pursuing him because detectives in Mexico, in March 2007, searched his house and found $205.6 million, in cash. They checked all the notes to see if they were genuine – a tedious process that took forever and in the process uncovered fifty-two fake 100-dollar bills. The haul was in a locked room upstairs off the main bedroom and the dollar bills were in three-feet-high and six-feet-wide piles, or else in suitcases on wheels, metal lockers and briefcases. They were all neatly arranged by denomination and weighed close to two tonnes. The crazy amount was described by Karen Tandy, head of the US Drug Enforcement Administration, as 'the largest single drug-cash seizure the world has ever seen'. To put it in context: the next highest was $50 million, hidden behind a false cabinet, in Colombia. Then came: $18 million in California; $5.7 million in Australia; $2.6 million in Canada, after the police fished a suitcase out of a harbour near Vancouver Island when they saw a man hurl it into the water as they approached his boat; and $1.5 million in Alabama where they found four bags stuffed full of notes in a lorry cab and the driver claimed not to know they were there. Mexico City's trove was off the scale. The cash seized at Ye Gon's house was stored by the authorities for ninety days, to see if anyone came forward to claim it. As no one did, the government said it would use the money to fund drug addict rehab programmes and to tackle organized crime. Alas, since this was Mexico there could be no happy ending and two federal agents, Josue Hernandez and Anibal Sanchez, who raided the house, were later found beaten and shot to death in southern Mexico, where it was said they were gathering further intelligence on drug traffickers.

The plunder vied for space in the house with Baroque tables, leather couches and Oriental rugs. On one wall there was a copy of Picasso's anti-war paean *Guernica*, in a bathroom there were child-size toothbrushes for Ye Gon's young son, and in the master bedroom, the boy's school photo and a drawing by the boy of mountains accompanied by a fond message to his parents, '*te quiero mama, te quiero papa*', I love you Mummy, I love you Daddy. There was also a velvet Fabergé case, a DVD of the action movie *The Corruptor* (starring Mark Wahlberg and Chow Yun-fat about the NYPD trying to break the drugs trade in Chinatown, and a turf war between rival triads), a syringe and an empty holster for a Beretta pistol.

Mexican academics have made studies of this 'narco style' and 'narchotecture' and they explain that the focus on glitz and material possessions signifies escape – that the occupant is boasting to the world, but also reinforcing the message to themselves that they've made it; they've climbed to the top, away from Mexico's sometimes grinding poverty, and they've risen up that ladder, despite the embedded corruption of many in the ruling class.

As a drugs linchpin, Ye Gon was expected to have an extravagantly luxurious home, but he also demanded it of himself as it provided solidity, belonging and achievement. 'They find in the narco world everything they cannot find anywhere else,' said José Manuel Valenzuela, a sociology professor at El Colegio de la Frontera Norte, a research institute in Tijuana. 'It's not just about money. It's about power.' It goes without saying that it's not in any good parenting guide to expose your children to drug trafficking, but in narcoland the children's toys sit next to the AK-47s. Partly, they fear kidnapping and, said Professor Valenzuela, they see their children as an important constituent of narco life because, as parents, they wish their legacy to be sustained through their children. In the meantime, they want those they love and trust to enjoy the fruits of what they've worked for. They're sweet and family proud, in other words. 'Narcos are much more complex than people think,' said Valenzuela. 'They're not monsters or aliens from another planet. They have a big part of the same social values as everyone else.'

As well as the mountains of US dollars at Ye Gon's house, the police seized 17 million Mexican pesos, 200,000 euros, 113,000 Hong Kong dollars, 180 Canadian dollars, 11 Centenarios (Mexican gold bullion coins made of 37.5g of pure gold), jewels, eight vehicles (including six Mercedes-Benz cars) and eight firearms, among them an AK-47 assault rifle. Ye Gon, forty-four years old, fought a nine-year battle to avoid extradition from the US before being sent back to Mexico in 2016, where he is now in jail, and has maintained his innocence, insisting that he is not involved in drug trafficking and money laundering, that the cash was destined for use in Felipe Calderón's presidential campaign and he was looking after it for safe-keeping. He is just an 'honest pharmaceuticals executive', living a quiet life, who has become an 'ultra-successful business entrepreneur.' As part of his defence he alleged that Mexico's future labour secretary, Javier Lozano, who was working on Calderón's campaign, forced him to safeguard the millions, threatening to kill him if he failed to do so. He claimed Lozano turned up at his house and made it plain what would happen to him if he did not do as he'd been ordered. 'Cooperate or *cuello*,' Ye Gon quoted Lozano as saying, with a throat-slashing gesture highlighting the Spanish word *cuello*, for 'neck.' The cash was in duffel bags and he was told to look after it. An associate of Lozano later delivered more of the money.

First of all, why Ye Gon, why was he singled out to look after hundreds of millions of dollars? Second, where did Lozano get that sort of money from? Third, what exactly was it meant to be used for? The answer to that one apparently is that the dollars would finance Calderón's election push and would then be used to carry out 'terrorist' activities if Calderón lost. Four, why was Ye Gon let in on such a dastardly plot? So it's like this, he said, 'so these notes here, they're for the adverts and posters; this section over here, they're for the bombs.' Really? Mexican government officials didn't buy it either, calling the allegations preposterous. Lozano flatly denied the accusation. Calderón said it was 'pure fiction.' Not so fast, though. Surveys by Transparency International, the internationally respected Berlin organization that monitors corruption, show that Mexicans regularly rate their government a 4.4 on a corruption scale of one to five, with five being the most corrupt. In true local fashion, in relation to Ye Gon, soon after his arrest Mexican car bumper stickers popped up: 'I believe the Chinaman.' The US and Mexican authorities said nonsense, that Ye Gon was a major link in the drugs chain, partnering Chapo and co. in the production and importation of crystal meth into the US.

Born in Shanghai, Ye Gon emigrated to Mexico in 1990 and, for a time, he imported Chinese trinkets – when police raided one of his warehouses they found women's purses and artificial Christmas trees – then he moved into pharmaceuticals. He gained legal residence in Mexico in 1997 and worked for two years as a technician at Laboratorios Silanes, a firm owned by President Vicente Fox's close friend and political backer Antonio López de Silanes Perez. At a ceremony, President Fox, guest of honour at the HSBC Torre opening ceremony and the man who unveiled the giant, coded fresco in the lobby, personally awarded Ye Gon a certificate of Mexican citizenship. Ye Gon was always smartly dressed, quiet, courteous and

reserved and he created his own pharmaceutical importing and brok-
ing firm, Unimed Pharm Chem. He maintained his plan was to grow
Unimed into Latin America's largest pharmaceutical manufacturer
and he was well on his way to achieving that when he was arrested.
What is certain is that he became one of Mexico's largest importers
of pseudoephedrine and ephedrine, the chemicals that are used to
make nasal decongestant and over-the-counter common cold treat-
ments. They also have another, illicit, use – as ingredients in the
manufacture of crystal meth or 'ice'. He was dealing with Chinese
suppliers and Ye Gon agreed to buy from them 50 tonnes of what was
billed as hydroxybenzyl-N-methyl acetethamine annually. They
would also help him design and construct a new 14,000-square-
metre plant, ostensibly to manufacture pseudoephedrine, at Toluca,
in Mexico. Over the years Ye Gon brought in vast cargoes, far in
excess of the amounts he was legally allowed to or was required to do
for making something to stop a runny nose like Sudafed. Acting on
a tip off, agents were told he was supplying the Sinaloa, who had
moved into crystal meth in its usual efficient manner – they supplied
the drug to their dealers to hand out to their customers as free sam-
ples, to get them hooked.

The police launched 'Operation Dragon' to follow and target Ye
Gon, to damage the supply of crystal meth in the US. The authorities
in Mexico and the US suspected Ye Gon of being involved in the
trafficking of people as well as drugs and they reckoned Ye Gon
arranged for 100 Asian citizens, supplied by his Chinese partners, to
travel to Mexico to work on the plant. When they raided the new
factory at 175 Miguel Alemán Boulevard, in San Pedro Totoltepec, in
Toluca, they realized it could have been a higher number. Inside a
large warehouse they discovered part of the building had been turned
into lodgings to house those in charge of the building project. In
another section, they found beds and overalls for the construction
workers and they were told that 300 Asian men had been working on
the Toluca site. Now there was no trace of them – they had all

disappeared. Ye Gon was thought to be at the centre of an international network, sourcing chemicals not only from China but from Europe and India, hiring containers destined for Unimed to journey via the port of Long Beach in California that were then sent on to Mexico. There, when they boarded the ships, investigators found what they claimed was hydroxybenzyl-N-methyl acetethamine. When they tested them, the loads turned out to be a derivative of pseudoephedrine. Agents believed that in total he was importing 81 tonnes of pseudoephedrine. Ye Gon said the shipments were legal and were coming from a company called Emerald Import & Export in Hong Kong, but that firm did not exist. A worker at Toluca said the plant received daily shipments of a white hard chemical substance that was then heated with hydrochloric acid to form a white crystalline powder of which they produced over 600 kilos a day. Each evening, it was bagged and driven away by Ye Gon or his personal driver, but despite making so much of the white powder every day none of these details appeared in the Unimed books, because at Toluca the employees and suppliers to the plant are paid in cash.

As well as his palatial house in Mexico, Ye Gon owned homes in Naucalpan in Mexico, Las Vegas, Los Angeles and in China. He told one currency exchange that the money came from another of his companies that produced the raw materials used in making veterinary medicines and that the cash was to pay his suppliers for that business in US dollars. His cousin, Ye Yongqing, was busted as being part of the same racket and received twenty-five years for taking part in organized crime, synthetic drug production and activities involving the use of illicit funds. A court in Toluca found that Yongqing was a member of the ice-trafficking organization run by his cousin, Ye Gon, and they were connected through a company formed in Toluca with money from their criminal activities. What was the bank for Ye Gon and Unimed? The same one as his Sinaloa customers, HSBC.

Until the alarm was raised in 2007 the bank enjoyed a close relationship with Ye Gon and his Unimed business. Oddly, the company was looked after by the bank's personal finance section – the part of HSBC that deals with individual, private customers – as opposed to the commercial banking arm.

JUST AT THE moment police entered Ye Gon's house in Mexico City, finding hundreds of millions of dollars in cash, Ye Gon was spotted in Las Vegas and then tracked to New York.

Ye Gon was well known in the world's gambling capital, and in less than four years, he'd blown a staggering $125 million at a handful of casinos, but mainly at the Las Vegas Sands resort, which operates the Venetian and Palazzo casinos where he liked to play baccarat for $150,000 a hand. In Vegas speak, Ye Gon was a particular sort of VIP known as a 'whale' – a hopeless gambler but also hugely wealthy. He was every casino operator's dream, someone who would turn up and kiss goodbye to a small fortune, seemingly without blinking, and over the course of several years he did it again and again. Making valuable gifts to high rollers such as Ye Gon and even reducing the amounts whales owe casinos after running up big losses, known as 'discounting,' is standard at Las Vegas's major resorts. Nor would a gift of a luxury car be out of the question for a top customer. While in Las Vegas, it later transpired, Ye Gon had transferred $45 million in cash to The Venetian from banks and money exchanges in Mexico and elsewhere. In addition, the casino loaned him $35 million to use at their tables. The high-stakes gambler has also lost another $40 million at other neighbouring casinos. As well as being attached to the largest ever drugs cash seizure, Ye Gon now had a second, dubious world record to his name: the biggest all-cash upfront gambler in Las Vegas history. As a result of Ye Gon's excesses at the tables the casinos fell over themselves to indulge Ye Gon, providing him with complimentary hotel rooms, private jets, meals, limousines, girls. The Las Vegas Sands gave him a Rolls-Royce. While there, investigators claimed, he told his mistress, Michele Wong, a former employee of the Mirage Hotel Casino, that he was laundering money for Mexican drug traffickers, which might explain why Wong used money he gave her to buy her $1.1-million Las Vegas home, jewellery, two Mercedes-Benz cars. She also used $500,000 that Ye Gon wired her to buy air-conditioning units and transformers, which she then shipped to his pharmaceutical plant in Mexico. The pair first met when she was a casino host at The Venetian's nearby rival, The Mirage, and he was a high-rolling customer. Their relationship turned romantic a month after she was fired in January 2005. She would later say that Ye Gon gave her up to $1.5 million over the course of their relationship, and that Ye Gon was the father of her son.

In the course of their romance, Ye Gon told her that he was being blackmailed by drug dealers to launder 'dirty money' in Las Vegas along with being involved in a Mexican politician's terrorist plot. The deal he claimed to have struck with the cartel was that he would launder the money in Las Vegas and gamble with the money as well as purchase high-value items in Las Vegas. It was certainly the case that, using Ye Gon's money, Wong paid off her mortgage within about three months of buying the house. Investigators seized title records for the house that showed Wong put a $305,108 down payment on the house and obtained a $853,500 loan to cover the rest of the cost. Wong last saw Ye Gon when he flew to Las Vegas from Orange County, California, on a private jet provided by The Venetian resort.

By law, every US casino with revenues of $1 million is obliged to alert the authorities if they suspect anyone is playing with illegal money, and as a result of the 2013 investigation into Ye Gon the Las Vegas Sands was subsequently fined $47.4 million by the US Attorney's office for failing to do its duty over him. They were given ten days to pay or else face prosecution for failing to file Suspicious Activity Reports for Casinos, or SARCs, which are required when a customer is involved in a transaction the casino knows, suspects, or has reason to suspect 'had no business or apparent lawful purpose or was not the sort in which the particular customer would normally be expected to engage, and the casino knew of no reasonable explanation for the transaction after examining the available facts.' US Attorney Andre Birotte Jnr said of the fine that 'what happens in Vegas no longer stays in Vegas'. Said Birotte: 'For the first time, a casino has faced the very real possibility of a federal criminal case for failing to properly report suspicious funds received from a gambler. This is also the first time a casino has agreed to return those funds to the government. All companies, especially casinos, are now on notice that America's anti-money laundering laws apply to all people and every corporation, even if that company risks losing its most profitable customer.' For its part, the Las Vegas Sands, while maintaining it was unaware of Ye Gon's alleged criminal activities, acknowledged that 'in hindsight . . . the Venetian-Palazzo failed to fully appreciate the suspicious nature of the information or lack thereof pertaining to Ye Gon . . .' To make matters worse for the casino, even though under arrest and having had his piles of bank notes seized, Ye Gon refused to pay back the $35 million credit. The net result is that The Venetian effectively lost $37.4 million on betting on Ye Gon (the casino took in $45 million, lent him $35m, still making a profit of $10m but was fined $47.4m). The deficit was large enough to erase all annual executive bonuses at The Venetian and its shares also took a beating. Not that Ye Gon was necessarily counting. In all, he earned at least $350 million over a three-year period while running Unimed.

Ye Gon did not dispute that figure or his gambling losses, but the wire transfers to Las Vegas Sands came from companies and individuals that on the face of it did not connect to Ye Gon, which made it harder to connect him directly to the cartels. While the wire transfers were prolific – he also sent funds from Mexico to a Las Vegas Sands subsidiary in Hong Kong for onward transfer to Las Vegas – in many instances, Ye Gon's wire transfers lacked sufficient information to identify him as the beneficiary. Added to which, while in town the Las Vegas Sands also allowed Ye Gon to transfer funds several times to an account that did not give any clue it was linked to The Venetian, and further investigation revealed that one account in particular was connected to an aviation account used to pay pilots operating the company's private aircraft. The police investigation concluded that 'when casino personnel asked Ye Gon to wire the money in larger lump sums, as opposed to breaking it up incrementally, and use consistent, listed beneficiaries, Ye Gon stated that he preferred to wire the money incrementally because he did not want the government to know about these transfers.' He liked to break up the payments so as not to attract unwanted attention – in other words, he was carrying out a classic version of the 'structuring' practice used by the cartels.

While the investigation into Ye Gon focused on establishing his connection with the drug cartels, by following the money the authorities in the US were able to show that the primary international bank that allowed him to send wire transfers across the world to support his 'stucturing' strategy of sending small amounts of cash, undetected, from account to account across multiple borders, was HSBC.

For three years Unimed carried out numerous cash deposits, huge amounts of transactions and payments in and out, with no evidence of where the money was coming from, and in all that time did not disclose any gross income – none of which was red-flagged by anyone within HSBC. It was only when the connection was made between Ye Gon's Mount Everest of cash in his house and his accounts held by HSBC that the full scale of the horror of what might emerge came to light within the bank. In March 2007, Paul Thurston, the HSBC chief of Mexico, sent an urgent email: 'This is a very serious, and high-profile, case which has potential reputational damage to the HSBC Group, and must be given the highest priority.' In the urgent hunt for how this had happened it was uncovered that Ye Gon and Unimed were originally clients of Bital – the bank without compliance – and they were seamlessly kept on by HSBC without any checks carried out on either party. At the time of the takeover the accounts were not designated 'high risk' even though there had been several instances where unusual transactions had alerted the bank's attention. There was even an instruction within HSBC Mexico to end the relationship with Unimed altogether, and while the flag had been raised, nothing had been done about it and it was only when they read about the cash trawl and his arrest that the HSBC bankers found the accounts were still open.

As soon as they realized how damaging this discovery could be for the bank, Thurston personally intervened and ordered a review by Graham Thomson, head of the bank's internal audits for Latin America. Thomson reported back. He had uncovered three things: poor client-checking procedures; lack of documentation and filing; and 'lack of a compliance culture.' This carried remarkable similarities with the Bagley email – except that Bagley's missive warning the bank that its prospective Mexican purchase did not do compliance had been years previously. In that intervening period, during which time HSBC were in sole charge, absolutely nothing had changed. Further internal digging revealed that whenever concerns about Ye Gon and Unimed were raised internally, assurances were given that all the documentation was fine and everything was above board, when patently it wasn't. It appeared that, at the time, no one higher up asked for evidence of Ye Gon's compliance and no one ever doubted what they were being told until the whole mess was out in the open. When pressed, the bank employee who vouched for Unimed said he'd been lied to by colleagues and as if that was not bad enough, it transpired that site visits to Ye Gon and Unimed to check that all was fit and proper, which were listed and dated in HSBC files as having occurred, had not taken place: they were pure fabrication. Within a month, it became clear that this was not a local issue that could be swept under the carpet, and in April 2007 the high command in London was told what had been discovered. Matthew King, head of HSBC Group Audits, sent an email to the CEO, Geoghegan, that, 'the review has revealed a number of weaknesses. A series of inaccurate, and possibly fabricated, visit reports seem to have been filed by the business which resisted any reporting of suspicions a number of times. For its part, the Money Laundering Department failed to act as a proper check and balance. I have suggested a thorough review of processes within the Money Laundering Department and of the Money Laundering Committee to ensure they are robust . . . There are also a number of personnel decisions to be taken.' It is easy to imagine that this might have caused a collective panic at the top of the bank, that the hierarchy would demand to know what the hell was going on, where else had this carry-on occurred? But no, they neither sought to find out what was going on, nor, it appeared, did they bother to tell colleagues anywhere else in the sprawling global group what had happened. Everywhere in HSBC from Hong Kong to the US was kept completely in the dark about events at HSBC in Mexico. The inescapable conclusion as to why the bank failed to set in motion a crackdown seemed to be that by the time Ye Gon's mountains of cash were being discovered, HSBC were so stretched across the numerous projects of expansion they simply did not have the time or resources to spare to focus on one bad apple thousands of miles away. There were simply more important things to concentrate on. Annual profits were up 5 per cent at $22.1 billion. There was a lot happening. There was Household to bed in and the US home loans market was starting to prove problematic. There was consumer lending, courtesy of Household, to develop and roll out, commercial banking had been made a priority and they were busy building an investment bank to take on Goldman Sachs and Morgan Stanley, and there were new lands to conquer.

There was, though, another diversion, one that provoked enormous consternation at the top of the bank. In December 2006, soon after Green stepped up from CEO to executive chairman, his cerebral air came under attack. On becoming executive chairman, Green paid a courtesy visit to the major City fund manager, Threadneedle Investments, and Michael Taylor, who was retiring as its chairman, publicly declared himself unimpressed. Taylor had a forthright style. Interviewed in the *Daily Telegraph*, he said: 'We had Stephen Green in here two weeks ago, and, cor, he was asleep on the job is how I would describe it. He's just not up for it.' This was a shattering, and virtually without parallel, public assessment of a head of a bank in a world where any outspoken criticism was, and remains, extremely rare, because this is an industry where institutional investors and their leaders publicly mind their Ps and Qs, not least because they are afraid of causing the share prices of their investments to fall. At the time of the conversation with Green, Taylor spoke for £840-million worth of HSBC shares, but so disheartened was he by what his firm saw that he hit out.

He was being asked about shares over the year and those that had outperformed. 'One of the disappointments for me is HSBC,' he said, and went on to castigate Green. At the bank, Green and his colleagues were stunned, and attempted to shake it off, reassuring the main shareholders and calling the media. The bank's response to this public tongue-lashing was immediate and unequivocal and they leapt to their man's defence, issuing a statement: 'In Stephen Green, we have a world-class chairman who we are enormously proud of.' Journalists were briefed that this was meant to have been a 'high-level' and 'strategic' discussion with Threadneedle, not focusing on specific issues. But there was no mistaking that this was a deeply personal blow, wounding and jarring, and it was not something Green could easily recover from. And it got worse when, in the spring of 2007, as the world's largest-ever cash seizure was being made in Mexico City at the house of an HSBC client, the bank's shareholder register was indicating the presence of a new name: Knight Vinke Asset Management from New York and the investment management firm appeared to be building a sizeable stake in HSBC. Urgent inquiries revealed that Knight Vinke was buying on its own account and working with CalPERS, the California Public Employees' Retirement System, but there were other US institutional investors involved as well. In all, some 22 million HSBC shares were bought, and the group was thought to have call options over another 13 million. In the everyday business of a bank as enormous as HSBC this kind of move was relatively common, but the difference with Knight Vinke was that not only was the holding large enough for them to be taken seriously and for Green and his team to take notice, what was of real concern was that Knight Vinke was an 'activist investor'. Companies like Knight Vinke scour the world for quoted companies where a shift in strategy will lead to a greater return and a rise in the share price. They buy some shares, then set about rattling the board's cage with an agenda for change, feeding the press and share analysts, openly challenging the directors to follow their lead, and unlike normal institutional City and Wall Street shareholders they do like to make as much public and private noise as possible. They had clearly seen something in HSBC's strategy that they thought they could take advantage of and turn a profit on.

In 2007, while HSBC were busy expanding their empire, Eric Knight, the boss of Knight Vinke, mounted a withering public assault on the bank, and in particular its new executive chairman. Tall, stooping, youthful-looking, Knight came with a strong reputation. Ex-Eton and Cambridge, formerly a merchant banker, he speaks softly and slowly, with great care. When I met him in London, I was struck by his charm; he gave the impression that by laying into the bank's leadership he really was doing them a favour. He had previously taken on two of Europe's biggest companies in Suez and ICN Pharmaceuticals and wrought change. 'I like working with Eric because he does his homework,' said the chief of one large backer. 'He is able to do things and say things publicly that we cannot say. There has been a gap in the market; it's the lack of assertive owners.' And now HSBC, a bank that for so long had done things its way, was in the firing line and it did not like this development one bit; the senior management was deeply troubled. An urgent meeting was held with Knight in New York on 12 June 2007, as the police were crawling all over Ye Gon's empire in Mexico City. The meeting did not go well and resulted in an 'open letter' from the investment firm to Green. Knight called for the board to undertake a 'fundamental review of the Group's strategy.' He said it could not be conducted by Green and must be led by someone impartial. To rub it in, they told the ex-McKinsey man that they'd hired a firm of management consultants to assist them. What was irking Knight were recently awarded incentive arrangements for the bank's chiefs, including Green. They could receive shares up to seven times their annual salary for achieving agreed targets in shareholder returns and earnings per share over the next three years, 'of which 30 per cent (i.e., approximately two times their annual salary) vests for very modest performance'. He accused the bank of 'complacency'. Addressing Green direct, Knight wrote: 'Whilst we recognise and appreciate the value of your experience with HSBC, we believe that, at this point in time, it would be best for the Group that the Chairman be a non-executive and recommend that this be implemented by the next Annual General Meeting.' In other words, we think you should not be in charge.

Knight is relentless, a terrier, albeit a big-framed one with brushed-back hair and chubby cheeks, who likes to wear a double-breasted pinstripe suit. He did not back off and followed this diatribe with others, writing to all HSBC shareholders lambasting Green's appointment, repeatedly calling for him to give up the day job and be made a part-time non-executive chair. 'Continuity of management is all very well, but it can result in paralysis, which is what happened here.' He accused HSBC's management of being 'complacent', and of making a series of strategic mistakes, as he put it, 'flag planting' in different countries with a series of takeovers. Knight called for the review to be led by Simon Robertson, the senior independent on the board. Robertson was the archetypal, old-style London merchant-banker grandee who was ex-Kleinwort Benson and Goldman Sachs, another Old Etonian, debonair, silver-tongued with slicked-back hair, and similar to Knight in that he too favours tailored chalk pinstripes and colourful braces. Robertson is gregarious, socially well-connected, someone who skied with the Royal

Family at Klosters, sat on the board of the Royal Opera House, and chaired Rolls-Royce. In other words, he understood high-level man-oeuvring, inside out.

The impact of Knight's onslaught on HSBC management and Stephen Green, especially, cannot be understated. The strike was intensely personal and also hugely time-consuming. The bank's above-the-fray directors simply were not used to dealing with an attack such as this, one that dared to question their very ability to manage, to set the bank's course how they wished. Green and his immediate circle were shellshocked, although they were relieved when Robertson went into bat for them and used his silky negotiating skills and his ability to schmooze investors to both allay their concerns and to calm down Knight. While Robertson applied his balm and HSBC accused the messenger, there was no doubt, however, that Knight's charges were credible and they were given weight when Legal & General, one of HSBC's most influential shareholders, threw their support behind Knight, the disruptor. Knight Vinke's assault, coming soon after Taylor's pointed critique, shone an awkward light on a bank that liked to cite sound Scottish principles as the bedrock of its success. While the bank's chiefs were trying to fend off Knight's salvoes and rally round their beleaguered leader, elsewhere in the HSBC 'family' it was business as usual. In Mexico, Chapo was having a ball.

SEVEN

The Third Taboo

I became interested in scrutinizing the powerful because I watched a film called *All the President's Men*. Like many others, I was transfixed by the spectacle of two reporters, Bob Woodward and Carl Bernstein played by Robert Redford and Dustin Hoffman, bringing down the leader of the free world, the president of the United States, without firing a shot. It has stayed with me ever since, as did the book of the same name about the Watergate break-in, the subsequent cover-up and Richard Nixon's demise, and as did the phrase: 'Follow the money.' If you want to get to the Mr Big, the person really in charge, if you want to establish the truth, you trace the money trail. More recently, in the TV crime drama *The Wire*, detective Lester Freamon says: 'You follow drugs, you get drug addicts and drug dealers. But you start to follow the money, and you don't know where the fuck it's gonna take you.' There was a fascinating exchange between Barack Obama and David Simon, creator of *The Wire*. Simon, a former journalist, a police reporter, recalled how he first saw a police force in drugs-scarred Baltimore who believed they could 'arrest their way' out of the drugs problem, that they could makes lots of street-level arrests, and the trade and the spin-off crime and issues it caused would simply disappear. This stance was being repeated in inner cities across the US. All that occurred in practice was that those caught with intention to supply ended up in jail and became more hardened. In the meantime, others were all too willing to take their place. No real progress was being made; quite the contrary. Insufficient attention was paid to those more difficult to snare, those higher up the chain. Too little firepower was focused on following the money.

Ed Vulliamy, the author and writer, who has written extensively on the Mexican drug wars and the relentless spread of narcotics and resulting violence in the US, put it very well when he wrote of the Obama administration having broken two taboos that had long impeded honest discussion. First, Barack Obama and his colleagues spoke for the first time of 'co-responsibility' for the narco-war in northern Mexico. In other words, it was not simply only Mexico's problem but was the result of America's (and Europe's) never-satisfied appetite for illegal drugs. The second was that the White House acknowledged another role played by the US; another aspect of co-responsibility. This was the so-called 'Iron River' of guns smuggled from the US to the Mexican cartels, which were used in the shootings and caused so much of the bloodshed. Said Vulliamy, that was all very well, but there was a 'third taboo' that had yet to be broken. This was the question of the money, the narco-greenbacks, the $323 billion a year. What happened to it? Where did it end up? How did it reach the cartels and how was it then fed back into the economy? How was it being laundered? What financial institutions were facilitating the process? Former customs special agent Lee Morgan told Vulliamy: 'Kinda strange, ain't it, how Washington's got all this technology, but never goes after the money?' Down the years, the DEA, FBI and the Mexican authorities launched operation after operation against the trafficking of drugs and the cartels, against the dominant player, the Sinaloa. Many of the projects were assigned masculine, determinedly aggressive codenames, so we had Operations Intercept,

Golden Flow, Condor, Casablanca, Michoacán, Baja California, Nuovo Leon-Tamaulipas, Chihuahua, Solare (a.k.a Project Reckoning), Wide Receiver, Fast and Furious, Narconetos, Imperial Emperor. These were just some of the major ones and each project followed a similar pattern. After each there was a triumphant press conference, the repetition of a set of statistics, number of arrests, total amounts seized, locations affected and their monetary worth. Photographs were issued of the apprehended bricks of drugs and assorted, terrifying-looking weaponry, and headshots of those arrested. There were self-congratulatory quotes proclaiming that this was a great day for security, for law and order, that the drugs traffickers were in retreat and that no one was above the law. What was never mentioned was that the supply of drugs would carry on as normal, often with barely a glitch; the users would still get their crack and crank, and people would continue being murdered. And drugs dollars would go on being laundered, same as before.

The DEA's 2007 operation 'Imperial Emperor' chose as their main target a man called Victor Emilio Cazares, a close lieutenant of Chapo. Like so many coordinated sweeps, the project was born out of frustration. At the time, the Sinaloa's drugs were rampaging across the US, through the cities and towns of the west, south-west, south-east and east. The DEA was looking to break concentric circles of distributors, couriers, packers and stash houses, so it brought together different police and law enforcement agencies under the Imperial Emperor banner. As for the origin of the name: Imperial is the name of the sand dunes and border country in southern California, Emperor was Cazares. At the time he was responsible for overseeing a smuggling network that over three years brought more than 40 tonnes of cocaine into the US, netting a profit of $200 million. Cazares had been arrested before, as a young illegal immigrant in Bell, near Los Angeles, with a bag of drugs. He claimed he was a 'landscape gardener with a cocaine habit that he was determined to kick'. His probation officer subsequently wrote that Cazares's 'plans are to work and become a Christian.' Instead, he chose shipping drugs over landscaping as his preferred career path and went on to rise up though the cartel, ending with a 25-acre estate outside Culiacán, where he was regarded in the local community as an upright farmer and employer. So honest did he appear that the Mexican government paid him subsidies to keep cattle, and he hired locals to pick his vegetable crops, paying them twice the going rate. Ever faithful to what he told his probation officer, the respected Cazares built a church in the grounds. However, his main source of wealth and his real job was as overseer and organizer of the drugs pipeline into the US for his boss, Chapo. Cazares could have been a senior executive of a large manufacturing company, charged with running the transport fleet. Like Chapo, he was a thorough manager, attending to every last detail. If a cargo was seized, the operative had to fill in forms and account for what went wrong. If Cazares thought their excuses were genuine and the bust was down to police skill, the loss was allowed to pass; if he thought it was their fault and, worse, they were lying or keeping it for themselves, then terrible retribution was exacted. And, where Cazares and Chapo were concerned, in their organization, retribution consisted of something a lot grimmer than a written employer's warning, the foregoing of a bonus payment or missing out on promotion. In 2007, the DEA announced that Imperial Emperor had succeeded in dismantling 'distribution cells that ranged from the South West Border to cities throughout the United States', resulting in 402 arrests and the seizure of 9,512 pounds of cocaine, 27,229 pounds of marijuana, 18,465 marijuana plants, 705 pounds of methamphetamine, 227 pounds of 'ice', 11 pounds of heroin, 100 weapons, and $45.2 million in cash. It was a mammoth operation. 'The following agencies joined forces with DEA for this twenty-two-month Organized Crime Drug Enforcement Task Force (OCDETF) investigation coordinated by DEA's Special Operations Division (SOD) and provided invaluable assistance to the successful outcome of this investigation: Federal Bureau of Investigation, US

Immigration and Customs Enforcement, Internal Revenue Service, California Department of Justice Bureau of Narcotics Enforcement Inland Crackdown Allied Task Force, Inland Regional Narcotic Enforcement Team, Los Angeles Interagency Metropolitan Police Apprehension Crime Task Force, California Regional Narcotics Suppression Program, Torrance Police Department, Long Beach Police Department, San Bernardino County Sheriff's Department, California Highway Patrol, Signal Hill Police Department, Southgate Police Department, Huntington Park Police Department, Baldwin Park Police Department, Riverside Sheriff's Department, West Covina Police Department, Glendale Police Department, Los Angeles District Attorney's Office, and the United States Attorney's Office for the Central District of California.' Simply reading that roll-call alone is enough to make you want to lie down. All that coordination required to take on one organization with one boss.

Karen Tandy, the then-head of the DEA, said: 'Today we ripped out this empire's US infrastructure from its commanders and transportation coordinators to its local distribution cells across the country, stripped it of $45 million in cash, and tossed it into the dustbin of history.' In fact, despite Tandy's bragging, it would be five more years before Cazares was arrested and he was eventually stopped purely by chance at a road checkpoint in 2012, in Mexico, near Guadalajara. In 2012 he was extradited to the US and in 2016, finally jailed. The press release was headlined: 'Sinaloa Cartel Trafficker Victor Emilio Cazares Gastellum Sentenced to 180 Months in Prison'.

After all that effort, all those agencies and all those agents putting their lives on the line, Cazares made a plea bargain and was sentenced to fifteen years. Cazares's remark to the judge passing sentence in San Diego carried a familiar refrain. 'I am very sorry for my actions of my past life. When I get out I'm going to live here and join a church and work for God. I want to live in a house surrounded by my children and grandchildren the rest of my life.' One of the positive outcomes of the plea bargain was that it allowed the DEA to better understand how Cazares banked and used his dollars, once the drugs were sold, as US prosecutors came to see that Cazares's sister Blanca, known as 'the Empress,' allegedly ran a money-laundering operation involving currency houses and bank branches in Mexican border towns and cities. She also owned a string of businesses, including a toy factory, a real estate agency and a restaurant that were used to wash the cash. No sooner had operation Imperial Emperor ended than Operation Xcellerator began. Lasting twenty-one months, starting in 2007, if anything, Xcellerator was even bigger in scope and resources than its predecessor and more than 200 enforcement agencies took part. At the end, in 2009, as with Imperial Emperor, the Justice Department was euphoric: 'Operation Xcellerator has led to the arrest of 755 individuals and the seizure of approximately $59.1 million in US currency, more than 12,000 kilograms of cocaine, more than 16,000 pounds of marijuana, more than 1,200 pounds of methamphetamine, more than 8 kilograms of heroin, approximately 1.3 million pills of ecstasy, more than $6.5 million in other assets, 149 vehicles, 3 aircraft, 3 maritime vessels and 169 weapons.'

Eric Holder, the US Attorney General, was bullish: 'International drug trafficking organizations pose a sustained, serious threat to the safety and security of our communities. As the world grows smaller and international criminals step up their efforts to operate inside our borders, the Department of Justice will confront them head on to keep our communities safe.' There was no doubt who was principally in their sights. It was the Sinaloa, it was Chapo. Holder's colleague at the DEA, Michele Leonhart, said: 'Today we have dealt the Sinaloa drug cartel a crushing blow in one of the largest joint international law enforcement efforts ever undertaken.' Xcellerator began in Imperial County, California, but went nationwide, 'to 70 distribution cells of the Sinaloa cartel in communities in 26 states, from Washington State to Maine.' They took in major cities but also small towns, like Stow, Ohio. On the surface, Stow was a suburban community of 35,000 inhabitants with small businesses, good schools and universities. Below, it was 'a conduit for criminals running cocaine. Just underneath the surface of this peaceful city, the Sinaloa cartel had been sending cocaine through this community's airport, ferrying dozens of kilos from California to Stow on a regular basis. This cocaine ended up not just on the streets of larger cities like Cleveland and Columbus, but also in surrounding small towns, and onto the campuses of schools in the region.' If it could occur in a place like Stow, it could happen anywhere. Said Leonhart: 'The spread of the Sinaloa cartel is a direct threat to the safety and security of law-abiding citizens everywhere.' Theirs was a monster, using the drugs money, the laundered proceeds, to grow ever bigger. 'The money generated from their sales of illegal drugs is used to fund other criminal activities, extending their violent enterprises further into our heartland.' The Americans were under no illusion as to the size of the enemy. 'During this operation, we also saw the extent and scope of the Sinaloa cartel's international network, including multi-hundred kilo cocaine shipments to traffickers in Canada; a super meth lab that's as sophisticated as we've seen anywhere; and presses capable of producing 12,000 ecstasy pills an hour.' What the Sinaloa did with their cash was moving up the enforcement agenda. 'We are committed to defeating those that thrive on the suffering of others, and we are determined to take away from them not just their drugs, but their money, and their freedom . . . Rest assured that, while this is DEA's biggest operation against the Sinaloa cartel and their networks to date, it won't be our last.'

While Imperial Emperor and Xcellerator were making hundreds of arrests of operatives and dealers, Chapo remained in business, in hiding, as strong and as active as ever. These were mere blips in his progress. As a result, HSBC, his dollar laundromat, continued on its own sweet, profit-making way. At the same time, at HSBC, the bank's Investor Relations, or IR, team were reporting ecstatic reviews from share analysts for Mexico. They had taken the leading stock-watchers on a junket all the way to Mexico City and were rewarded with top marks in the analysts' circulars: 'HSBC at its best: Mexico – An oasis of growth' and 'If only it was all like Mexico.' The investor relations team had reported to the board that one analyst declared: 'Taking a deposit-rich franchise with a retail focus, the Group cleans up the balance sheet, adds state-of-the-art systems and a much broader product range while respecting local culture.' Analysts at Citi, the IR executives informed the board, were full of praise: 'The 2002 purchase of Bital and subsequent investments have created a business generating a return on investment of 30 per cent, which considering its size probably makes it HSBC's best acquisition since the 1992 purchase of Midland Bank.' But while the board was concerned with Eric Knight, and patting themselves on the back about their foresight in buying into Mexico, the Latin American country was provoking consternation elsewhere in the bank, in compliance.

Those who work in this very necessary but unglamorous area within banking have always had to deal with the stigma of being seen to obstruct rather than lubricate the money-making machine. In an ideal world, many bankers would tell you, they would not be employed at all, but reality is not like that, so banks have to maintain teams of people to check the rules are complied with. They profess that they welcome them and need them, but you just know they're saying it through gritted teeth.

In July 2007, a worried John Root, in compliance in HSBC in London, emailed Ramon Garcia, the Mexico head of compliance:

'A number of items jump out from your most recent weekly report (02JUL–06JUL), but everything pales in comparison with the [money laundering] items on page 4. It looks like the business is still retaining unacceptable risks and the [anti-money laundering] committee is going along after some initial hemming and hawing. I am quite concerned that the committee is not functioning properly. Alarmed, even. I am close to picking up the phone to your CEO.'

Root referred to a client matter and said it was reminiscent of HSBC's dealings with Ye Gon. '[It] looks like another [Ye Gon] type of situation . . . What is this, the School of Low Expectations Banking?' Continued Root: 'So, [Ye Gon] is strike one. [It] is strike two. Let's now look at strike three. (I hope you like baseball.) The [anti-money laundering] committee just can't keep rubber-stamping unacceptable risks merely because someone on the business side writes a nice letter. It needs to take a firmer stand. It needs some cojones. We have seen this movie before, and it ends badly.'

In October 2007, the Mexican bank regulator, the CNBV, asked to meet with Thurston, the HSBC Mexico head, who summarized the meeting in an email to Geoghegan. He wrote:

'At their request, I met today with the Head of Banking Supervision, and the Supervisor for HSBC, from our regulator, the CNBV, following their on-site examination of various aspects of our business, including cards, money laundering, and treasury operations . . . They walked me through a presentation pack which firstly set out specific points . . . but then moved on to more general concerns of the CNBV with HSBC in Mexico. These centred on:

– weaknesses in internal controls . . . slow progress in tackling [Know Your Customer] data problems and anti-money laundering procedures.

– corporate culture, where they comment that . . . HSBC has driven growth in credit products and launched new products without adequate controls . . .

They also expressed concerns at senior management having dual responsibilities for Mexico and the region, stating that 'there are many concerns on how management will be able to implement strong controls within the bank in Mexico, while keeping an eye on other countries.'

On 27 February 2008, Bagley conducted an exit interview with HSBC Mexico's head of anti-money laundering, who was being replaced. According to Bagley's summary note of the meeting, Leopold Barroso said that, while in his position, he felt civil and criminal 'litigation exposure' due to 'the continued poor controls in the bank, the fact that there were allegations that 60 per cent to 70 per cent of laundered proceeds in Mexico went through HBSC Mexico, and because he did not think that senior management had any commitment to robust anti-money laundering controls.'

Barroso indicated: 'It was only a matter of time before the bank faced criminal sanctions and cited a number of cases.' Bagley wrote: 'It was clear that LRB [Leopold Barroso] felt very strongly that relevant business heads within [HSBC Mexico] had absolutely no respect for [anti-money laundering] controls and the risks to which the Group was exposed and had no intention of applying sensible or appropriate approaches. Again, he cited a number of examples where, despite strong recommendations with the CMP [Compliance], business heads had failed or refused to close accounts or indeed on occasions file SARs [Suspicious Activity Reports]. He thought that there was a culture that was pursuing profit and targets at all costs, and in fact had seen no recent improvement in the standard of controls or the types of decisions being taken.'

And yet, while a picture was starting to emerge of an empire that was out of control, of some parts doing their own thing, and there was a growing number of people inside the bank who suspected that the Group was heading for criminal charges, the bank's group management was still more concerned with growing the bank, cost-cutting and producing ever greater profits. Even the requests for an increased head count to deal with the handling of significant volumes of alerts within the bank were ignored, since the bank was going through a phase of driving returns and keeping staffing levels to a minimum. This was especially true where compliance and anti-money laundering were concerned. The upshot was that at the time that the head of anti-money laundering in Mexico was leaving and denouncing a lack of resources, in the bank family, at a time, in hindsight, when it was clear that they needed to be doubling their efforts in anti-money laundering in Mexico, HSBC continued ratcheting down costs and slashing resources.

Meanwhile, in the command room of HSBC the drive to become world number one and prove Eric Knight and his supporters wrong continued, and in the bank's US arm they launched the '1509' initiative to achieve a return in equity of 15 per cent by 2009. This translated into the '$100 Million Dollar Cost Challenge', which was as straightforward as it implied: to take out costs of $100 million. At the time, HSBC in the US had millions of customers and more than 16,500 employees overall, but the entire compliance department numbered fewer than 200 full-time employees; the anti-money laundering section was only part of that, and much of its work was outsourced thousands of miles away, to India. As 'Project 1509' got underway staff hires were frozen, leading to complaints and sackings. The hiring freeze began in September 2007, when compliance had a head-count of 198 full-time employees and the compliance head, Carolyn Wind, asked for six more recruits and was told by David Dew, the chief operating officer of HSBC in the US: 'This increase will be almost impossible to justify and therefore I must ask you to please cancel the open positions and ensure that your [full-time employees] as at 31 Dec 2007 does not exceed 199.' Tellingly, the compliance department got in touch with their peers at other banks and discovered that at three major banks comparable to HSBC they all had greater numbers of staff. They also found that while their section was raising Suspicious Activity alerts at the rate of three or four a month, their contacts in the other banks were hitting thirty to seventy-five a month, and at one international bank, it was 250 per month. It was obvious to anyone who was willing to take a closer look that HSBC was grossly under-equipped to prevent money laundering. After her request for additional staff was turned down, Wind moved her requests higher up the chain and raised it with the HSBC board for North America. In response a colleague, Janet Burak, sent a supportive memo saying she was bothered at the 'inappropriate concern' shown to Wind's pleas. A month after the board meeting, Wind, a seasoned head of compliance for the US, was sacked, leading to Wind firing off a letter to HR: 'David [Dew] and I disagree on the extent to which my organization can withstand cost cuts and still maintain an effective compliance risk mitigation program. I also believe in an open dialog with the Board and its committees, which may go against the desires of some in the organization.' Wind later told investigators she believed she was fired for speaking out internally about the lack of compliance resources. As Wind was on her way out of HSBC another compliance executive put a request in for 'first-level checkers'. She said: 'We're strapped and getting behind in investigations . . . I'm told I cannot hire first-level staff unless it's offshored . . .' And if there was any doubt that these concerns were not getting to the highest levels of the company, it would be dispelled by a note from the top, from Geoghegan, to the regional CEOs: 'We have agreed that we will have a headcount freeze until the end of the year.' In the face of this response, some staff at the bank in the US still refused to take 'no' for an answer. Having received Geoghegan's reply, two senior executives sent in separate asks. Michael Gallagher explained: 'I have expressed considerable concern for some time over the lack of resources both in compliance and within PCM [Payments and Cash Management] to adequately support KYC [Know Your Customer] and related regulatory requirements.' At the same time, Lesley Midzain, the US chief compliance officer, said she would like four extra full-time staff: 'Given the hiring freeze in global businesses . . . this has continued to be an area of notable risk and regulatory attention and which needs some stabilization for Compliance resources.'

The fundamental philosophies that Stephen Green adhered to in his pursuit of global dominance for HSBC were set down in his paper 'Managing for Growth', and they were: 'grow our revenues by building a world-class, ethical, sales and marketing culture'; and 'be a low-cost producer by increasing productivity and managing costs strategically.' While the word 'ethical' came first, there was an ever-more fraught struggle between absolutely complying and being a total stickler for rules, versus making money. Compliance staff were constantly having to fight their corner. In December 2008, Warren Leaming, who worked in compliance in Group headquarters in London, wrote to the head of HSBC Mexico warning 'the presumption' still seems to be 'in favour of the businesses' views' and that 'needs to change to a more compliance-oriented balance.' Executives were constantly having to weigh up commercial value against reputational risk. Inevitably, faced with the prospect of producing greater returns for the bank and for themselves personally that would be reflected in their end-of-year bonus against blocking business, they were tempted to opt for the former. It was a question of weighing up the certainty of earning more money, against the chance – only a chance – of the bank and them being caught and causing damage to the bank's image. This was all a far cry from Green's declared allegiance to 'ethical' capitalism. The man who so decried the Faustian pact was inviting his subordinates to make one of their own on a regular basis.

As HSBC Group Management were busying themselves with getting bigger and growing profits, absorbing their purchases, expanding on all fronts, driving 'sell, sell, sell' and stripping out costs with a headcount freeze and encouraging initiatives like the '$100 Million Cost Challenge', Mexico had descended into chaos. On 1 December 2006, when HSBC's bosses were filling their diaries with seasonal parties and receptions and the bank's preacher executive chairman was looking forward to one of the busiest periods in the Christian calendar, the elected federal deputies in Mexico's Congress were brawling on the floor of the chamber and the pictures of the politicians, some of whom were well known to the HSBC executives in Mexico, grappling and slugging were transmitted around the world. The cause of the anger was the just-finished presidential election, which the rightist Felipe Calderón had won, although the left claimed that their candidate, Andrés Manuel López Obrador, was robbed of victory. When the time came for the swearing-in, Calderón's supporters surrounded the podium to prevent Obrador's lot from grabbing it and preventing the oath-taking. Among the guests were the former US president George Bush Senior and Arnold Schwarzenegger, the Governor of California. Bush had six secret service men surrounding him and Ioan Grillo, there as a reporter, asked Bush what he thought of the pandemonium. 'Well, I hope that Mexicans can resolve their differences.' Arnie had no bodyguards and Grillo asked The Terminator the same question. 'It's good action!' was his in-character response. It was already a major story but Schwarzenegger's comment added glitter and Mexico's fighting politicians led bulletins across the world.

The sight of the 'good action' should have rung more alarm bells in HSBC Tower, but the inhabitants were otherwise too busy to worry about what was happening in one of the outposts of their empire. Ten days after the inauguration, the newly installed President Calderón took 'good action' of his own: he formally declared war on the drug cartels and he flooded the drug traffickers' districts with heavily armed troops and masked police. They used armoured Humvees backed up with helicopters and the word that went out was that no quarter would be given. The talk was of 'reconquering territory' and 'recovering the calm day-to-day life of Mexicans.' For the second time in recent memory pictures of machine-gun-toting soldiers and police pouring into rural towns and villages flashed around the globe. In all, Calderón ordered 50,000 men into the borderlands, although Chapo remained elusive, as did most of his key lieutenants except one: Hector 'Whitey' Palma was among those paraded in shackles in front of the TV cameras and extradited to the US. The Americans loved what they were seeing and, again, it was headline news, as in early 2007, the US President George Bush Jnr congratulated Calderón and promised to assist in the war.

The two presidents met in the Mexican city of Mérida and agreed the 'Mérida Initiative': the supply of $1.6 billion of US training and military hardware over the following three years. Mexico would also receive thirteen Bell helicopters, eight Black Hawks, four transport airplanes, as well as scanners and phone-intercepting equipment. In August 2007 came another development: the Sinaloa and Los Zetas agreed a ceasefire. The two sides met in Monterrey, in northern Mexico, and Chapo agreed to back off after three years of fighting. The terms agreed were that Los Zetas would still control Nuevo Laredo and the eastern state of Veracruz; he and his organization would keep the west and they got to add the smart Monterrey suburb of San Pedro Garza. However, any hope that peace between the two gangs would end the violence was soon dashed when word travelled round that Chapo had done a deal with Calderón, that he would be left alone as undisputed king of the Mexico drugs trade in return for handing over associates and pointing enforcement agents in the direction of other cartel leaders. Factions turned on each other and on the police. Murders that had been running at the rate of 200 a month rose to 500 and massacres became commonplace, as did shootouts and even grenade attacks. World TV zoomed in on the extraordinary level of carnage, while Mexicans knew not to venture outdoors at night but generally got on with their normal routine. The actual drugs trade, the smuggling into the US and bringing the proceeds back into Mexico, that went on as usual. As did the depositing of cash in the bank – HSBC remained open for business, not closing its doors, despite Black Hawks flying overhead, and bodies, often headless, being dumped on street corners.

Despite a 'war' having been declared in Mexico that directly affected the safety of their staff in the banks across the country as they ran the gauntlet of threats and kidnapping and being told so by their country boss, and the local anti-money laundering chief fearing that the bank was breaking the law, in Canary Wharf HSBC management had what they regarded as more detaining issues. On the back of an investor taking a pop at the executive chairman and Knight Vinke demanding change, the Studzinski experiment had not worked, not least because 'Studs' was not convinced as to how committed HSBC was to forming a proper investment bank. As a result, he left to join Blackstone, the private equity firm. This left Green and Geoghegan and the senior tier in a major firefight and they tried to persuade the industry that their bank still retained 'bulge bracket' aspirations, and that not only did they intend to make good on their promise to stand side by side with Goldman Sachs and co., but that they had the right people and structure to pull it off, despite what people inside and outside of HSBC were saying. The exit of the charismatic Studs meant there was the additional headache of trying to persuade those who he had recruited not to follow him out of the door. But it was to no avail as many of the new recruits left anyway, with one top HSBC banker simply saying on departure that he had realized 'that this re-creation of Morgan Stanley was not going to happen and decided that enough was enough.' The dream that Green and co. had had in 2003 as they assessed potential to expand their global empire far beyond boundaries that HSBC had ever considered was coming apart.

As a result of Studs' leaving, Stuart Gulliver was put in charge of trying to keep a hold on the investment bank goal and he changed the business model of the company again, further adding to the company's identity crisis, shifting away from being highly paid advisors on deals to being financiers, playing to HSBC's strength as a massive, global bank. The bank, he said, would be 'emerging markets-led', in other words, they would focus on the potential of places like Mexico.

Another piece in the HSBC world-conquering jigsaw also went missing as Household ran into trouble. In early 2007, at Canary Wharf at the top of the HSBC building, they'd noticed a rise in defaults on subprime loans in the US. While at the time the US housing crisis was not yet front-page news, and most people had yet to understand what subprime meant, or the effect it would have on global markets, at HSBC this kind of quantifiable damage was a problem that could be identified on a spreadsheet or on Geoghegan's impressive state-of-the-art wall monitor, and they took it extremely seriously. A hastily commissioned internal audit report summarized the following action plan: '1. Fix the problem. 2. Protect the HSBC brand. 3. Make a new business plan.' The cause of the high-level nervousness was a rise in US interest rates coupled with a drop in house prices. All US mortgage lenders were affected but especially those at the bottom of the market, subprime, where, thanks to the Household acquisition, the once high and mighty HSBC now plied its wares. In response, HSBC raised their US bad debts provision to $10.6 billion and Green, still licking his wounds from the Vinke-led disruption, was apologetic and told shocked investors: 'This wasn't supervised as closely as it should have been.'

Geoghegan was equally forthright: 'Mistakes were made, people went for growth rather than quality.' The duo and their colleagues reacted impressively quickly to a problem that they clearly understood and sat much more comfortably in their skill-sets as bankers. This was the kind of firefighting that was much more typical for a banker's brief than dealing with murderous drug cartels laundering money in countries that they rarely visited. They drafted in management consultants and conducted a strategic review of the North American operation, which was then presented to the board in November 2007, by which time the subprime crisis had become a full-blown global catastrophe, with Bear Stearns on the verge of collapse. The report recommended drastic measures, including cutting the number of branches, the old Household network; focusing on large cities in the south of the US, from California to Florida, along with New York, Chicago and Washington; reducing consumer lending; moving out of subprime; streamlining the entire business. The unexpected outcome of the report was that Household, acquired amid great fanfare for $14.2 billion in 2003, was effectively consigned to memory and the HSBC in the US that emerged after the crash in 2008 looked much more like the bank it had once been. Perversely, the exposure to the subprime market via Household and the rapid extrication from the subprime market as a result of acting quickly on the report's recommendations made it look, as more and more banks were forced to go under or turn to government for bailouts in 2008, as though the bank had acted presciently. When the dust settled after the biggest financial crisis since 1929, HSBC appeared to have emerged relatively unscathed. Woe at the top of HSBC turned to preening and self-congratulation. 'There is no doubt that the Household acquisition allowed us to position the bank better for the crisis that was coming,' says Geoghegan. The bank suffered some losses, said Geoghegan, 'but we took far less than any of our competitors did, and in the US, by admitting we saw a problem, we were then able to move swiftly to fix it.' The then-Shadow Chancellor, George Osborne, publicly congratulated HSBC, saying the bank was reaping the benefits of its 'prudence.' Writing in *Euromoney*, Abigail Hoffman pronounced that 'HSBC has had a good crisis.' Doug Flint, the bank's finance director, said the crisis showed that HSBC was 'not too big to fail, it was big enough to cope.' Perhaps the glorying wasn't such a surprise. After all, the British are good at this sort of thing. They were able to turn the rout at Dunkirk into victory; at HSBC, this was the banking equivalent.

EIGHT

HSBC wises up, sort of

Benjamin LeBarón and Luis Widmar were US citizens living in Galeana, Chihuahua. After one of his family members was kidnapped, LeBarón became outspoken in the community against kidnapping and cartel violence. At least twenty armed Sinaloa sicarios stormed LeBarón's house in the middle of the night and abducted him and his brother-in-law, Widmar, in front of LeBarón's wife and five screaming children. Chapo's thugs then beat the men and executed them; next to their bodies left on the side of a road was a sign stating that the murders were in retaliation for Sinaloa members who had been arrested. Rodríguez Hernandez was a photographer for a newspaper in Mazatlán, Sinaloa, and, in another act of revenge by the cartel, was murdered at a restaurant while eating with his wife and child. Rodríguez had photographed police officials with Sinaloa members. In another case, Eliseo Barrón Hernandez, a reporter for a paper in Torreón, Coahuila, who exposed ties between the Sinaloa and local police, was beaten and abducted in front of his two daughters. Later he was shot in the head and dumped in a ditch; following his death, Chapo's butchers hung five banners in prominent spots in

Torreón, one saying: 'We are here, journalists. Ask Eliseo Barrón. El Chapo and the cartel do not forgive. Be careful, soldiers and journalists.' Sinaloa sicarios stormed Sergio Saucedo's home and kidnapped him in front of his wife and children; they tortured and murdered him, cut his hands off, and placed them on his chest. Hugo Hernandez, aged thirty-six, was taken to Sinaloa after being kidnapped in neighbouring Sonora state. A week later, his torso was found in a plastic container on the streets of Los Mochis; elsewhere another box turned up holding his arms, legs and skull. His death was videoed and his corpse cut into seven pieces in total. His murder was a warning. To make sure it was understood, his face was sliced off and stitched onto a football. It was left in a plastic bag near the local government offices in the town hall. There was a greeting note with the football: 'Happy New Year, because this will be your last.'

These were just a very small fraction of the killings carried out by Chapo's crew over the years, but they serve to indicate their cruelty and sheer brazenness. Chapo and Carrillo Fuentes were engaged in a fierce turf war. At a meeting to restore the peace, Chapo put his hand out to Fuentes, who ignored it. Soon after, armed assassins lay in wait for Fuentes and his unsuspecting wife and gunned both of them down as they left a cinema in Culiacán. 'Chapo said he was going to kill him,' was the simple explanation from a member of the Sinaloa. Julio Beltran Leyva, a Chapo ally, disobeyed an order not to send a shipment of cocaine from Acapulco. A hit squad attacked Beltran Leyva, firing so many rounds at him that his head was left dangling from his neck. A corrupt police official, known as Rafita, who worked for rival drug lord Arturo Beltrán Leyva, was slain outside his home. Sicarios working for Chapo killed Rafita after luring him out of his house by pretending they had hit his young son with a car. The boy did not realize anything had happened and continued on his way to school. Meanwhile, they executed his father. These, and many, many more slayings, were carried out by the Sinaloa, acting on Chapo's instructions.

It was not as if, over the years, the Mexican authorities did not try to combat the Sinaloa cartel's power. In 2008, Chapo had been on the run for seven years, and in the face of increased criticism that their tactics of fighting the war against the drug cartels with troops and police alone was not working, the authorities moved firmly against the bank they were certain was making it possible for Chapo and the Sinaloa to operate. They followed the money. As one of their most senior regulators said, for years they had watched and waited – in expectation that things would improve, that HSBC would reform. But nothing changed. Instead, as the cartel continued to grow and spread, the bank's role deepened and widened, and over the years they had got to know all about the specially made cases of cash, the Cayman Islands and the non-existent branch; they knew about Ye Gon, and the currency exchanges. They'd been aware for years, prior to its sale, that Bital had been bad. 'Banking in Mexico had been mismanaged, it's true, but Bital was lousy. It was, though, a powerful franchise, it was worth having, in the sense it had a lot of branches and a lot of clients.'

By 2008 the authorities felt frustrated and ultimately let down by HSBC as they tried to bring an end to the drugs wars and put Chapo back behind bars. It had not always been the case that they were frustrated. Indeed, when HSBC arrived in Mexico banking supervisors had thought that this new, big foreign owner with its great talk, history, management know-how and smart techniques would weed out the bad apples at Bital. 'There was no secret that Bital did not do compliance. HSBC knew that. We reasoned that HSBC would bring their capital and their expertise.' They were disappointed. Said the regulator, 'it was a disaster.' Instead, what they found was that there was a marked disparity between HSBC's senior management, said the regulator, and the bank on the ground; between the image that HSBC sold and the truth. The self-styled 'world's local bank' was not that at all. 'They never got across the operation. Never. Their people would come and go. They never ever tried to speak Spanish, they never spoke the language. They gave the impression of not knowing why they were here and not wanting to be here. They had no idea about building teams and processes. You could tell their guys were lost. They didn't grasp what was really happening; there was a disconnect between what they were thinking was happening and what was actually happening. They didn't get around; their IT was poor, their controls were non-existent.' Almost immediately on acquiring Bital the Mexican authorities noticed how the senior HSBC executives drafted in from overseas and put in charge didn't buy homes in Mexico City. The senior regulator went to dinner with one of the bosses. 'He had an apartment that had been used by many of their people because they knew they were not going to be here for long. They didn't look for a house – which is a pity, because Mexico City is a nice city to live in.' The regulator added: 'He had the same furniture as the previous guy. It seemed dumb, it told you they were not here to take over the bank and make it a success.' This failure to put down roots in the country was indicative of the bank's attitude to the country and its people, and it rankled. 'The leaders were sent in, they'd see it as some sort of burden to be sent here. They'd stay for two years, then leave. There was never really anybody who took it on as a proper job, to make a successful bank.' As the problems with the cartels escalated and the Mexican authorities came to better understand how the HSBC network was a hindrance rather than a help to their attempts to rein in the cartels, they approached the bank and the supervisors conducted an on-site inspection of the bank's branches, resulting in a meeting in October 2007 with Paul Thurston, head of HSBC Mexico. When that did not lead to any discernible immediate reaction (all it mainly did was provoke internal HSBC strife about lack of resources, when the Mexican authorities were seeking meaningful, urgent proof that the bank was taking money laundering seriously) they cracked down. They paid more visits to the bank's outlets, they observed and inspected, they asked to see branches' ledgers and they quizzed the staff and kept a record of all their findings. The findings were damning.

'We'd spent a lot of time with a lot of people,' said a senior Mexico bank supervisor. 'We'd been into branches, we looked at files, we conducted random inspections of files, we were really worried.' What was alarming was that HSBC did not appear to be responding. 'We were doing all these inspections, we were talking to them all the time, meeting their people, saying they needed to put in controls and change, and get on top of it, but none of it was solving the problems.' In February 2008, as the world watched events unfold in the City of London and on Wall Street, as Northern Rock in the UK was being nationalized, and a month before Bear Stearns was bought out by JP Morgan, a draft report was hand-delivered to HSBC by the heads of CNBV and Mexico's Financial Intelligence Unit expressing serious concerns about 'the very high level of [money laundering] risk' at HSBC Mexico. The report found that deficiencies in HSBC Mexico's internal controls had not fallen but increased; 55 per cent of the files sampled by regulators were incomplete; high-profile risk clients were not properly supervised; 'know your customer' updates for high-risk customers were missing; and HSBC Mexico had delayed closing suspicious accounts. One example they gave was of a $2.8-million account kept open for an entire year after it was supposed to have been shut. But that was not all, as the Mexican authorities increased the pressure on HSBC to act. In the same report they said that much of the billions of dollars of drug cartel money laundered through Mexico was in US dollar deposits in personal banking accounts held and maintained by HSBC. The bank had opened and maintained hundreds of thousands of these US dollar accounts, and it was claimed that they had not been properly scrutinized, if at all. When asked about them, senior HSBC Mexico executives were dismissive, defaulting to their 'sell, sell, sell' instruction, the need to drive the P and L, and regarding them as a 'cheap' source of revenue. The report presented to HSBC showed that from 2004 through to 2008, HSBC

Mexico had accepted over $16.1 billion in US dollar cash deposits in Mexico. To give some context to this huge figure, the authorities pointed out that this enormous sum eclipsed the amount of US dollar cash deposits at financial institutions with market shares multiple times greater than HSBC Mexico's.

The Mexican authorities were seriously unhappy with HSBC and expected them to respond. This cash, it was shown, was then sent to the US through an internal scheme called 'Banknotes', under which HSBC in the US bought and sold physical dollars. The Mexican agencies knew this because they had observed billions of dollars being taken in convoys of armoured cars from Ciudad Juárez on the Mexican side, over the Bridge of the Americas across the Rio Grande, to El Paso and the HSBC branches in Texas. Over their counters in Sinaloa state alone, HSBC staff had accepted more than $1.1 billion in dollar bills. 'It was evident that all these dollars could not be from tourism or legitimate shopping', said a Mexico banking supervisor. Turning up the heat, the report charged HSBC with failing to provide requested information, claiming the files or basic account documents could not be located. The FIU produced a chart highlighting how HSBC's response record was worse than that of other Mexican banks. The authorities cited three major money laundering cases – Ye Gon, and the exchanges Casio de Cambio Puebla and Sigue – where 'many transactions were carried out through HSBC'. In their investigations, officials said, to be sure that the message was clear, they had uncovered clear instances of money laundering that HSBC had not reported. The verdict of the investigation was damning and the accusations kept coming, when claims that the bank had made of being unable to lay its hand on account documents were shown to be false when the authorities found copies of them, easily. 'These last cases may imply criminal responsibility of HSBC and its personnel – such as that relating to false statements to administrative authorities and complicity – that the law enforcement and judicial authorities must investigate.' As well as the CNBV and FIU, in early

2008, the central bank, Banco de México, also started showing an interest in HSBC's affairs and wanted an explanation as to why HSBC Mexico's dollar exports were significantly larger than its market share suggested. On 18 February 2008, in a meeting between HSBC Mexico's CEO, Paul Thurston, and the heads of CNBV and FIU, the authorities again raised concerns about the volume of HSBC Mexico's dollar deposits and exports. This time they dropped a bomb and revealed that they had an audio tape of a Mexican drug cartel leader saying that HSBC was 'the place to launder money'. They did not say who it was and still won't – possibly for fear of compromising those who made the recording – but people I've spoken to who have heard it say there's no doubt: he was saying HSBC.

Receiving such a horrifying testimonial, you might suppose, would cause an almighty ruction at the top of the HSBC Tower at Canary Wharf. God's Banker and his senior team might put Risk and their flag-planting and quest for extra bigness to one side for a while and throw themselves into sorting out Mexico. Instead, HSBC management's first reaction was characteristic of the wounded establishment player: rather than accepting the criticism and jumping into action, the instinct of the mighty, all-knowing bank was to try to shoot the messenger. On hearing of the report, the immediate response from headquarters was not to ask whether the allegations were true, but simply 'why now?' In reply, on 23 February 2008, Thurston sent an email to Geoghegan, copied to Stephen Green and three other senior executives: 'Firstly, to answer your question of why is this being raised now? The intelligence that we have been able to gather is that with President Felipe Calderón declaring war on the drugs gangs, crime and corruption, the judicial authorities have heightened the focus on financial investigations and have been putting increasing pressure on the bank regulators because the banks have been seen as not providing good enough support.' Thurston said that HSBC was in the firing line because, 'HSBC has historically, and continues to have, a worse record than the other banks, so we have become a focus of attention. The new Head of the FIU has told us that his staff have told him that HSBC has been the most difficult bank to obtain accurate and timely data from for the past four years.' The implication was not to worry because the claims were not as awful as they appeared – HSBC, seemingly, was being picked on because it did not comply with petty bureaucratic box-ticking. In fact, said Thurston, perhaps to calm his boss, HBSC Mexico had taken more corrective action than the regulators were aware of. The issues raised were because of an account documentation problem, but that would be addressed, in part, by a new centralized electronic imaging system which was taking effect Mexico-wide later that month. In addition, he wrote that 'stronger disciplinary procedures' were being introduced for branch managers who signed off on account openings without personally ensuring all the correct documents were obtained. On the core bulk cash deposits issue, Thurston wrote that the anxiety stemmed from the US and was a general concern, 'not aimed specifically at HSBC,' about 'the flow of US banknotes from Mexico and the potential linkage to drug-related activity.' Significantly, he did not address the charge that HSBC was the go-to bank for money laundering, but neither did he dispute it. This may have stemmed the tide for a while, but the momentum against HSBC was building to such a degree that the Mexican authorities were not going to be fobbed off so easily. Five months later, on 30 July 2008, a senior compliance official in HSBC Group again warned of the lack of controls and widespread corruption at HSBC Mexico. In his warning he recounted to the bank's global head of compliance an interview he had with a seasoned sub-director in HSBC Mexico's anti-money laundering department. The HSBC sub-director had reported that over 1,000 high-risk accounts had recently been identified, and that there was 'little or no accountability in high-risk regions for managers who knowingly accept suspect clients.' He was 'alarmed at the gap between what [HSBC] said about integrity and proper [anti-money laundering] controls, and what is actually happening out in the field, particularly in states close to the US border.' The HSBC senior compliance official then warned that the sub-director's 'misgivings should of course be treated confidentially. I don't want my sources fired or killed. (No exaggeration here – more people are dying in the drug wars in the north of the country than are being killed in Afghanistan or Iraq).' In a sign that the message about the level of changes that needed to be made wasn't getting through at head office, there was a collective shrug. They now recognized that there was terrible blood-letting taking place in the north of Mexico, in the borderlands, but the bank did not acknowledge its own role in helping the perpetrators of the gore. Much to the frustration of the Mexican authorities, despite their reports and warnings and HSBC's reassurances that the issues would be addressed, throughout 2008 the bank carried on accepting cash deposits that could only have come from the sale of drugs.

This pattern of behaviour continued throughout 2008, the only difference this time being that the Mexican authorities were keeping a very close eye on the bank's activities. In November 2008, a compliance officer again reported to the head of compliance about likely widespread money laundering occurring at accounts opened in branches along the US-Mexico border, including Ciudad Juárez. The compliance officer noted a recurring pattern, where customers were declaring anticipated monthly account activity of $300, but then depositing millions of dollars in cash per month, usually in branches far from the border, in clear contravention to the rules that the bank had promised to enforce on their customers. Employees were accepting cash deposits far in excess of HSBC Mexico's $100,000 per customer maximum without obtaining authorization from superiors as required. Indeed, the compliance officer stated that in 'my investigation so far, NOT ONE SINGLE PERSON ha[d] heard' [his emphasis] of this policy. The compliance officer further warned that even when money laundering accounts were eventually 'closed', they stayed open for months while the account holders continued to clean millions of dollars through the system. The compliance officer

concluded that '[I]t is my opinion that we are not "Preventing" anything,' and that '[w]e are allowing the organized criminals to launder
their money . . .' Despite warnings from regulators in late 2007 and
February 2008 that HSBC was the preferred financial institution for
drug cartels to launder money, and despite the numerous internal
alerts throughout 2007 and 2008 of massive money-laundering
schemes and employee corruption, HSBC Mexico accepted over $4.1
billion in US dollar cash deposits in 2008. This was a record amount
for HSBC Mexico, exceeding by over $1 billion the amount of dollars
deposited and exported in the four years prior, which was around $3
billion. This was more than double the amount of dollar cash exports
of banks that had much higher market shares than HSBC Mexico.

However, it appeared that finally HSBC were wising up to the
endemic nature of the problem that needed fixing. On 26 November
2008, a meeting took place between HSBC and the Mexico bank
supervisor, CNBV, and, on the following day, the head of compliance
at HSBC Group was alerted to CNBV's ongoing concern 'that whenever there is a serious [money-laundering] scheme HSBC seems to
be involved.' By chance, Geoghegan had flown to Mexico City to meet
the Minister of Finance and corporate clients as part of one of his
round-the-world trips. It was supposed to be a fly in, fly out, glad-
handing, pro-consular visit, but instead he was asked to see, without
notice, the country's bank supervision chiefs, including the President
of CNBV, Guillermo Babatz; head of CNBV bank supervision, Patri-
cio Bustamante; and head of CNBV anti-money laundering, Pablo
Gomez, and their officials. The three supervisory chiefs laid it on the
line with Geoghegan, who was the first person from the top of HSBC
Group Headquarters they were able to spell out the details of their
concerns to in person. They were 'very concerned' about the US
dollar accounts at the 'Cayman Islands branch of HSBC Mexico' and
the 'sheer volume of US dollars that [HSBC Mexico] repatriates' to
the United States. They told him that between January and September
2008 alone, HSBC Mexico had sent $3 billion in cash to the US,

which represented 36 per cent of the market and double what the biggest bank in Mexico, Banamex, owned by Citi, had repatriated. Geoghegan didn't need reminding that these numbers couldn't stack up, since HSBC Mexico was only the fifth-largest bank in the country. The officials were also gravely concerned that whenever there was a serious money-laundering case, HSBC was involved, and, they added ominously, that the 'USA authorities are concerned at the very high levels.' One of those present recalled: 'It was a very uncomfortable meeting. Michael Geoghegan looked genuinely shocked. Instead of paying a nice visit to the Minister of Finance and some clients he heard this – he wanted to bite our heads off. He was saying, "you've alarmed me, you've surprised me."' A reeling Geoghegan appeared to be thinking aloud when he said 'our whole business in Mexico is not as valuable to us as our reputation.' The penny, or should that be peso, was finally beginning to drop. 'Judging by the internal emails, the chief executive was meant to have known what was going on, but I don't think that was true, not by how he was looking.' Instructively, the most significant remark made at the meeting was that the Americans at a high level were circling, and it was perhaps this, more than the details spelled out by the Mexican regulators, that made Geoghegan sit up. The Mexican agencies had got wind of heightened US interest, in particular the growing conviction in Washington that HSBC was out of control, that it was a major conduit for Sinaloa drug money, and by dropping this into his lap they ensured that he wouldn't be able to ignore the matter.

The Mexican government and bankers had had a long, fruitful relationship with Washington born out of necessity to keep them informed as the drugs wars had escalated and receded over the decades. As long ago as 1986, when, after the murder of Kiki Camarena, President Ronald Reagan had intensified the war on drugs, including closer cooperation with Mexico and funding to help fight the drugs cartels, the relationship, albeit unequally, had seen the development of lines of communication into the White House. Throughout their

investigations into HSBC the Mexicans had been in regular touch
with their US counterparts and kept them fully informed. Far from
being lackadaisical, as is sometimes portrayed when it comes to
moving against laundering, Mexico City was by now all over how
HSBC was being used by them, by the Sinaloa, and was increasingly
fed up and angry. The concern in the US was coming from one of the
most efficient and powerful agencies in the land: the Office of the
Comptroller of the Currency, or OCC. The bureau's job, simply, was
to 'ensure a safe and sound federal banking system for all Americans.'
It's the nation's bank regulator and supervisor and has sweeping
powers to move against banks in the US, national and foreign, that
engage in unsafe and unsound banking practices. The OCC is one
of those federal institutions that Americans from an early age are
taught to revere, and is part of the national fabric, the historical bind-
ing, like the flag, anthem and Mount Rushmore. For a country that is
sworn to nurture business, the Office occupies a prestigious place –
providing Americans and non-Americans with the certainty that US
banks are reliable and trustworthy. Its foundation dates back to the
US Civil War and the belief of President Abraham Lincoln and Treasury Secretary Salmon Chase that the newly united states needed a
single, unified banking system. That led to the National Currency Act
of 1863, followed by the National Bank Act, which created the Office
of the Comptroller of the Currency to administer the new regime.
Arguably, without the OCC there would be no mighty, universally
recognized and accepted dollar. Under the law, a bank applied to the
agency for a charter from the federal government and the bank could
then buy US government bonds, producing income for the government. The bonds were deposited with the US Treasury, which would
provide the security for the new paper currency issued by the banks –
the notes could be redeemed in exchange for gold or silver. The new
currency was the dollar and because it was backed by the bonds, it
acquired security and stability. In 1913, the Federal Reserve Act

created a separate body to manage the dollar, but the OCC kept 'currency' in its title.

The OCC were well aware of complaints levelled at HSBC and had previously had run-ins with them in 2003 and 2006 over its compliance and anti-money laundering procedures. One recurring consternation was the HSBC US operation's poor-quality management in this area. In 2007, Lesley Midzain was hired to replace Carolyn Wind – the compliance chief who was fired after she complained about lack of resources – but the federal officials were unimpressed with the newcomer. Prior to being placed at the helm of the bank's US anti-money laundering programme, Midzain had no professional experience and little familiarity with US money-washing laws. In later testimony, the US central bank, the Federal Reserve, wrote that Midzain did 'not possess the technical knowledge or industry experience to continue as the [anti-money laundering] officer.' The Fed observed that she 'was interviewed by OCC examiners from another team and they supported the conclusion of the OCC resident staff that Midzain's knowledge and experience with [anti-money laundering] risk is not commensurate to HSBC North America's high-risk profile, especially when compared to other large national banks.' In 2009, the OCC reached the same conclusion. The bureau wrote to HSBC, echoing the Fed's criticisms. 'Ms. Midzain was selected as the Compliance Director . . . although she does not have the qualifications or the experience to manage a program at an institution with the size and amount of . . . compliance risk that HSBC has. She is a Canadian lawyer (a barrister and solicitor) . . . She is also a member of HSBC Group's executive development program. Ms. Midzain's assignment has been her first assignment outside of Canada as a part of that program . . . During its 2009 compliance management examination, the OCC determined that Ms. Midzain lacked the experience and expertise . . .' The view from within HSBC was that Midzain was an intelligent, talented, qualified lawyer, destined for greater things within the bank, who could easily take US anti-money laundering in her stride – or in other words, a classic case of HSBC adopting its 'one size fits all, move everyone around, we can take charge anywhere' policy. Where HSBC believed they were employing a master cohort of executives who could be dropped into any situation in any place, and rule, the Fed came to the conclusion that the Midzain appointment displayed a lack of understanding or care about compliance. More than a whiff of complacency over the technical requirements of the role of compliance, the Fed felt that for HSBC dealing with money laundering rules was regarded as a hindrance and not something requiring specialist knowledge or competence. Or, worse, that since it did not go to the bottom line, and did not make the bank money, it was not a priority. To be clear, HSBC was not alone in that opinion and it remains the prevailing attitude across banking and much of big business that those whose role it is to apply the rules – whether they're health and safety, environment, financial – generally come second to the frontline hitters. The upshot for HSBC US was that the bank felt that they could parachute a Canadian into the US operation and that she would be able to pick up the local rules and procedures, not to mention the nuances and subtleties. The reaction of the supervisors in Washington was not dissimilar from their colleagues in Mexico City faced with executives sent in from abroad to manage HSBC Mexico. The mega-multinational was again exhibiting a marked disdain for local and important sensibilities.

In response to the Federal Reserve and OCC criticisms, HSBC did remove Midzain from the anti-money laundering post, but not quite. She was retained in the more senior job of head of HSBC US's compliance department, which meant that she was still the boss in this area and continued to exercise control over the anti-money laundering team who reported to her. As far as HSBC was concerned, Midzain was on their 'executive development program' – and that put her onto a fast-track management footing. The implication was clear:

the American public servants could moan as much as they liked, but HSBC knew better.

In 2009, HSBC US hired a new anti-money laundering chief, Wyndham Clark, a former US Treasury official, who was required to report to Curt Cunningham, an HSBC US executive who freely admitted to having no anti-money laundering experience, and through him to Midzain, whom the Fed and OCC had already found to lack anti-money laundering expertise. Shortly after he arrived, Clark began requesting additional resources and after thirty days at the bank, Clark sent Cunningham a memo with his observations, noting that HSBC US had an 'extremely high-risk business model from [an anti-money laundering] perspective,' and had experienced recent high turnover among management in the department, and had granted only limited authority to him, Clark, as head of the anti-money laundering unit to sort it out. In response he did get three new hirings and commented: 'Clearly a positive, although I understand that these were requested quite a while ago. I hope that isn't the typical response time.' Replied a colleague: 'Oh, this was express time. Trust me on that. Usually the response is "no".' Clark tried to overcome the lack of staffing by using temps and contractors to answer the OCC inquiries and address the anti-money laundering deficiencies. By the time he formally left in August 2010, Clark was using nearly 100 temporary employees and contractors, and had requested fifty additional permanent full-time compliance personnel. Understaffed and under pressure, compliance and anti-money laundering staff constantly battled alert backlogs while requesting extra resources. These requests, if answered at all, generally resulted in additional temporary staff dispatched only when the backlogs grew to unmanageable levels. As the backlog increased, tensions rose. Clark, the anti-money laundering director who had been on the job only a few months, wrote: '[W]e are in dire straights [sic] right now over backlogs, and decisions being made by those that don't understand the risks or consequences of their decisions!!!!' He became increasingly concerned that the bank was not effectively addressing its dirty money problems and he met with the Audit Committee of the HSBC North America board of directors and informed the committee that he had never seen a bank with as high a money laundering risk profile as HSBC US. He also warned them that anti-money laundering resources were 'insufficient versus current risks and volumes'. Clark wrote to a senior HSBC colleague: 'With every passing day I become more concerned . . . if that's even possible.'

Less than a year after taking the job, Clark resigned. He sent an email to the group compliance head, David Bagley, explaining his reasons. '[T]he bank has not provided me the proper authority or reporting structure that is necessary for the responsibility and liability that this position holds, thereby impairing my ability to direct and manage the [anti-money laundering] program effectively. This has resulted in most of the critical decisions . . . being made by senior management who have minimal expertise in compliance, [anti-money laundering] or our regulatory environment, or for that matter, knowledge of the bank where most of our [anti-money laundering] risk resides. Until we appoint senior compliance management that have the requisite knowledge and skills in these areas, reduce our current reliance on consultants to fill our knowledge gap, and provide the [anti-money laundering] director appropriate authority, we will continue to have limited credibility with the regulators.' After Clark quit, the bank hired Gary Peterson, an existing anti-money laundering consultant to the bank, as HSBC US's new anti-money laundering supremo.

Around the same time that Clark departed, Midzain also went, leaving open the post of chief compliance officer. That post remained vacant until HSBC US hired Eric Larson who, in turn, left after fifteen months. The bank then asked Peterson to serve, not only as HSBC US's anti-money laundering director, but also as its compliance head, and as HSBC North America's regional compliance officer. The upshot of all this was that in five years, HSBC US had four chief compliance officers and five anti-money laundering directors.

And yet, for all the manifest woes and discontent inside and about the company – from employees, investors and regulators alike – in 2008, Green, Geoghegan and their colleagues reached the summit of their achievements set out six years previously, and HSBC was acknowledged as the world's biggest bank. Despite staff struggling with compliance and money laundering and endless complaints about lack of resources and seemingly non-stop procession of resignations from key but unglamorous roles, HSBC had become World Number One, with annual profits of $19.13 billion. *The Economist* declared it 'the largest banking group in the world'. *The Banker* named HSBC the 'world's most valuable financial brand'. Bank of America and Citi were beaten. Managing for Growth had triumphed. In their own version of the game of Risk, which had included High Noon, the 'sell, sell, sell' mantra, the move into commercial banking, cutting costs – they'd all come good. There had been some hiccups along the way. Household was best forgotten, although it meant the bank was in a good place ahead of the crisis, and investment banking and the hiring of Studs and 700 bankers, that was another miss. Otherwise, though, it was strong, resilient, ideally placed to expand further.

Elsewhere, however, dark forces were quietly massing. In the US, a new development intensified OCC's focus on the HSBC laundromat as the OCC became aware of two separate federal investigations into possible massive-scale money laundering through accounts at HBSC. The first investigation was by the US Department of Homeland Security's Immigration and Customs Enforcement (ICE) unit investigating possible washing of illegal drug proceeds, the second a US Attorney in West Virginia investigating a Medicare fraud. Senior OCC officials in Washington arranged to meet with the ICE representatives, and on 1 September 2009, a meeting in Washington was attended by the OCC deputy general counsel Daniel Stipano, Deputy

Controller in charge of Large Bank Supervision Grace Dailey, OCC senior legal counsel who specializes in anti-money laundering, James Vivenzio, the OCC anti-money laundering examiners of HSBC in the US, and the ICE investigators. After the meeting ended and the ICE representatives had left, the OCC officials remained behind to discuss supervision of HSBC in the US. The lead anti-money laundering official overseeing HSBC in the US said that during his tenure the bank had been the subject of eighty-three warning notices, and he had twice recommended issuing to the bank a heavyweight 'Cease and Desist' order. Stipano, the OCC's number two lawyer, asked for a thorough review of HSBC in the US in relation to money laundering, which took concerns about HSBC to another level. Behind the scenes, moves against the bank were gathering pace. Following Stipano's intervention, the OCC doubled its efforts and drew up a plan to investigate HSBC and, in anticipation of the move, recruited additional staff to deal with the paperwork. In March 2010, the OCC issued a 'Supervisory Letter' stating that HSBC had failed to file Suspicious Activity Reports, or SARs, on time and the bank had allowed a backlog of over 17,000 of these alerts to build. While basking in the glory of the previous year's global triumph, HSBC had just received its first formal suggestion of possible law-breaking. The agency went on to claim that 98 per cent of the SARs fell into the most extreme 'high-risk' category and 14 per cent were at least six months overdue. The OCC gave the bank a deadline of 30 June 2010 to clear the 17,000. The number one bankers in the world were put on notice. Soon after delivering the Supervisory Letter, the OCC's main official charged with supervising HSBC in the US, Sally Belshaw, and the head of Large Bank Supervision, Grace Dailey, met Geoghegan and the bank's North America chief, Brendan McDonough. The bankers were told that the Washington bureau had identified serious anti-money laundering deficiencies 'throughout the bank'. Belshaw wrote a note: 'He [Geoghegan] asked when I thought things went bad.'

To this day, compliance chiefs at other banks are astonished by this failure to recognize the enveloping crisis in its midst. 'There are areas they should have picked up on: the volume of cash deposits and their lack of proportionality; the backlog of suspicious transactions which was mounting; the number of new accounts opened in the Cayman Islands and the absence of documentation . . . these were all warning that their systems were open to abuse and were being abused', said the former head of compliance at a US investment bank. Belshaw noted, 'Grace and I described the spotty history of the bank relative to [anti-money laundering] compliance.' They went on to tell Geoghegan how, in the past, whenever the OCC raised an issue, 'management reacted to our findings and took corrective action.' But in recent years this had changed, and it was remarked that there had been a marked, negative shift in attitude. 'This, however, culminated in a systemic concern that we ultimately characterized as ineffective management . . . We believe that over the years, the people and program did not advance to keep pace with the risk . . . Talent left the organization and was not replaced by people with sufficient technical skills to lead. Succession/bench strength for the compliance area is now inadequate . . . The backlog issue is a symptom of these management weaknesses . . .' By now Geoghegan, the chief executive of HSBC worldwide, second to Green, the executive chairman, had heard the same story of failures within his bank in person from the Mexicans and now direct from the Americans: their bank was a gift to those wishing to rid themselves of dirty money. He had also been informed, straight, why this had occurred. They'd grown the bank too big to manage – or rather, while they were growing the bank so big they did not attend to how it was actually being managed. But it wasn't over, as Belshaw and Dailey continued. The two women highlighted 'findings of weakness in [know your customer] in several areas: bank notes, wire activity, domestic and international customers. We highlighted our recent concerns/questions about management's ability to address the backlog problem (and violation) given weaknesses we are seeing in data integrity in reports, quality of alert dispositioning, and the lack of independent review/oversight of that process.' They laid it on the line: 'Our supervisory letter requires that backlogs be completely corrected by June 30th. We emphasized that not only must the number be addressed, but they must be effectively dispositioned (qualified reviewers guided by appropriate policy/process, adequate documentation, appropriate/timely SARs filed), and an ongoing system of controls must be in place to ensure the process is sustainable. We will be requiring qualified, independent verification of that as part of the process.' The reaction of the bank's most senior management to the letter was calamitous.

NINE

The whistleblower who wasn't a whistleblower

Everett Stern had always wanted to join the Central Intelligence Agency. More specifically, since he was a teenager he had dreamed of being in the CIA's National Clandestine Service, as a spy, collecting intelligence on enemies of the state. Stern was born in New York City, grew up in Florida and went to college at Florida Atlantic to study for an arts degree. A relationship ended, and he decided to fulfil his desire to serve his country, to travel, to nail those who wanted to do America harm, so he applied to become a spook. He was interviewed but failed to be accepted. It was a shattering blow, a life's dream up in smoke, and instead he went on to complete an MBA at Stetson University in May 2010. After that, and stuck for something to do, he saw an online advert for a bank that was looking to boost its anti-money laundering programme. Intelligence gathering . . . money laundering, it had the similar whiff of intrigue and excitement. The bank was attractive, too: HSBC, which was global, substantial and clearly going places – a journey that he wanted to be a part of. He filled out the forms and was called for interview. To his delight, he was taken on, aged twenty-six, to start in the bank's offices in New Castle, Delaware, in its expanded anti-money laundering push. HSBC had asked the consulting firm, Deloitte, how it should best deal with the growing litany of issues surrounding the bank and money laundering. The US authorities had been leaning on the bank to bring in external 'independent' experts to help and Deloitte, with revenues of $26.6 billion and 170,000 staff in 2010, was more than an auditor, its usual description as one of the 'Big Four' firms that audit accounts worldwide. It had several business arms, including Financial Advisory Services, or FAS, which covered compliance and money washing checks for clients. HSBC, which should have tackled anti-money laundering in-house many years earlier, had found itself, thanks to the authorities in Mexico and the US, crawling all over it asking awkward questions, needing to bring in outsiders for assistance. These experts were supposed to act objectively, not for the bank or in tandem with HSBC, which is something that the authorities were particularly insistent on.

Deloitte's FAS unit was selected to assist HSBC because it had built up a nice business advising other banks in the same specialist and reputationally dangerous field of anti-money laundering. In 2004, FAS had been called in after the New York State Banking Department and the Federal Reserve Bank of New York had identified weaknesses in Standard Chartered's anti-money laundering processes at its New York branch. Deloitte was meant to behave independently of Standard Chartered, but years later, it turned out they hadn't. Subsequently, Deloitte were hit by a $10-million fine from the Superintendent of the New York State Department of Financial Services, Benjamin Lawsky, and he was so annoyed that he had barred Deloitte's FAS from accepting new consulting engagements at financial institutions regulated by his office for twelve months. Lawsky found that Deloitte, 'Did not demonstrate the necessary autonomy required of consultants performing regulatory work'. At the behest of Standard Chartered, Deloitte removed a recommendation aimed at rooting out money laundering from its written final report to his department. In addition, said Lawsky, Deloitte had broken New York banking law by disclosing confidential information about other banking clients to Standard Chartered. It transpired that a senior Deloitte employee had sent emails to Standard Chartered workers containing two reports on anti-money laundering issues at other Deloitte client banks. 'Both reports contained confidential supervisory information, which Deloitte FAS was legally barred from disclosing to third parties.' Deloitte was supposed to be maintaining distance, making sure Standard Chartered reformed its ways; instead, it had been doing the bank's bidding and sharing with it confidential regulatory information. However, it was not just Standard Chartered who had been up to no good since, in the UK, Deloitte also appeared to be uncomfortably close to Lloyds Bank and the processing of customer claims for payment protection insurance. PPI, as it was known was mis-sold by UK banks on a gargantuan scale to people who did not want or need it; the insurance policy was supposed to provide cover for loan repayments if the customer fell seriously ill and could not work or lost their job. Lloyds – the biggest PPI seller in the UK – was fined £4.3 million by the Financial Services Authority for not settling PPI claims promptly. Lloyds admitted to 'issues' in the handling of PPI complaints and fired Deloitte, which operated the unit. The news was accompanied by a story from an undercover newspaper reporter who claimed that when he went through training to join the bank's PPI complaints centre he saw staff being taught how to 'play the system' against customers. This included choosing to ignore the risk that fraud may have been committed and knowing that most customers gave up if their complaint was rejected first time around. The Standard Chartered brief was similar to the one that Deloitte had with HSBC. Under pressure from the Feds, the same firm that had worked with Lloyds was drafted in to help HSBC deal with its money laundering compliance issues. The solution Deloitte came up with for HSBC was simple: to throw bodies at the problem to clear the backlog at speed.

Clark, the US Treasury official who joined HSBC in 2009, struggled to add three full-time staff to what was then a department of 130 full-time staff for the whole of the US. By the time he left, in August 2010, he was using nearly 100 temps and contractors and had put in a request for fifty more full-timers. Within a further month of his departure, the tally shot up again – to more than 400 full-time employees, which was an impossible number to train sufficiently in the huge complex world of fraudulent money transfers.

New Castle is charming and quaint, home to 5,000 or so people, full of wide walks and historic old buildings. Located on the Delaware River, it's ten miles, a six-minute drive, from the state capital of Wilmington. To walk around it is to step back in time to the Colonial era, and New Castle has the distinction in the US of coming second only to Williamsburg, Virginia, for the number of preserved houses and municipal buildings from that period. What distinguishes New Castle, Wilmington and Delaware as well, however, is the sheer number of banks, finance and trust companies and multinationals that base themselves here. It's a strange contrast: sleepy old state with towns of cobblestones, brick mansions and tall ships along the waterfronts, antiquities and collectibles on one side; then serious, modern company offices with corporate signage and blackened-out windows on the other. The corporates are here because Delaware offers them total secrecy. When HSBC moved its legal US head office address from Buffalo, New York, to New Castle in 2004, it was in effect relocating to the American mainland's equal in the offshore Cayman Islands. In 2009, the year before the OCC issued its 'Cease and Desist' order, Delaware headed the world list of most opaque jurisdictions. The tiny East Coast state saw off the likes of Switzerland, Luxembourg, British Virgin Islands, Panama and the Cayman Islands and it was ranked number one for the place that afforded the best protection to anyone who did not wish to disclose that they were the beneficial owner of a company. That's why it is still home to 50 per cent of the US's quoted firms and 650,000 companies, which works out as around one company per Delaware resident. If this has a familiar ring, that's because Delaware, like Cayman, specializes in the creation of shell companies.

The ranking of number one – best or worst, depending on how you prefer to look at it – comes from a mammoth, 1,800-page study, the Financial Secrecy Index, which took eighteen months to compile and was put together by academics, accountants and investigators for Tax Justice Network, whose verdict on Delaware was that it was: 'The world's top secrecy jurisdiction. Register a company here and no one will ever know. If you have overseas income, it will be tax exempt.' The state, long the base of 46th President Joe Biden, and not far from Washington, DC, may appear benign but it sells corporate secrecy, and it does not make public details of trusts, company accounts and beneficial ownerships. Delaware also allows companies to base themselves there or give it as their legal address with virtually zero disclosure. Similar to Ugland House in Cayman, Delaware has its own hum-drum office building which is the legal home to 285,000 separate businesses: 1209 North Orange in Wilmington. Delaware state officials insist that it is not secrecy that attracts so many companies and individuals to register businesses in their fine state; rather, it is their brilliantly fair and efficiently run judicial system.

Cayman and Luxembourg were publicly upset at being highly placed in the Financial Secrecy Index, both appearing in the top five. Cayman Finance, the islands' business representative body, fumed: '[This] report [has a] selective bias and [is] totally discredited, and will be seen as such by everybody in the financial world.' The Luxembourg Bankers' Association (ABBL – Association des Banques et Banquiers) moaned: 'The ABBL does not consider Luxembourg to be a "secrecy jurisdiction". In both penal and fiscal matters, Luxembourg already co-operates more fully on an international basis than 80 per cent of countries in the world.' John Christensen, a director of

Tax Justice Network and a joint author of the report, was unimpressed: 'The secrecy jurisdictions are found in North America, the former British Empire and Europe. These are the regions which have driven the neo-liberalization project that has skewered financial markets and turned them into criminogenic markets. They can attract capital with no questions asked.' His colleague, Richard Murphy, a senior adviser at Tax Justice Network, chipped in: 'Two million corporations are formed each year in the United States, more than anywhere else in the world. Delaware, in turn, is the biggest single source of anonymous corporations in the world. Why go to the Caymans when you can just go down the street?'

In 2013, The *New York Times* published an op-ed headed 'Delaware, Den of Thieves?' by John Cassara. 'Outside of crimes of passion, criminal activity is typically motivated by greed. As a special agent for the Treasury Department, I investigated financial crimes like money laundering and terrorism financing. I trained foreign police forces to follow the money and track the flow of capital across borders. During these training sessions, I'd often hear this: "My agency has a financial crimes investigation. The money trail leads to the American state of Delaware. We can't get any information and don't know what to do. We are going to have to close our investigation. Can you help?" The question embarrassed me. There was nothing I could do.' Cassara said that in the years he was assigned to the Treasury's Financial Crimes Enforcement Network, or FinCEN, he observed many formal requests for assistance concerning Delaware. Its image was 'tawdry ... synonymous with underground financing, tax evasion and other bad deeds facilitated by anonymous shell companies—or by companies lacking information on their "beneficial owners", the person or entity that actually controls the company, not the (often meaningless) name under which the company is registered.' It is all very reminiscent of Obama's point of criticism about the Cayman Islands. Said Cassara: 'Our State and Treasury Departments routinely identify countries that are havens for financial crimes. But, whether because of short-sightedness or hypocrisy, we overlook the financial crimes that are abetted in our own country . . .' Obama, it turns out, did not need to single out faraway Cayman – there was a place just a short drive away, along Interstate 95 and US 202.

A few days before Stern started working at HSBC in Delaware in October 2010, believing that he was finally going to be living his dream of going after the bad guys, the OCC issued its 'Cease and Desist' order requiring HSBC to strengthen multiple aspects of its anti-money laundering effort. They've issued one to HSBC before, in 2003, in the period after 9/11 when the feds got tough on money laundering. This is the second. It's a 'sort yourself out, or else' instruction – the 'or else' being that the OCC has the power to investigate further and can force the shutting down of the bank in the US. Ultimately, it could have moved to have the bank's charter withdrawn and that would have meant that HSBC would have had to withdraw from the US market completely, which would have been a calamity. Some argued that HSBC got off lightly with this instruction from the OCC. Here, after all, was a major corporation that in recent years, after that first order was issued in 2003, was warned multiple times about its lax compliance procedures and had been made fully aware of the concerns surrounding its activities – yet had done absolutely nothing to stem the tide. Whichever view is correct, the thirty-one-page 'C and D' order makes for grim reading: a backlog of over 17,000 alerts identifying possible suspicious activity that have yet to be reviewed; ineffective methods for identifying suspicious activity; failure to file timely Suspicious Activity Reports with US law enforcement; failure to conduct any due diligence to assess the risks of HSBC affiliates before opening correspondent accounts for them; a three-year failure by HSBC US, from mid-2006 to mid-2009, to conduct any anti-money laundering of $15 billion in bulk cash transactions with those same HSBC affiliates, despite the risks associated with large cash transactions; poor procedures for assigning country and client risk ratings; failure to monitor $60 trillion in annual wire transfer activity by customers domiciled in countries rated by HSBC US as lower risk; inadequate and unqualified [anti-money laundering] staffing; inadequate [anti-money laundering] resources; and [anti-money laundering] leadership problems. This was the world of HSBC that young Everett Stern, keen, ambitious and desperate to prove himself, was about to step into.

Everett Stern comes across as earnest, fast-talking, bespectacled, well built, with a sharp, razor hair cut around the sides. With his confident delivery and penchant for wearing a conservative suit, white shirt and plain tie, polished shoes and a patriotic US flag in his lapel, he sounds and looks the official, military sort. On his first day on the job he was asked to report to a low-rise building leased by HSBC close to a shopping mall. 'There were folded-up cubicles and the walls were unpainted', he told Matt Taibbi of *Rolling Stone*. It didn't seem like a bank office – most of the people there were wearing jeans and t-shirts and that's because its main function is as a call centre for the bank's credit card operation. Stern's job was 'compliance officer', for which he was paid $54,000 a year and he received no training. 'I had to go to the library to take out books on money laundering. That's how bad it was.' Frequently, he got so bored that, having finished his daily workload early, he and a colleague would head out the back and throw stones into a nearby quarry. The large room he was shown into in the office was mostly eerily deserted. There were about a dozen people there, hunched over screens, he recalled, and there didn't seem to be anyone in charge and certainly no sense of urgency. 'If we asked for any more work, they got angry.' The New Castle anti-money laundering operation was split in two, between regular HSBC staff monitoring current transactions and those drafted in to work on 'look-back', to tackle the backlog of alerts, which Stern was attached to. He soon realized that no one was that interested in what was being done because whenever he raised a potential issue for investigation his superiors became irritated, seemingly wishing he hadn't bothered them. Perhaps it is hardly a surprise that this was the case. After all, Stern was a member of a team sitting in a bank building in Delaware, named the number one location in the world for financial secrecy, charged with looking into thousands of transactions made via the same bank, overseen by his colleagues in HSBC, that were designed to stay secret. To add to the circular nature of it all: Deloitte, the global brand advising HSBC on how best to deal with anti-money laundering, how to break apart secrecy, also had its name on offices in Delaware and in Cayman. Far from being a glasshouse of rigorous investigation and analysis, New Castle in practice was a cosmetic device to convince the authorities that HSBC was taking money laundering seriously. Crucial to that image, of course, was reducing the number of backlog cases of suspicious transactions. The bank had to bring down the pyramid of alerts, but it only had to mark them as read and looked at, not follow up each one with an investigation. Far from the place where Stern had thought he had come to help catch the bad guys, in reality New Castle was little more than a box-ticking exercise to keep the authorities at bay. 'There were multiple backlogs' of alerts, said Stern. 'The name of the game was to close as many as you possibly can.' Confirmation of the office's actual role came not long after Stern joined when his 'target monitoring team' was suddenly reinforced by young workers moved across from the bank's Household credit card processing business. The 'sell, sell, sell' boys and girls were relocated to anti-money laundering after Household was wound down, but they weren't interested in fraud, and certainly didn't care to the degree that Stern did about doing his job well. Stern later claimed that you could walk into the building and that there would be a very high chance that the person you spoke to wouldn't have a clue what money laundering was. Their priority was not busting apart criminal deposits and payments but planning their social lives.

Early on in Stern's time in New Castle he received the edict from Deloitte that those working on clearing the backlog, rather than monitoring current transactions, had a set target of seventy-two transactions to clear a week. It is hard to say why it was such a precise number, but seventy would have been fourteen a day, which works out at two an hour, a neither overly nor under ambitious number. As for Stern's exact brief it was straightforward enough to follow. When something that might be suspicious occurred on an account, it attracted an alert on the system. It could be anything from a name or address that didn't seem right, or someone wiring $9,999 to stay under the $10,000 notification limit, to the use of round figures. If an alert was flagged, the bank was supposed to immediately investigate, and it was Stern's job to undertake that investigation, which meant finding why the alert was raised and checking it out. Or that at least is what he thought his job was. If the bank didn't clear the alert, it created a 'Suspicious Activity Report,' which was handed over to the US Treasury Department to be investigated, so the question was how deep did the scrutinizing of the New Castle employees go? 'Basically, if a company had a website, you could clear them,' said Stern. Meanwhile, above them, management was sending big-upping emails. 'Great job by some Delaware professionals in the early part of the week,' said one. The email was headed: 'The 60-plus crowd,' in praise of those who had cleared more than sixty suspicious transactions that week, proof that the bank was doing what the OCC had ordered, well advanced towards hitting the magic seventy-two. It was all about speed and volume: when teams had cleared so many transactions, when they passed a target, they would be rewarded with a catered lunch. Stern was more diligent than the others, but his efforts were not appreciated. 'They didn't like all this digging around.' On one occasion Stern successfully identified one suspicious transaction by drawing up a spreadsheet to track names with different spellings. This way he could show how someone at the bank could deliberately make the slightest change to a spelling to by-pass a security filter. Except that when he reported it, instead of praising him a boss asked: 'How much time did you spend on the Excel analysis?' Stern had always been very good with computers and spreadsheets in particular, and thinking that it would be appreciated by the senior management, he offered to design a template for producing uniform reports about alerts. The next morning, his superior came back with his answer: 'I appreciate the effort, like the product, however what I will say is this: I struggle with the fact you indicate (Everett) you spent the entire morning working on this. The only thing we should be focusing on right now is clearing alerts . . .' At weekly meetings, Deloitte went through how many cases had been cleared and questioned delays and those contractors who were held up as too slow on the job were dismissed.

Meanwhile, alone and feeling increasingly underappreciated for doing his job too well and being belittled for it, within only a few months of starting work Stern joined the list of those who had grown frustrated at HSBC's disregard for bringing its crooked customers to justice. 'I realized they'd hired me because I was an idiot. It was all for show.' Eventually he had had enough: enough of being fobbed off; enough of seeing suspicious transfers that included everyone from the Mexican drug cartels to Hamas and Hezbollah being repeatedly ignored by his superiors and he did the only thing that he could think was his duty to do: he emailed his former recruiter at the CIA to tell them what was going on. It was an agonizing decision. 'Before I sent the email I was tossing and turning. I knew I had to do the right thing, to make a stance for what was right.' Even so, it was not easy. 'I was reminded of what my dad taught me that Emerson said: "To know even one life has breathed easier because you have lived. This is to have succeeded."' He couldn't sleep, couldn't make up his mind, and had no one he could turn to for advice. It was a momentous step, one that would lead to personal ruin in working in banking and financial hardship. Finally, at two o'clock in the morning he pressed the 'Send' button. Such a move is extremely rare because any whistleblower knows they are unlikely to work again in their chosen industry, particularly in the closed world of banking where the rule of omerta has always been prevalent. Any whistleblower has to weigh up the momentous nature of what they are doing with the fact that if they are discovered, they will lose friends, be ostracized, or worse, regardless of claims by politicians that they have passed laws to protect them. The reality is that once they have blown the whistle they're finished where they work, and often where they live.

In October 2011, a year after he joined, Stern left the bank. 'I came into this job with such energy,' he said. 'I was like a balloon that got popped. I was really excited for the job.' By 2012, a year after his departure, and his action out in the open, Stern was reduced to 'sleeping on a cot in a 400 square feet apartment. People don't see that, and they don't see the struggle you go through right before you blow the whistle.' Within finance, the code of silence is especially strong and it is just not done to break ranks and to speak out. The fact that Stern chose to do so not only speaks volumes of his courage but also his natural outsider status – he broke the rule of omerta because he had no idea that it existed since he didn't grow up inside a banking family. The industry is built upon discretion, upon maintaining confidences – and that extends to the employees talking about each other, sharing information about their place of work. Partly, as well, historically it is a male-bonding thing – in that heavily macho culture speaking out is akin to self-imposed social exclusion. The boys' mantra of 'what happens on tour, stays on tour' applies just as much to the masculine atmosphere of the trading floor or banking hall. The omerta is engrained throughout the organization. Even getting a banker to say something in public on a positive subject can be a painful experience and every utterance they make is tightly controlled, and I know this from my own personal experience. On one occasion, to sit down with a bank chief entailed me jumping through five sets of hoops, explaining to various PRs what I wanted and providing guarantees that only just stopped shy of being written in blood that I was not going to turn 'hostile' or ask a question from leftfield, and even then what the banker said to me was so bland as to be almost unprintable. On another occasion, I was passed through eleven different staff members before I was shown into the corporate dining room with a bank CEO. This culture is in the DNA – it's impressed upon new recruits and constantly reinforced, and no one, absolutely no one, talks to or contacts the media without prior approval, much less the CIA! Which is why Stern's decision to speak out was so remarkable.

But what shouldn't be forgotten is that HSBC, not for the first time, were responsible for making a crucial mistake in having hired outsiders to do their grunt work and throwing bodies at the money laundering problem in the belief that in their crude, muscling manner, they could simply make the problem go away. In opening their doors to people who were not from the banking family, they inadvertently admitted into their midst people like Stern, a self-styled 'disrupter, advocate and patriot'. In the normal course of hiring the bank's recruits would have to endure round after round of interviews. They would be vetted and approved, their CVs examined, their characters analysed and those who made the grade immediately were expected to return the honour at having got the job with unwavering loyalty because from the moment they were accepted they became a part of the family. In this instance, HSBC, working through Deloitte, which was running the project, threw their usual caution to the wind and to address the OCC's concerns as rapidly as possible and avoid any further threats of a 'cease and desist' they went out and recruited people who were not interested in them, who did not see themselves as signing up to a glorious career with the world's largest global bank. They were being paid – by the hour in many cases – for a one-off assignment. They weren't even reporting to HSBC staff but to equally disinterested middle-managers drafted in from Deloitte. That's how it felt, and that mood of disinterest and lack of appreciation was compounded by the soulless nature of working in the New Castle premises. All of which added to the sense that it was not the quality of the work that was going to be appreciated, but simply the quantity – people like Stern were there to shift as much of the backlog as possible in the quickest time.

In the short time that Stern had been there he was turning up information that he didn't know what to do with, and it was with this in mind that he emailed his contact at the CIA, even though they had rejected him once already. 'I remember being a candidate for the National Clandestine Service, now called the Directorate of Operations [DO]. It was a shame I was rejected before I joined HSBC Bank. I still got to serve, though, by passing critical national security information to the CIA for over a year while working at the bank.' And the information that he shared with the ICA showed that when the bank did boost resources, they filled the building with people from their own credit card business, people who had been fired from their jobs on the understanding they would be immediately rehired to go into anti-money laundering. All they were doing, said Stern, was 'clearing transactions all day long', often without giving them so much as a second glance. He was alarmed by the amount of money laundering he was seeing, and the bank's failure to prevent it. Stern was not alone in what he observed and experienced at New Castle. Other contractors, when pressed later, described the HSBC/Deloitte operation as 'more cosmetic than concrete', and as 'a factory . . . There was a lot of pressure to get investigations closed'. One contractor said that when an investigator couldn't track down information on a counterparty to a particular transaction, the investigator was told to close the case even if it seemed suspect. Another said he was 'extremely, extremely disappointed with the way it was handled. There was a lot of pressure to get investigations closed.' Another simply pointed out that many suspicious cases were 'buried.' In one example that was later highlighted in the investigation into HSBC's activities, a contractor reported that he wanted to find out why thirteen parties had wired a total of $1.3 million into an HSBC account in Hong Kong on the same day. When he asked a Deloitte supervisor to request that the Hong Kong office provide information about the customer, he was told that decision rested with the HSBC manager in charge of the account. The information was not provided, and the same contractor said he was later fired for not clearing enough alerts.

As for Stern, he disputes the verb 'to whistleblow' in his case. 'I was not a whistleblower. That suggests you blow the whistle and stop.' Stern is not like that, he kept going and kept informing. 'I'm a fighter, I was trying to change a culture and to make a significant, positive change to society.' He was severely criticized as a result. He later gave a long interview to ABC News explaining his position. 'They said it would be out in two weeks, but they never aired it. The media needed to report on this story, but they've shown extreme apathy and a lack of reporting integrity in regard to this story.'

What drove him on, he said, was his outrage and purpose. 'By removing and lessening moral responsibility we create a problem. That problem needs to be hit at source, which means individuals taking personal responsibility. And it means if it is not going right, then reporting it – because that is the right thing to do.' Stern had no truck either with those who play down financial fraud, business illegality, as somehow not so serious, even when it was clear that the proceeds were being used to finance drugs, weapons, terrorism. 'White-collar crime is not white-coloured. It's red-collared and the red is blood.' Sometimes, 'the enemy is the high-ranking CEO in a business suit.' After he left the bank, like most people in his position, Stern was effectively barred from banking, and did shifts as a waiter at a branch of PF Chang's. 'I was reduced to working as a waiter. I went from working at a Chinese bank to working at a Chinese restaurant. My MBA education was worth $2.15 an hour plus tips.' But what he set in motion would have a profound impact on HSBC and he was able to do what neither the authorities in Mexico or the US, or those concerned within the head offices in London had been able to do. He had shone a light on HSBC's banking activities that was so bright that by the summer of 2012, the CIA's inquiry had broadened to the bank's money-laundering operations in the Middle East, Iran, Sudan, North Korea and, of course, Mexico.

Meanwhile, Stern's own journey after HSBC took a very different course. In 2014, he started his own private intelligence agency, Tactical Rabbit, in Pennsylvania, where he lives. 'Tactical Rabbit was founded in response to what I perceive as the inability of financial institutions to properly verify their customers, hedge fund investment decisions being made without factoring in non-traditional data, and terrorists and organized crime syndicates increasingly using the financial system against the public,' stated Stern. In other words, it's like a private version of the CIA. They supply 'actionable business, legal and national security intelligence. Our main mission is promoting justice and defending the United States.' His firm 'does what others cannot do and goes where others cannot go while providing gold standard intelligence collection and analysis, top-notch advocacy, and world-class consulting services. These three pillars form the basis on which we design and implement tactical and long-term strategic solutions tailored to achieve individualised success for our valued clients. Tactical Rabbit uses sophisticated, proprietary investigative tools and techniques that enable us to dig deep, and dive down the right rabbit hole.' Stern maintained that his team is comprised of former 'CIA Field Operation Officers, FBI Special Agents, DEA Special Agents, Secret Service Agents, NSA Contractors, US Special Forces.' In his life after HSBC he steered campaigns against the threatened closure of Sweet Briar College, a private women's college in West Virginia, to highlight racism by a member of the Palm Beach County Sheriff's Office and to show a glitch in the Medicare payments system. In each one he relied on information supplied by an insider. In August 2013, he joined an Occupy Wall Street working group called Alternative Banking to publicize his allegations against HSBC, frustrated at the lack of progress with the CIA's investigation. He publicly declared that HSBC committed anti-laundering violations through the end of his employment in 2011. 'Financial institutions can misbehave,' said Stern, 'but my tough team of experienced investigators at Tactical Rabbit will work to keep them in line.' Said Stern: 'Our own banking system and money is being used against us . . . Under my leadership, Tactical Rabbit will force Wall Street to abide by the highest ethical standards. The games are over.

This is not a fire drill.' In April 2015, Stern announced his candidacy for the United States Senate as a Republican candidate for Pennsylvania, challenging the incumbent Pat Toomey for the Republican primary in the 2016 election. Subsequently, Stern stood down, saying he'd injured his left leg in a car accident, so he couldn't walk long distances and campaign effectively. In October 2021, Stern called a press conference. He was pitching for the US Senate again, for the GOP in Pennsylvania. He opened, though, with this: 'I'm here today not as a candidate running for US Senate, I'm here as a citizen who is genuinely concerned about our country, sincerely concerned about the undermining of our democracy.' He maintained he'd been contacted by a shadowy group who wanted to use his firm to obtain information on officials in a number of states, to put pressure on them to force them to hold election audits to support Donald Trump's claims that the 2020 ballot was fraudulent. 'They wanted to gather intelligence on senators, judges, congressmen, state reps, to move them towards the audit,' Stern said. 'The word "move" was emphasized tremendously. It was clear to me what they wanted was not traditional opposition research – what they wanted was to extort and to literally move people towards the audit with dirt.' He claimed he was told to 'accomplish the mission even if you have to use domestic terrorism.' Stern said he was in touch with federal law enforcement about the request. What motivates him is that 'I take action and take personal risks for the greater good of society. I come from nothing when my opponents come from a sheltered high society. I know what it is like to lose everything. I also know what it takes to pick yourself off the floor and make something of yourself. I want to help people that are on the floor and think they can't get up. If I can go from sleeping on a cot in a 400 square foot apartment and waiting tables to running for US Senate, then anyone can achieve anything.' At the time, HSBC had little inkling how true this was.

TEN

The dam begins to crack

If you wanted someone to play a New York police detective in a movie, you could do worse than ask Frank DiGregorio to play himself. Lieutenant DiGregorio, to give him his full title, or 'Frankie D' as his fellow cops know him, is everything you imagine a NYPD veteran to be. He's ebullient, gravelly-voiced, a fast-talker with a sharp New York wit. His face is weather-beaten, the result of years of shark fishing. Now in his sixties, he began as a beat cop, pounding the hard yards in Brooklyn and Queens. He spent the 1980s trying to break organized crime's stranglehold on the waste industry. Latterly, his specialty is major league money laundering, in particular the washing of drug proceeds, earning him promotion and a threat on his life. In 2005, DiGregorio was seconded from Queens to the Homeland Security Investigations El Dorado Task Force, or HSI EDTF in the acronyms of US law enforcement jargon, and the task force comes under the ICE, or Immigration and Customs Enforcement, remit. Named after the mythical South American city of gold, El Dorado is an umbrella body set up in 1992 with a declared aim 'to dismantle and disrupt money laundering and criminal financing organizations operating in the New York/New Jersey area utilizing the tools and resources of all participating agencies.' The organization draws its 250 investigators, researchers, intelligence analysts and prosecutors from thirty federal, state and local agencies. Its anonymous redbrick offices in midtown Manhattan, on the west side, near Chelsea Piers, occupy an entire block – the car park was used as the US government's central command after the 9/11 attacks on the nearby World Trade Center and the seals of all the various agencies hanging on one wall inside make for an impressive sight.

The idea was that by forming one unified band the various task forces wouldn't tread on each other's toes, or worse, that an agency did not arrest another's undercover officers or wreck their sting operation or duplicate their efforts. When they pooled resources, every time they seized assets the captured goods were shared among the agencies involved, to help fight further crime and to combat the impact of the crime in their home territory, such as heroin and opioid addiction. They targeted everything and everyone, from drugs and human trafficking to fraud, weapons smuggling, cybercrime and slavery. Every resource was at their disposal, from computer hacking to wire taps to old-fashioned watching and following – initially, Frankie D had to postpone our meeting because he was out, engaged on surveillance of a suspect. DiGregorio is an expert on the Black Market Peso Exchange method of laundering, the one that sees the cartel convert dollar bills into pesos via trading, seemingly legitimately, in normal everyday goods. He's a senior member of the task force, a team supervisor, and he tells it how it is. In 2007, the authorities become aware of large amounts of cash being routed via courier companies through Miami and Houston airports. When they traced the delivery orders, they found that they originated in New York. They followed the cash to its end destination in HSBC in Mexico and Frankie D was assigned to investigate along with two younger agents, Graham Klein and Carmelo Lana. Following the money trail, the team tracked a man called Fernando Sanclemente as he drove around

NYC collecting the proceeds of drugs sales. In one evening, he stopped on a street corner in Queens, spoke to someone for about thirty seconds and left with a yellow plastic bag and on the same night he visited a Dunkin' Donuts, out near La Guardia airport. They watched as a black livery mini-cab pulled up and the driver handed him a black bag. They carried on following him to Laurel Hollow in New York, where they stopped him. When they searched him, they found the two bags contained $154,000 in cash and a search of his apartment revealed accounts and papers consistent with someone laundering money.

Sanclemente, they discovered, was reporting to Julio Chaparro, and the more they looked at Chaparro, the more they realized that he was a major player leading a double life. One was Julio Chaparro, a respectable forty-eight-year-old father of four who owned three toy factories in Colombia. The other was Julio Chaparro, a vital cog in the drug-trafficking wheel, a go-between, funnelling enormous amounts of cash for suppliers between New York and Colombia via Mexico. Central to his network was HSBC Mexico. 'We identified cash that was going over the US border into Mexico, then into the Mexican banking system,' said DiGregorio. 'Some of it was then coming back into the US, in the form of wire transfers.' What they uncovered was classic money-washing. 'The bank was crediting US individuals and US business accounts for South American exports. There were six links in the chain – at the bottom was the Colombian farmer, in the middle was the money broker and at the top was the cartel. The man [Sanclemente] was working for the money broker and US exporter.' The amounts involved were far in excess of what you would expect from a toy business: they tracked $500 million in cash, and when Chaparro was indicted they alleged that between 6 October 2008 and 13 April 2009 – barely more than six months – he'd overseen transfers of $1.1 million. They set up sting, fake accounts and in so doing realized that where HSBC, both in Mexico and the US, was concerned, the controls the bank was obliged by law to observe were at best relaxed, at worst non-existent or even being deliberately by-passed completely.

Chaparro was arrested in Colombia in 2010 and extradited to the US in 2011. In one legal filing, US prosecutors said, Chaparro used accounts at HSBC Mexico to deposit 'drug dollars and then wire those funds to . . . businesses located in the United States and elsewhere. The funds were then used to purchase consumer goods, which were exported to South America and resold to generate "clean" cash.' The prosecution accused him of 'basically putting the orchestra together' and investigators saw 'him as a major player in terms of cleaning a lot of money.' His lawyer, Ephraim Savitt, admitted that Chaparro was a middleman, but said that he was merely the 'page turner of sheet music for the conductor' of the orchestra. Chaparro pleaded guilty to a money-laundering conspiracy count and got six years, and was ordered to forfeit $500,000 and the $154,000 seized by DiGregorio's team. The pursuit, however, did not end with the toy factory owner. DiGregorio and his colleagues were now hunting down much bigger players – a chase that culminated in a visit by Frankie D and his colleagues from the sidewalks of Brooklyn and Queens to London, to the world headquarters of HSBC.

At the same time, in a very different part of the US from crowded, never-sleeping NYC, another law enforcer was taking a close interest in HSBC. In Wheeling, West Virginia, they're rightly proud of Oglebay Park. Once the country estate of Cleveland industrialist Earl Oglebay, the landscaped 2,000 acres were donated to the people of Wheeling for 'public recreation.' The open space has got everything: championship golf courses, skiing, riding, outdoor theatre, swimming, tennis, nature walks, arts and crafts, gardens, a planetarium, shopping, endangered species in the 'Good Zoo', an arboretum, holiday cottages, a spa, conference centre. Its 'Winter Festival of Lights' is a traditional must-see. Oglebay has a genuine claim to fame in government finance and park management circles as 'the only self-supporting public municipal park in operation in the United States'.

The centrepiece of the park is the Wilson Lodge hotel, which includes the Ihlenfeld Dining Room decorated with large, picture windows overlooking bewitching countryside and a lake. Charles Ihlenfeld practised law as a prosecuting attorney and town mayor in his native Wheeling for fifty-six years until his death in 1989. He was, if anyone was, 'Mister Wheeling'. Ihlenfeld sat on numerous public and community bodies and was a leading local Democrat and a philanthropist. After the death of his wife in 1984, he arranged for a gift to Oglebay Park to fund the expansion and renovation of the public dining area at Wilson Lodge. Ihlenfeld had intended it as a memorial to his wife, but after his death, the couple's sons, William and Charles, requested that the dining room be dedicated to both their parents.

William was a lawyer, like his father, as in due course was his son, also William or 'Bill'. Born and raised like them in Wheeling, Bill grew up in a family that knew the difference between right and wrong, and regarded putting something back into the community and looking out for the underdog as second nature. 'I remember paying attention to what my father and what my grandfather did. I remember always noticing the public service they performed in local government or state government. I remember them both always helping people. I know I wanted to do something along those lines. I wasn't quite sure what.' His mother had been a language arts teacher, and for a while, after being forced to concede he would not achieve a childhood ambition of making pro-ice hockey player, he tried journalism. At Ohio University he studied journalism and he was offered an internship at WOWK-TV in Charleston, West Virginia. 'While I was at WOWK-13, the station covered a high-profile trial gavel to gavel. It involved the murders of a mother and daughter from Cabin Creek, West Virginia, and I had a front-row seat. I was captivated by the process, and I quickly realized the importance of prosecutors. My interest in journalism morphed into a love for the criminal justice system and a desire to be a prosecutor.' He could, though, have been a journalist. 'My professors told me that they thought I would do well but that it would be a long road before I reached any level of success in journalism. That's when my dad reminded me that law school was an option, and I took him up on that suggestion.' Ihlenfeld enrolled instead for law at West Virginia University College of Law. The profession is in his genes: he became president of the competitive Lugar Trial Association that saw students practise trials against each other; and he adored the trial advocacy course taught by the Professor of Law, Charles DiSalvo. 'He knew the names of every single person in the class, all seventy-five of us. One day early in the semester in civil procedure, he went around the room and without the help of a seating chart identified every one of us. This sent a message that he cared enough about us to know who we were and also that we better do our homework because he could call on us by name at any time.' DiSalvo had a profound impact on Ihlenfeld, both as university teacher and as career mentor. 'Professor DiSalvo taught us not to try cases we didn't believe in with all of our heart. He also taught us how to prepare for trial, and his guidance helped me immensely in trying hundreds of cases as a state and federal prosecutor.'

Ihlenfeld got his law degree in 1997 and went home to Wheeling as an assistant prosecuting attorney in Ohio County, West Virginia, and in 2010, he was the US Attorney for the Northern District of West Virginia. Smartly dressed, lean, fit, married to Rebecca, with young children, church-going, fiercely proud of where he grew up, he was the local John Grisham hero prosecutor. His roster was domestic violence and sexual assaults. 'This caseload was my assignment for three years, so I became very familiar with the challenge of prosecuting cases where the victim doesn't wish to cooperate. Without my most important witness, I quickly became an expert in the rules of evidence. I learned them backward and forward, especially the exceptions, and spent so much time with the rule book that I might as well have cuddled up with it in bed at night.' Over time, he moved into drugs as a prosecutor, dealing, to start with, with the bottom end, the bit players, the juveniles, caught in possession and selling. 'The handling of cases involving teenagers was enlightening and helped me better understand the concept of restorative justice. I learned that simply prosecuting and punishing a young person is not enough. You must also take steps to look "behind the curtain", so to speak, and determine why he committed the crime and what can be done to help steer the child down a different, better path.' This is what set him on his course, as US Attorney, to trying to tackle Northern West Virginia's spiralling dependency on opioids and heroin. He struck at it every which way, including creating the US Attorney's Addiction Action Plan, an unprecedented initiative that brought together educators, health care professionals, business leaders, clergy, recovery specialists and law enforcement officials. 'I quickly realized that the traditional approach of arresting, convicting and incarcerating was not going to be enough to get the job done. It's not easy and it will take time, but we can do better than we are. We can move faster than we're moving.' He sought funding to combat the drug epidemic and he worked on Project Future, an initiative that educated youth about the science behind addiction and the importance of making good decisions. He was also part of the creation of a scheme to provide defendants with the opportunity to avoid imprisonment and a conviction on their record if they successfully completed a tough recovery programme.

Subsequently, Ihlenfeld volunteered for numerous community organizations that support victims of crime and the visually impaired, including, Upper Ohio Valley Sexual Assault Help Center, West Virginia Coalition Against Domestic Violence, Wheeling YWCA's Family Violence Prevention Program, The Seeing Hand Association and The Martinsburg Initiative. He led a team of College of Law students to Southern West Virginia to support flood relief efforts, helping victims repair their homes and providing them with essential supplies. Ihlenfeld also volunteered for Legal Aid of West Virginia, representing the disadvantaged who required a lawyer on a pro bono basis. He said then: 'I give back to causes I'm passionate about and that have a need. I not only provide financial support to these groups, but I also give my time, and I do that because community service runs in my family. I also do it because God has blessed me with so much that I feel like He expects me to give some of my blessings back to those who are less fortunate.' From the beginning, drugs were a recurring theme for US Attorney Ihlenfeld. It was unavoidable. 'I had no idea the drug problem would take up so much of my time . . . Nationwide, drug cases prosecuted by US Attorney offices take up about 30 per cent of the overall case load. In the Northern District of West Virginia, 60 per cent of the cases we have prosecuted have involved the drug problem. I'm proud of that, but on the other hand I wish that number would come down. I'd love to see us knock that number down closer to the national average.' He pursued the suppliers while trying to assist the addicted. 'You make an impact when you take down a drug traffic organization as opposed to the conviction of one person . . . Those addicted aren't stopping because their dealer is gone. Instead, they will seek the drug out through an additional dealer and there are many willing to fill that spot of supplier.'

Another speciality was health-care fraud, and in one of his schemes he established a group to better identify federal criminal violations related to health-care fraud. 'We took a data-driven approach to the prevention of health-care fraud in West Virginia to proactively evaluate health-care reimbursement data of medical providers in the state. By using advanced statistical analysis, we were able to identify potentially fraudulent billing patterns and uncover waste and abuse more efficiently.' This is how he snared Dr Barton Adams.

It's just over 100 miles from Wheeling to Vienna (population 10,000), also in West Virginia. Vienna 'Pride of the Valley' is set in the Ohio River Valley, amid the mountains (West Virginia University's sports teams are the 'Mountaineers'). It's peaceful, rugged, country, but also home to the Grand Central Mall, with eighty-five stores, making the shopping centre the finest in the region. The quiet, family-oriented, wholesome, well-being-minded district of trails and parks, outdoors recreation and trim buildings belies a dark shadow. It is hard to believe but Wood County, in which Vienna sits, topped the US national overdose death ranking in 2017 with 363 recorded overdose calls to 911. Local Sheriff Steve Stephens said: 'That's roughly an overdose a day. There's a reason there's a Walmart in Vienna . . . because there's enough business, same thing with the drug business. As long as there are addicts and people that want to buy it, we're going to continue to have this problem.' Above the town, cut into the hillside, is a residential dead-end road, Brentwood Heights, where the homes are neat, suburban, two-storey. It was here that Dr Barton Adams lived with his wife Josephine and their children, in a rented house. Neighbours later said they thought there was something strange about the Adams in that they kept themselves to themselves, did not mix, and he had a habit of driving his car straight into the garage and closing the door. In a closed community like Brentwood Heights, every small detail is noticed and judged.

Adams, a doctor of osteopathy, had opened a clinic, Interventional Pain Management, in the town. He was not what he seemed, however – instead of the all-caring medical doctor anxious to help relieve pain in his patients he was a big-time fleecer, a scammer, devoted to making fraudulent health insurance claims to Medicare and Medicaid. His box of tricks included billing twice, charging for ultrasound scans and pain-relief injections that were not performed and getting patients to sign for medical services they never received. Eventually, the police caught up with him and US Attorney Bill Ihlenfeld began to uncover a web of accounts and transactions all designed to launder money through Adams's bank, HSBC. In total, Adams and his wife channelled $3.7 million via a web of accounts and shell companies. Josephine set up a shell company in the British Virgin Islands, called Keyfield Limited, and opened an account at HSBC in Hong Kong in the company name. Through this system, money would be churned into accounts in the US before ending up in HSBC accounts in Canada, China and the Philippines. Ihlenfeld said Josephine enjoyed a 'luxurious lifestyle' and 'took trips around the world, stayed in fancy hotels, and had plans to retire overseas, until the whole scheme collapsed.'

In 2013, Adams, aged sixty-one, received fifty months in a federal prison for health-care fraud and tax evasion, and was ordered to forfeit $3.7 million to the government and to repay $3.1 million to the health-care firms he had defrauded, including Medicare and Medicaid. His sentence was on top of the four years he'd already served, having been in jail since 2009 for contempt of court in connection with the investigation. Ihlenfeld realized the not-so-good doctor's case was just 'the tip of the iceberg' in terms of the volume of suspicious money flooding through HSBC. What so alarmed Ihlenfeld was the bare-faced, unsophisticated nature of what Adams and his wife were doing. It was crude, simplistic, easy-to-spot and, you would think, impossible-to-ignore money laundering, yet HSBC was apparently unperturbed, and seemingly did nothing to close them down. He accused HSBC's compliance department of being systemically flawed. The 'laundering practices – which [even] Moe, Larry, and Curly [the comedy Three Stooges, beloved of slapstick movies] would dismiss as too transparent – would not be detected by HSBC regardless of who the customer was, or where any transaction occurred.' From his Wheeling, West Virginia base the US Attorney decided to dig deeper into the global bank. Ihlenfeld and his assistant, Michael Stein, worked with agents from two offices of the Treasury Department: Ryan Korner and Jason Gandee from IRS Criminal Investigation and Financial Crimes Enforcement Network (FinCEN). 'They were among the first to expose HSBC's illegal money-laundering activities and the immense dangers they presented to our nation,' said Ihlenfeld. 'Our investigative team was outstanding, and it uncovered what was happening before any other law enforcement agency in the nation. Despite the fact that the criminal conduct was occurring right under the noses of federal agents and prosecutors in New York, it took a team of Mountaineers to figure it all out and to bust one of the world's largest banks.' What especially riled him was that 'HSBC was helping to fuel West Virginia's [drugs] problems.' In all, his team spent 5,543 hours looking into HSBC. Their inquiries roamed well beyond West Virginia, across the major cities of the US, to Asia and Latin America. 'What began as a routine look into a West Virginia doctor for health-care fraud turned into the discovery of billions of dollars in money laundering . . .'

Farther south in Mexico City, attitudes against HSBC were hardening. Repeated meetings and warnings had produced no tangible results and the bank supervisory authorities began assembling a legal case against HSBC, one that would result in the largest fine in Mexican history, of $28 million. 'It was as high as we could go,' said a senior regulator and one of those closely involved. The CNBV homed in on a charge of non-compliance with anti-money laundering systems and controls and, having gone through the files, the supervisory body narrowed its rap sheet down to specifying 1,729 unusual transactions, failing to report thirty-nine unusual transactions, and twenty-one administrative failures. While a $28 million fine was something that HSBC could easily absorb due to their huge global profits, what was of much greater concern was that, unbeknownst to HSBC at the time, the authorities were feeding the information they uncovered straight to the Department of Justice and OCC in the US. 'By September 2010 we'd had another inspection of HSBC in Mexico. Nothing had changed. We sent the results of our three inspections to Washington; they'd asked through the proper channels and we sent them. That resulted in the OCC "Cease and Desist" order. Every detail that they had came from Mexico, they came from our inspections – we shared them with the OCC, the Department of Justice and the Feds.' The Mexico official said this with a degree of hurt because they felt that the general perception outside the country was that they were bothered about money laundering, that they did not do enough to close down the cartels, and this kind of issue was endemic to a country rife with corruption and therefore it was specifically 'Mexico's problem'. The truth, alas, was they had to live with the daily barbarity, and their fear of repercussion was very real. The tendrils of the Sinaloa and the other cartels were everywhere and they reached into pretty much every aspect of society, from the politicians running the country to the poorest farmers just trying to put food on the table.

Matters were not helped, of course, by the corruption of some politicians, police and officials. Sometimes, though, their apparent willingness to voluntarily aid the drug traffickers was the result of intolerable pressure – they knew the gangsters would kill their families if they did not do as they were told. Frequently, they would take a bung, from a desire for personal enrichment – Mexico is still very poor in parts, public sector wages are low, and they see those at the top in business and politics enjoying power and wealth. That's not to offer an excuse, but to explain why dismissing this as 'Mexico's problem' doesn't get to the heart of the problem. Make no mistake: to pursue one of the biggest corporations in the world, the bank with the giant glass tower in the heart of the capital, the one with the lions outside, with expensive and brilliant lawyers on call, and unlimited amounts of funds, the one with political leaders in its thrall, is a brave call for a public servant. How far things had come from 2002 when Mexico was welcoming HSBC to the country with open arms, its president turning up to cut the ribbon on its new headquarters and unveiling a mural ostensibly showing how a bank like HSBC could benefit Mexico. Now the politicians representing the same offices of government were eyeballing senior HSBC executives across tables and building a legal slam dunk against them and their omnipotent corporation. No sooner did they inform the bank it was being penalized in 2010 than HSBC did the usual and reached for its expensive, slick lawyers. The bank started fighting the Mexican bank supervisors in the courts, in secret, to try to get the fine overturned. The charge became sub judice. 'We were in court with them, we couldn't say we were fining them,' said a senior supervisor. That year HSBC published its annual group accounts without any mention of a contingency for the Mexican fine. 'We asked them "why not?" They say they don't need to, it is such a small amount for the group. "We don't need to disclose it." ' Said the supervisor: 'Even if the amount was small, the issue it relates to is not small. It is serious.' The bank's attitude to the level of the fine was not only indicative of the arrogance of HSBC, but it also showed a cynical, Goliath mindset. The bank was trying to have it both ways – on one level it was not bothered, instructing hugely expensive lawyers to help them fight the fine, while in the process, buying time and running up hefty legal bills for Mexico, adding to the pressure on public officials to drop the penalty. What they didn't know, however, was that while they were dismissing the Mexican fine in the US the El Dorado Task Force investigation was gathering pace; Everett Stern was passing over information to the CIA; and in West Virginia, Bill Ihlenfeld, aided by his small team, also had HSBC in his sights.

El Dorado could draw upon the powerful Washington-based Asset Forfeiture and Money Laundering Section (it has power of veto over any indictment or proposed settlement) of the Department of Justice. The Drug Enforcement Administration and the Immigration and Customs Enforcement, a unit of the Department of Homeland Security, were also taking part. In all, if the OCC and financial regulators and the office of Cyrus Vance, the New York County District Attorney and other federal departments are included, there were ten different sets of officials, enforcers and investigators now looking at HSBC, most of whom were based in the corridors of power in New York, in Manhattan, and in DC, worlds that HSBC knew well and respected much more than their counterparts in Mexico. In West Virginia, by taking on the global financial colossus of HSBC, Ihlenfeld was in well over his pay grade, but he stuck to his task. His superiors at the Department of Justice were not impressed and instructed him to back off, sparking a classic, farcical bureaucratic face-off – of the sort that would do the BBC TV comedy series about Whitehall in-fighting, *Yes Minister*, proud. While drug dealers continued to flog their wares, while innocents carried on dying, and while dirty cash poured over the counters and through the networks of the world's most profitable bank, America's public servants were determinedly fighting among themselves. The scrap began because Ihlenfeld, the ambitious lawyer who had been brought up in a family with a tradition of propriety, who was taught by his professor at law school to go after cases he believed in with all his heart, to prepare his prosecutions thoroughly and who could see the daily harm wreaked by drugs in his district, point blank said 'no', he would not back off the prey that he had in his sights. His response to the request to desist was to double down and he drafted a list of what he said would be no fewer than 175 criminal counts against HSBC and its executives for money laundering. Again, the Justice Department told him to stop, to let the El Dorado Task Force go after HSBC, but again he refused, and instead made the hugely bold move of asking for an arbitrator to adjudicate. In late 2010 he drafted a letter to Gary Grindler, the acting Deputy Attorney General, in which he stated that there had been a breakdown in the relationship between his office and Washington. 'We have made several offers to amicably settle this dispute by dividing the investigation in a way that guaranteed the two investigations would never interfere with each other.' He went on: 'Despite our best effort, all of our offers have been categorically rejected. None of our proposals has even induced a counter-offer.' Wrote the mountain region DA: 'As a general proposition, there is no reason why the professionals from different DOJ components cannot work together for the common good. This particular situation is no exception.' The irony, of course, was that the El Dorado Task Force was meant to stop this precise sort of occurrence – but only if the agencies concerned were federal or in the New York and New Jersey area. Ihlenfeld, in his office, in Wheeling, West Virginia, did not fall into either category – although the drugs problem, the suppliers and the bank they were using were the same. In normal circumstances the various demarcations and actions on the government side would only serve to highlight the difficulty of an under-resourced, sprawling public service machine with its competing interests and jurisdictions attempting to tackle a sleek corporate powerhouse. Except HSBC may have looked like a sleek corporate powerhouse but the bank was itself full of conflicting fiefdoms and territories, and layers of management.

What narked Ihlenfeld was that his office was much further down the track in investigating HSBC while El Dorado's inquiry was 'just starting' so, 'even if DOJ's budget was unlimited, it would be wasteful for' the competing group to replicate what his team has done already. They were behind in terms of what they knew – he pointed out the El Dorado team did not realize that HSBC operated a bulk cash processing centre 'within walking distance' of their offices until West Virginia prosecutors told them during the mediation. However, Ihlenfeld's heaviest fire was directed towards HSBC, who he accused of running a 'systemically flawed sham paper-product designed solely to make it appear that the bank has complied' with the Bank Secrecy Act and was able to detect money laundering. In an echo of Everett Stern, he drew attention to HSBC's failure to report suspicious activity on hundreds of billions of dollars in business from 'high-risk' sources where some 73 per cent of accounts with foreign correspondent banks were rated 'standard' or 'medium' risk and so weren't monitored at all. In one example, the bank 'summarily cleared as many as 5,000' internal alerts of suspicious activity from correspondent customers in Argentina after lowering the country's risk rating. They highlighted failings in the bank's back-office operation. In its 'remote deposit capture' business – an operation that electronically sends cheques around the world – HSBC 'failed to detect, review and report large volumes of sequentially numbered traveller's cheques' from non-US sources. As the months progressed, the details of the extent of HSBC's activities came more transparently into view thanks to Ihlenfeld's work and it quickly became clear that HSBC had repatriated more than $106.5 billion in banknote deposits through foreign correspondent accounts, many of them in Mexico and South America, in a three-year period. And yet, 'since 2005, the bank has filed only 19 suspicious activity reports relative to the receipt of bulk cash and banknote activities.' By contrast, between 2005 and 2010, banks and other depository institutions filed more than 3.8 million SARs, according to FinCEN.

After all this, however, the in-house fighting over jurisdiction continued and Ihlenfeld's pleas to investigate still fell on deaf ears. The small-town attorney was ordered to leave well alone. 'We'd found money laundering at HSBC before any other organization in the US. We were a team of Mountaineers, but I made plans to indict the bank and its executives. I wanted to send a strong message to Wall Street. Instead, I was told to stand down by Attorney General Eric Holder and the Justice Department.' Fed up with the insistence to leave HSBC to the officials in New York and Washington, Ihlenfeld called it a day, but not without one final snap at HSBC. A withering parting shot from Ihlenfeld was to liken HSBC to another notorious episode in recent US banking history. Using an analogy that resonated around Washington and New York, and the bank regulatory community, the DA from West Virginia compared HSBC to Riggs Bank: 'HSBC is to Riggs, as a nuclear waste dump is to a municipal landfill.' It was a stinging, deliberately choice comparison. Riggs was founded in 1836, some thirty years before HSBC, in Washington. It was regarded as a smart, and more latterly as an old-money, WASP bank. Twenty-three US presidents and their families trusted Riggs with their financial affairs, among them Abraham Lincoln, Ulysses S. Grant, Dwight D. Eisenhower and Richard Nixon. Numerous other politicians and dignitaries banked there, as well as Washington embassies. In a phrase that could have come straight from the HSBC phrasebook of modesty, Riggs liked to call itself 'the most important bank in the most important city in the world.' The similarities did not stop with boastfulness. In 2005, all that grandeur and pedigree counted for nought as Riggs pleaded guilty to repeatedly failing to report suspicious transactions in bank accounts, including those belonging to the military dictator General Pinochet of Chile, the Saudi Arabian embassy and President Teodoro Obiang Nguema of Equatorial Guinea, infamous for running one of the most corrupt and brutal regimes on Earth.

Riggs was fined a total of $41 million for these cases and for having lax money-laundering controls. Under its agreement with the US government, the bank 'accepted responsibility for its actions' in helping Pinochet set up two offshore companies to hide assets and allowing him to deposit more than $10 million into its accounts, sometimes under assumed names, between 1994 and 2002. The bank also admitted to opening thirty accounts, with balances and loans totalling $700 million for government officials of Equatorial Guinea. 'This long-term and systemic misconduct was more than simply blind neglect,' prosecuting US Attorney Kenneth L. Wainstein charged. 'It was a criminal breach of the banking laws that protect our financial system.' Riggs was scrutinized by the US Senate Permanent Subcommittee on Investigations, which discovered that on at least two occasions between 2000 and 2002, a Riggs staffer went to the Equatorial Guinea embassy in Washington and collected suitcases holding $3 million in $100 bills, in plastic-wrapped bundles. The employee took the cash to a Riggs branch in downtown Washington and deposited it into an account held by a company in the Bahamas, controlled by Nguema. Another Riggs account set up after oil was discovered in Equatorial Guinea acted as a conduit for vast sums and the money was paid in by US oil companies. At one point, $700 million was in this 'oil account' controlled by Nguema, his ministers and their families from the impoverished country. The settlement that Riggs agreed to with the government in 2005 led to Riggs being sold to PNC Financial Services, based in Pittsburgh. The deal valued the bank at $779 million – roughly the amount washing through the

Equatorial Guinea 'oil account' – and no sooner did the sale go through than the Riggs name was taken down, to be replaced by PNC. It was an ignominious end to a sorry episode. The ranking minority member of the Subcommittee, Senator Carl Levin, called the Riggs affair 'a sordid story of a bank with a prestigious name, that blatantly ignored its obligations under our money laundering laws'. Daniel P. Stipano, deputy chief counsel for the OCC, insisted at the time: 'What happened with Riggs is unacceptable. It cannot be repeated.'

ELEVEN

Everyone's idea of a public servant

While investigators were closing in on the World's Number One bank in early 2012, Mexican and US agents were ramping up their hunt for the World's Number One drug baron, Chapo. Over the years they had received plenty of leads, many false, but in February that year they got a breakthrough when they 'flipped' a BlackBerry belonging to one of his closest associates and used it to trace several messages to a single phone that was being used in Cabo San Lucas, at the tip of the Baja Peninsula. They had a fix: it was Chapo. The FBI in New York also had thousands of intercepts for that number, but until they examined the BlackBerry they did not know it was the Sinaloa leader himself that they had been tracking. In March 2012, the US DEA and Mexico police put together a joint operation to take him down. Cabo, in the holiday seaside area of Los Cabos, is one of Mexico's swishest resorts, visited by Hollywood stars, US tourists and much favoured for international conferences. At the same time as they were moving in on Chapo, US Secretary of State Hillary Clinton, by coincidence, was also in Cabo, staying at the Barceló Los Cabos Palace Deluxe, for a G20 foreign ministers meeting. As the ministers talked over three-course meals and hundred-dollar bottles of wine, 300 hundred crack Mexico City federal police were, at the exact same time, sweeping into Cabo in strict secrecy. The target was a line of mansions on the seafront because they were sure that Chapo was in one of them. There were twelve houses in all, and they were each raided and searched in methodical order, but all they found were lots of irate wealthy US holidaymakers and retirees and there was no sign of the head of the world's most ruthless drug-trafficking organization. The coordinated raids were on the verge of proving to be one major embarrassment and yet the phone that they were tracking kept pinging, so the raid homed in again, this time on a cul-de-sac of three mansions on the outskirts of Cabo. The police swooped in as before and that should have been it for Chapo, since he was without his usual security and only had his closest bodyguard 'Picudo', his pilot, a cook, a gardener and a girlfriend for company. But, ever alert to danger, from the third house at the end of the road they watched as the police surrounded the first and then the second house on the cul-de-sac. As the police turned towards the third house, Chapo made his move and, together with Picudo, he literally ran down the beach and away from the hapless Mexican police, and he was gone.

The Associated Press reported: 'Mexican authorities nearly captured the man the US calls the world's most powerful drug lord, who, like Osama bin Laden, has apparently been hiding in plain sight. Federal police nearly nabbed Joaquin "El Chapo" Guzmán in a coastal mansion in Los Cabos three weeks ago, barely a day after US Secretary of State Hillary Clinton met with dozens of other foreign ministers in the same southern Baja Peninsula resort town.' The debacle became a national joke: how the police charged down the front door of Chapo's house without sending anyone round to check on the back. Sure enough, a new *narcocorrido* appeared. 'Se Quedaron a Tres Pasos' or 'They Stayed Three Steps Behind' was recorded by the Sinaloa band, Calibre 50, about 100 police officers storming the house and Chapo scarpering:

They stayed three steps behind Guzmán
They looked for him in Los Cabos
But he was already in Culiacán!

Chapo had indeed gone back to his native mountains, where he continued to run his criminal empire, and it would be two full years before the police closed in on him again.

Across the Atlantic, at HSBC there had been an abrupt change in leadership. In September 2010, Stephen Green was due to retire in a year's time and out of the blue he was secretly approached to be a UK government minister. Already, there was speculation within the bank as to when he might go. Suddenly and unexpectedly came the suggestion that he might like to be minister of state for trade and investment, and be made a 'lord' with a seat in the House of Lords. There was no open appointment process, according to Green, who said: 'I got the call out of the blue: "Would you want to be considered to be the trade minister?" to which I initially said "no". This came from Jeremy Heywood [Cabinet Secretary] on behalf of the Prime Minister and the conversation developed because I made the mistake of saying, "Not only do I not want to, but I can't think of anyone from the business world who would really want to do this," and he said, "Oh, why is that?" I said, "Well there's too much globetrotting, banging the drum and not enough, or at least the perception is, not enough real policy work attached to it: where is the strategy behind this?"' This urged Heywood to try harder; the two men talked again and Green then spoke to the Prime Minister, David Cameron. They talked about the 'strategy for improved trade performance and we ended up mocking up a job description and I ended up doing the job. So that's how I got into it and of course got put in the House of Lords for the same reason.'

This is the same Cameron and Heywood that would later be called out for allowing Lex Greensill, the Australian financier, the boss of the collapsed Greensill Capital, into the inner sanctum of Downing

Street, giving him a desk and a business card as an advisor to the Prime Minister. Here they were, earlier, with Green helping the HSBC chief write his own job description and rewarding him with the post of government minister and a peerage, which he could hold for the rest of his life.

The Coalition Government had been searching confidentially for four months, ever since the 2010 general election, for a senior business figure to become trade minister, acting as a bridge between commerce and Whitehall, to help sell Britain abroad. Lord Davies, the previous trade minister, had said that he was not interested in staying on. Sir John Rose of Rolls-Royce was one mooted name, but Cameron alighted on the HSBC chairman because he was attracted by Green's commercial seniority and global experience. What Cameron could see was that with Green in charge the bank had grown to be the biggest in the world, seeing off Bank of America, Citi and the other American giants. He could see that under Green the bank had made a string of acquisitions, had steered carefully through the absorption of Household and the move into investment banking – no matter that they had both ended in relative failure. The point was, HSBC had not only grown but had avoided the financial crisis by getting out of US subprime lending early. That was smart – no matter that it had no choice. The bank was a much bigger bank now, all credit to him. And it was getting bigger still, powering ahead. Within the corridors of power in Downing Street, HSBC was a badge of honour for Cameron's Britain. The Tories' Liberal Democrat coalition partners meanwhile were more impressed by Green's professed belief in ethical banking and the need for businesses to take corporate responsibility more seriously. The word from Downing Street was that Green's job would straddle the Department for Business and the Foreign Office, and his hiring reflected, 'the enormous importance this government places on forging strong international relationships to open new trade links, promote British business overseas and maximise inward investment to the UK.'

The notion of serving a coalition, and not one party, did appeal to the seemingly permanently conflicted, non-political God's Banker. 'I remember saying to the Prime Minister when we had our first conversation, "There's a couple of things you ought to know about me before we go too far down this track. One is that I'm not a member of the Conservative Party or indeed any party. And I'm a floating voter. I have voted for all three of the main parties over time. Is that a problem?" To which he said instantaneously, "Absolutely not and certainly not in the context of a coalition government." And so, I never did. I'm not a member of any political party although I sit on the Conservative benches in the Lords. I said plainly, of course, I'm going to take the Government whip. You can't be a member of the Government and not take Government whip, and there's a Coalition Government whip.' At no point did there appear to be any due diligence conducted. If there was and if officials had spoken to authorities in parts of the world where HSBC did its business, such as the US and Mexico, awkward questions might have been asked. As it was, the HSBC chairman was installed as a government minister and sworn in as Baron Green of Hurstpierpoint in 2011, jumping ship from HSBC just as it was starting to take on serious water. 'Hurst', as Hurstpierpoint is known locally, is a village in Sussex, close to where Green grew up in Brighton. Not everyone was so convinced by the appointment, however. His new brief, said one commentator, 'seems not to have been designed with Green in mind.' In Green's latest book, *Good Value: Reflections on Money, Morality and an Uncertain World,* he wrote: 'We need to be able to look ourselves in the mirror and ask two questions about our role in the global bazaar: how is what I am doing contributing to human welfare? And why am I specifically doing it?' Said the critic: 'It's hard to imagine his fellow ministers, let alone his new business audience, asking the question as they rush from one meeting to another . . .'

Green was entering government at a high ministerial level. He would be working with seasoned politicians who were adept at soundbites, at playing to the cameras, to the microphones and public opinion, often careless with their sweeping, broad-brush statements. Green was someone who liked detail, who would search for both sides of an argument. He hated the headline-grabbing quotes that were bread and butter for an elected politician. This was a new minister who once said how much he abhorred PowerPoint presentations because he did not like having to reduce granular analysis to simple bullet points and straight assertions. Yet, it was precisely that world, of grandstanding and showmanship, that he was now entering.

He was, though, no stranger to the inner, minute workings of the government machine, the one away from the spotlight, the engine that puts policy into practice. 'I did start my career in the Civil Service, so Whitehall wasn't a completely strange phenomenon.'

Even before he was tapped up by Heywood and Cameron, at HSBC a process to find a new chairman was discreetly underway, with Sir Simon Robertson, the senior non-executive director, heading the search. While Green stayed with HSBC until Christmas 2010, until the succession plan was finalized, the search for his replacement was brought forward. By tradition, the top job should have gone automatically to Geoghegan, the chief executive, and he was duly installed as favourite by bookmaker Paddy Power. However, the row about Green's promotion to chairman in 2006, defying the new corporate governance rules, unexpectedly still echoed through the higher offices at HSBC and there was pressure to play by the new code and to go outside. As a result John Thornton, an Asia specialist, ex-Goldman Sachs and also a non-executive director at HSBC (so not entirely external), was in the running. In the end, neither man got the post. They broke with the past but still went internal as it was decided that Douglas Flint, the bank's finance director, should take the role. With his elevation came the usual repercussions of these major changes at the top of any company. After he met Robertson, Geoghegan emailed him to say that he had decided to leave; he hid any disappointment at not getting the top job well. 'You can rest assured that I will remain HSBC's biggest fan,' he wrote to Robertson before congratulating Flint. The lifelong HSBC servant, the perpetual global traveller and motivational speaker at those mass staff gatherings, the chief bag-carrier and translator of Green's strategies, the person charged with putting the chairman's ideas into practice, who had the bank literally at his fingertips on a smart screen in his office, fell just short of making it to the very summit of the banking world. Flint was popular even before his appointment across the HSBC network, because he was smoother, more poised than Geoghegan, with a dry, sophisticated wit. Importantly, the investment community liked Flint, and they believed him to be a straight-talker, and critically, he was well-regarded and trusted by regulators. In other words, even though they were the number one bank in the world, they were still suffering from some of the bruises that had been inflicted in recent years, and Flint was seen as just the person to restore and rejuvenate HSBC's reputation.

By 2012, as Chapo just evaded capture, Green was safely installed in government, and among the trade missions he soon helped arrange was one by Prime Minister David Cameron to Mexico City in June of that year. It was the first visit by a British Prime Minister to the country in more than a decade and Cameron, accompanied by Green, led a twenty-five-strong business delegation, featuring senior executives of UK multi-nationals Diageo, Virgin Atlantic and Rolls-Royce, green energy suppliers and the pottery-maker Emma Bridgewater. The party met the Mexican President Felipe Calderón and Mexican business leaders, including Carlos Slim, and toured the trading room of Mexico City's stock exchange, even meeting officials and representatives from the same Mexican government that had tried to pull HSBC into line when Green was in charge. Cameron and Calderón held a joint press conference in the gardens of Los Pinos, the Presidential residence where Lord Green also spoke, of the need for Britain to prioritize Mexico over Brazil. He also said that Mexico's ranking in the World Bank's 'ease of doing business index' was higher than Brazil's, and yet Brazil was getting more attention in the British public mind than Mexico. Mexico, in other words, was the place to invest. To hammer the point home, he also pointed out that in that year Mexico outpaced Brazil in terms of GDP growth. 'This isn't just a flash in the pan. This isn't just something that will be true in the next year or two or three. No, this is going to be the trend for the next generation. The centre of the world's gravity is shifting from the west to east (and) from the north to south. Mexico is becoming . . . a diverse growing economy that is more and more interesting to British business.' At the very moment Lord Green was banging the drum for Mexico, in another part of Mexico City, the country's bank regulators were finalizing the bringing of the maximum fine allowed under local law against the very organization the UK trade minister chaired until recently. Officials from the agency were also steadily supplying more and more material about HSBC aiding and abetting the Sinaloa drug cartel to fellow criminal investigators in the US. One of those US bodies looking into HSBC was the Senate Permanent Subcommittee on Investigations, or PSI. As Lord Green was standing alongside Cameron pronouncing on better trade links in Mexico City, the Washington-based PSI was busy drafting a report on the bank and the period of his chairmanship. Much of the information relied upon by the subcommittee's inquiry team originated from those officials in Mexico City, from the same government that was entertaining the UK Prime Minister and his trade minister. The PSI is the Senate's crack investigative unit, a Delta Force of scrutineering panels, with a long, justified renown for being politically neutral, for not holding back, and for tackling the grandest, biggest corporations, and they had begun examining HSBC after the OCC's 'Cease and Desist' letter had been sent in October 2010. Held up as being above the hurly-burly of party politics, the PSI occupies a special place in the US psyche, one described by historian Arthur M. Schlesinger Jnr: 'While the conventional assumption is that the strength of legislative bodies lies in the power to legislate, a respectable tradition has long argued that it lies as much or more in the power to investigate.' Set up temporarily to examine profiteering in the Second World War under then Senator Harry Truman, the Truman Committee, as it was first referred to, established itself permanently with a series of high-profile, landmark investigations into tough subjects, from Nazi war criminals to racketeering to white-collar crime.

Under the chairmanship of Carl Levin, the subcommittee's stature rose higher still. The Michigan senator became the ranking minority member in 1999, and chairman from 2001 to 2003, and again from 2007. No target was too big or too grand or too powerful. Tax-cheating billionaires, corrupt foreign dictators, money launderers, mis-selling credit card firms, and corporate names like Apple, Citibank, Enron, Goldman Sachs – he and his colleagues went after them all. The PSI attracted its own moniker: Pretty Scary Investigations.

Born in Detroit, in 1934, Levin was one of three children in a Jewish family that believed passionately in behaving properly, in contributing to society, in assisting and respecting others. Levin described his parents and siblings as 'strong New Dealers' adhering to the principle of government to create opportunity and promote justice and fairness.

His father-in-law, an immigrant, left $10,000 in his will to the federal government. 'He knew he wasn't going to pay an estate tax – he was comfortable, but not wealthy – but as an immigrant he felt he owed a debt to America and he wanted to pay it one way or another. I tell that story, often on April 15, when wealthy people are complaining about their taxes.'

Levin studied political science at Swarthmore, the private liberal arts college, then went to Harvard Law. He made social law his vocation, as general counsel for the Michigan Civil Rights Commission, then Special Assistant Attorney General for Michigan and chief appellate defender for Detroit. Levin joined the Detroit City Council and became its president.

In a signal of what was to come, he was so angered by the slowness of progress in resolving Detroit's decrepit housing and urban decay that he took direct action, driving a bulldozer himself, 'to help raze some of the houses'. Levin was elected to the Senate in 1978 and when he retired in 2015, he was the longest-serving senator in Michigan's history.

Someone who worked for Levin and his subcommittee was Elise Bean. She said of Levin: 'He was the public servant everyone imagines when thinking of how Congress ought to work. He was tough and shrewd, with the integrity, smarts, and stamina to take on any opponent. His signature image was of a dishevelled, avuncular everyman, piercing blue eyes peering calmly over half-rim glasses perched on the end of his nose, refusing to avert his eyes from what he saw.' His 'level gaze, Midwestern decency, and willingness to combat wrongdoing even in the face of long odds', says Bean, were inspiring. She was hired as an attorney, then Levin made her staff director and chief counsel of the PSI. 'Because Senator Levin's favourite subject was financial chicanery, I learned more than I ever wanted to about money laundering, offshore gimmicks, tax dodging, accounting skulduggery, and derivatives double-dealing. Our investigations ranged from wrongdoing that fuelled crime, produced billion-dollar losses, or cheated average families, to dishonest practices that led to widescale economic mayhem like the 2008 financial crisis. And we did it while drinking Manhattans with our Republican colleagues.'

They worked out of the marble, limestone and grey granite Russell Senate Office Building in DC, next to the Capitol. In 2004, Levin said Riggs was 'a sordid story of a bank with a prestigious name, that blatantly ignored its obligations under our money-laundering laws.' And the OCC said Riggs could never be repeated. Barely five years later, in late 2010, Levin sanctioned the PSI probe into HSBC, an investigation that would turn up something far, far worse, that in the words of Ihlenfeld, the public service-minded West Virginia prosecutor, really was a 'nuclear waste dump' versus the Riggs 'municipal landfill.'

Or, as Bean put it, the HSBC case revealed a 'a rat's nest of improper conduct at the bank that shocked even our cynical ranks'.

HSBC had crossed the PSI's desks in relation to previous anti-money laundering investigations and the drums in Washington were now beating that all was not right with the giant bank, that it was a laundromat for drug traffickers, in particular the Sinaloa cartel. Bean and the subcommittee secretariat saw the OCC letter in October 2010. 'It was blistering, they were blasting the bank. When we asked Senator Levin if we could find out what prompted that blast at the bank, he agreed. Senator Tom Coburn [the ranking minority member] was equally supportive. Neither blinked an eye at taking on one of the most powerful institutions in the world.' An inquiry chaired by a man who, if you cut him open, ethics would be coursing through his veins, was taking on a bank that liked to think and proclaim it too stood for the same values, that believed it had a culture redolent with them, and declared as much, and that until very recently had been run by someone who actually preached and wrote about ethical capitalism. The PSI contacted the two main US regulators, the OCC and Federal Reserve, and HSBC and in 2011 the regulators turned over pretty much everything they had. 'They knew us from prior investigations,' said Bean, and they supplied copies of their examination reports, workpapers, internal memos, and copies of HSBC's documents they'd gathered. Emails from their investigative teams to HSBC were also sent to Washington. Faced with the PSI request, HSBC had a choice: to dig in and resist or to cooperate, and it was at this point that the mood shifted in HSBC and they chose the latter, said Bean, 'because HSBC was already in hot water with its regulators and couldn't afford to look like it was obstructing Congress.' But, to make doubly sure, the PSI issued a subpoena, forcing the bankers to comply. Bean, and throughout 2011 her investigators, received internal audit reports, analytical memos, bank records and some emails along with non-US documents where they were able to do so and collected material from other regulators and evidence from court cases. In all, said Bean, they secured 1.4 million pages of information.

Laura Stuber, who now works as Policy Director for the Attorney General of California, was Senior Counsel to the PSI at the time, charged with making sense of it all. 'It could have been a document dump, and HSBC were trying to bury us,' said Stuber. 'They seemed to have a view, "give 'em what they want and let's get out of this thing".' Stuber and the other investigators conducted interviews to help them make sense of the material that they had taken possession of with anti-money laundering and banking experts, as well as those with first-hand knowledge of the bank, and HSBC senior and middle managers. The verdict was far worse than they had supposed. 'It was shocking.' She summarized: 'For the most part everyone at HSBC adopted the pose of sticking their heads in their hands.' And Bean's conclusion? 'Downright scary.'

It was clear, said Bean, 'The bank knew a lot. There were accounts that had been ordered to be closed that hadn't closed, yet even after they were found still to be open no one forced them to close. They were supplying Cayman Islands accounts with billions of dollars, and when they wanted to close those accounts, they couldn't, because there was nobody there.' The PSI staff were encouraged to be methodical. 'Senator Levin was fantastic, he was a great boss,' said Stuber. 'He understood investigations, he understood that things don't happen within a month. He said 'take a year, take a year-and-a-half' to go through it. He gave us a lot of time to do our work. He had a deep interest in what we were doing and in those issues. He was a former prosecutor, so he was great at asking questions and doing the follow-ups.' She added: 'That's so lacking these days.' The writing of the report itself took two months. 'It was difficult,' said Stuber. 'Most investigations don't last as long as ours, they don't get the volume of documents that we got. What we did was fairly unique. The normal news cycle does not last as long as our investigation – they don't do investigations that last for more than a year.' For a start they had to

grapple with the sheer scale of the bank. As well as the offices worldwide, the staffing and customer numbers, said Bean, 'HSBC's stats
included $2.5 trillion in assets', which is a very difficult figure to get
your head round. Here's one way: think of the stash found at Ye Gon's
house. That was $200 million, and it weighs 2 tonnes. Now $2.5 trillion divided by $100 million is 25,000 tonnes. To give you an idea
that's about the same weight as the Statue of Liberty (24,600 tonnes)
or twice the Brooklyn Bridge (13,320) or two-and-a-half times the
Eiffel Tower (10,100). It was all being managed by one bank, one
chairman, one board of directors, one chief executive, one executive
management tier, one group compliance department. They had
spurred on HSBC, in no time, to be not just big but ginormous.
That's what they wanted, and that's what they got. But their Risk
gaming strategy, their High Noon pursuit of big, of 'planting flags'
and 'sell, sell, sell' had to come at a cost. If they did not meet that bill,
was society expected to pick up the tab or should they be made
responsible for what flowed from their ambition? This was the very
question that the PSI had to wrestle with.

Take the bank's operation in the US. HSBC first entered the US
market in the 1980s, when it bought several mid-sized US banks.
Said Bean: 'By 2011, it had 470 US branches across the country with
4 million US customers. More than that, HSBC US had become the
US nexus for the entire HSBC worldwide network. For example, of
the more than 600,000 wire transfers that HSBC US processed each
week, two-thirds of the US dollar transfers involved HSBC affiliates
in other countries.' Like trying to picture $2.5 trillion in assets, this is
a level of activity that is beyond comprehension, or reasonable monitoring. What was galling for a US Senate subcommittee was to hear
from an HSBC executive, said Bean, 'that the main reason HSBC
entered the US market was not to compete for US customers, but to
provide a gateway for its overseas clients into the US financial
system.' Those overseas clients included, as it turned out, Chapo and
the Sinaloa cartel. Said Bean: 'Bank documents also showed that, for

ten years, HSBC's compliance headquarters in London knew all about HSBC Mexico's severe [anti-money laundering] deficiencies but failed to alert HSBC US even though HSBC US was providing HSBC Mexico with free entry into the US financial system. It was a classic case of a US affiliate being abused by both its parent and a non-US affiliate.' Under its formidable chair, the PSI built up its own set of rules, 'the Levin Principles', which were in addition to the official code for running Congressional inquiries. There was the 'two-year rule' – 'whether the subject was worth two years of our lives, because that would be the minimum amount of time involved,' said Bean. The boss insisted they conducted original research. 'Senator Levin didn't want a regurgitation of what was already known. He wanted new information.'

They were instructed to 'focus on the facts', to use 'case studies' and not allow witnesses 'to spout generalities and platitudes', to always be bipartisan, to take their time, to listen to all sides, to maintain confidentiality (the questioning of witnesses was held in private and the notes of those sessions would not be made public), to produce a detailed report, and to 'use hearings to effect change'. The hearing would come after the investigation was complete, when the report was published. 'Human nature being what it is, we knew many witnesses would use the time to come up with solutions that could be announced at the hearing,' said Bean. The PSI team was ordered 'to take on the tough guys'. Levin was committed to taking them on, said Bean, 'the big institutions, the CEOs, the bullies no one else had faced down.' The final Levin rule was 'tackle the problems'. He was not prepared to allow his committee to come up with a report, hold a hearing or two, harangue a target and leave it at that, which was the pattern elsewhere in Congress. He saw the report, said Bean, 'as a road map' and they would push for change via legislation and reform of regulations, and strengthened codes of practice, and as well, 'we referred wrongdoers to law enforcement.' The effect of this, of Levin's steering, the PSI's reputation, its terrier-like investigators, its sheer lack of fear, was to stun HSBC.

On 16 July 2012, the PSI published its 334-page report, 'US Vulnerabilities to Money Laundering, Drugs and Terrorist Financing: HSBC Case History'. For this type of document it pulled no punches. Levin set the scene, emphasizing that in 'an age of drug violence on our streets' following the money had never been more vital. As he put it, 'stopping illicit money flows that support those atrocities is a national security imperative.' Then he inserted the blade into HSBC and twisted, accusing it of playing 'fast and loose' with US banking rules. Using the language of the narcotics trade, the Michigan senator portrayed the prestigious HSBC as 'a gateway into the US financial system' for people who do not belong there. 'Due to poor controls, HSBC US exposed the United States to Mexican drug money . . .' The bank run by Baron Hurstpierpoint, the UK trade minister, God's Banker and guru of ethical capitalism, had 'severe' deficiencies, including a 'dysfunctional' monitoring system, an 'unacceptable' backlog of alerts, 'insufficient' staffing, 'inappropriate' country and client risk assessments.

Levin said regulatory agencies should consider whether 'to revoke the charter of the US bank being used to aid and abet that illicit money.' This was a bank where the culture of compliance had been 'pervasively polluted'. In a swipe at Green and Geoghegan the senator noted that the bank's 'recent change in leadership says it's committed to cleaning house' but warned 'it will take more than words for the bank to change course.' This, as we know, was the same bank that was forever telling the world about its culture, how it was different (and better) than other banks. Its chairman, then plain Stephen Green, liked to talk about 'a great deal of commonality that runs through everyone who works here – which is that they subscribe to the same professional standards and have the same integrity and morality'. Green would maintain HSBC was 'an organization that does think carefully about its own values and culture, which we inherit from our predecessors over decades' and it was 'a bank that genuinely seeks to be an ethical bank . . .' Said Green: 'the culture of this bank is its most important asset.'

There are times when no amount of corporate PR slipperiness, no phrasing, no masking, no ducking and diving, can hide the truth. This was one of them. The bank, to use another phrase beloved of spin doctors, could not exert its usual hold over the narrative. HSBC received the report 24 hours ahead of publication, as is standard practice, which meant that they had no time to brief and attack and undermine the thumping PSI document. It was also privileged information, which meant that legally they were stuck. In anticipation of the publication of the report, Stuart Gulliver, who holds a degree in law from Oxford, and ran HSBC's stuttering investment banking side, and had stepped up to succeed Geoghegan as CEO, wrote to all the staff at HSBC to pre-empt the disaster: 'Between 2004 and 2010, our anti-money-laundering controls should have been stronger and more effective, and we failed to spot and deal with unacceptable behaviour.' There would shortly be a hearing, he said, that would 'reveal that in the past we fell well short of the standards that our regulators, customers and investors expect'. Said Gulliver: 'It is right that we be held accountable and that we take responsibility for fixing what went wrong.'

The hearing was set for the day after publication, 17 July, at 9.30 a.m. in Room SD-342 of the Dirksen Senate Office Building in Washington. Levin opened by mapping out how the Mexican drug traffickers took drugs into the US and smuggled dollar bills back into Mexico, to branches of HSBC 'which in turn took all the physical dollars that it got, transported them by armoured car or aircraft back across the border to HSBC US . . . completing the laundering cycle.' In just two years, 2007 and 2008, HSBC Mexico shipped $7 billion in dollar notes to HSBC US. 'That was more than any other Mexican bank, even one twice HSBC Mexico's size.' It was systemic. 'This is something that people knew was going on at that bank.' Faced with the wrath of the senators, the bank's tactics were to say *mea culpa*, to default to those twin defences of officialdom caught blinking in the arc lights, of 'hindsight' and 'lessons learned'. Six bank witnesses appeared. Over and over, they repeated those words, as if they had been rehearsing a pre-prepared script: 'hindsight' and 'lessons learned'. But it was not all grovelling to the review board, as they had another ploy up their sleeves, one designed to take the wind out of the PSI sails from the very start of proceedings.

The first HSBC witness was Bagley, the head of compliance. After twenty years with HSBC, he chose this moment of all moments to announce he was going: 'I recommended to the group that now is the appropriate time, for me and for the bank, for someone new to serve as the head of Group Compliance.' The cynical process of sweeping the bad news under the carpet by moving the most vulnerable targets out of the line of fire had begun. In fact, he wasn't leaving at all – in November that year he became head of compliance in HSBC private banking and he didn't depart, finally, until April 2013, nearly a full year after the report had been made public. Subsequently, he was made director of regulatory risk, fraud and anti-money laundering at the Co-op Bank.

While HSBC thought they were doing what was needed to placate the investors and the City by moving Bagley out of harm's way, Levin poured scorn on HSBC's approach. Turning to Paul Thurston, the former HSBC head of Mexico and now head of Retail Banking and Wealth Management at HSBC in Hong Kong, Levin asked: 'A number of you have talked about hindsight. These are contemporaneous emails. This is not something discovered in hindsight or learned in hindsight. This is something that people knew was going on at that bank. Why was it allowed to continue?' Thurston said that putting right the wrongs would take time and there were multiple problems. Cue Levin: 'These were problems which were known for years. This is not something which was looking back. This is something which year after year after year, starting in 2002, was known by this bank.' Michael Gallagher, the bank's former North American chief, also played the hindsight card. 'But with hindsight, it is clear that we did not always fully understand the risks of our businesses' and 'that we could have done much more and done it more quickly.' Senator Coburn was unimpressed. 'Looking at the whole of this, that to me is almost an unbelievable statement . . . It is almost like you were not aware that these things were happening?' The most telling testimony, however, was from Bagley. He may have been required to throw himself on his sword, but even in the coded, conservative language of the senior banker he made it plain where he thought the blame lay. 'We have learned a number of valuable lessons . . . One of these lessons concerns managing growth.' His choice of words exactly echoed the title of Green's masterplan, Managing for Growth. 'With the benefit of hindsight, it is now clear to many of us that the bank's business and risk profile grew faster than its infrastructure,' said Bagley. The bank got too big too quickly. 'The bank underestimated some of the challenges presented by its numerous acquisitions, and despite efforts to meet these challenges, we were not always able to keep up.'

The monster that was HSBC was out of control. The small central management had no idea what was occurring in all those countries where they delightedly planted the corporate flag. There were 'numerous affiliates around the world operating with a significant degree of autonomy' – a polite way of saying they were doing their own thing. Bagley, HSBC's own chief policeman, had no power. 'As the Head of Group Compliance, my mandate was limited to advising, recommending, and reporting. My job was not – and I did not have the authority, resources, support or infrastructure – to ensure that all of these global affiliates followed the Group's compliance standards.' Where did it all go wrong? It was down to the game of Risk. 'HSBC's growth accelerated rapidly. Some of the new acquisitions had operations that at the time of acquisition fell far short of HSBC's own compliance standards and expectation . . . With its roots in a far smaller bank in a very different global banking environment, HSBC's historic model, in retrospect, simply did not keep pace.' HSBC had grown so big and so quickly that it could not comply with the law. On behalf of the bank, Gulliver said he was 'profoundly sorry'.

TWELVE

All the way to the top

Frank DiGregorio wouldn't be drawn on what happened on the Brooklyn detective's visit to the headquarters of HSBC in London. 'It's protected by grand jury,' he said, so, alas, he cannot disclose precise details, but it is easy to get a sense of just how big a deal the HSBC scandal was for him. All he would say is that he and his police colleagues met 'people from the upper echelon of the bank – a lot of them aren't there anymore.' Did they see Green, Geoghegan, Thurston, Flockhart and Bagley? He wouldn't, couldn't, say. He explained that 'in any good investigation you try to interview everybody involved' and that was all. But what is easier to glean is that a team of detectives and attorneys from New York journeying all the way to London to interrogate the group management of HSBC is an indication as to how serious things had become, how deep the bank and its bosses were in the mire. In West Virginia, Ihlenfeld was also still champing at the bit to prosecute the bank but, to his frustration, he had been ordered to back off, and his investigative efforts were wrapped up into DiGregorio's El Dorado Task Force inquiry. The same was true of Stern – his drip-drip of information to the CIA about what he'd found had also been fed, eventually, into the one investigation. Now that was being assessed in total secrecy by the grand jury. The law enforcers were operating separately from Levin's panel and the enforcement agencies and the Senate subcommittee were on parallel tracks.

While Bean and her colleagues had been digging away, and reporting to Senator Levin, police and prosecutors in Washington and New York had also been amassing evidence against the bank. The Levin subcommittee had also supplied them with material. By the summer of 2012, the feds had been before the grand jury and the course was set clear for a criminal prosecution of HSBC. The file now lay with the Department of Justice, with the other agencies feeding into it. But the push soon took on a farcical dimension when the Justice Department realized that Benjamin Lawsky from the New York State Department of Financial Services was also circling. It turned into a classic internal governmental territorial battle to see which could be first to hit HSBC: department versus department, pride against pride. The compiling of a watertight case now plays second fiddle to egos. This, of course, played to HSBC's advantage. Lawsky had already gone after Standard Chartered for sanctions-busting and poor compliance, now he was stalking the much bigger HSBC.

On 24 August, one of the US government prosecutors moving against HSBC voiced his concern in an email to colleagues: 'There is a lot of late breaking news with respect to the investigation of HSBC . . . The various prosecutors and regulators are scrambling to get their investigations and enforcement actions completed with almost alarming speed, apparently in hopes of avoiding being beaten to the punch again by the NY Department of Financial Services. Unfortunately, this appears to be resulting in major fraying of the interagency cooperation on timelines . . .' Just as it seemed the net was tightening around HSBC it transpired that the Justice Department had started talking to HSBC about a possible quick settlement and plea bargain, a move designed to achieve victory for the people at the

Justice Department but described as 'crazy' in another email by a prosecutor who said it was too soon to be discussing terms when the full extent of the violations was not known. US Treasury records showed that the Justice Department's Asset Forfeiture and Money Laundering Section (AFMLS) – the unit responsible for enforcing anti-money laundering – was leaning towards a criminal prosecution of HSBC and a plea bargain. In a 4 September feedback note from a call between the agencies, Treasury officials were told: 'There were developments today in the interagency coordination related to HSBC that I think warrant bringing to your attention . . . DOJ (represented by [AFMLS Section Chief] Jen Shasky) stated for the first time that it is considering seeking a guilty plea from HSBC. DOJ is mulling over the ramifications that could flow from such an approach and plans to finalize its decision this week.'

On that same multi-agency call, listening in from London in disbelief at this latest turn in events were officials from the UK's watchdog, the Financial Services Authority (now the Financial Conduct Authority). If they had been in the dark as to what was coming, they weren't any longer. The Justice Department was weighing up between indicting the bank and seeking a plea bargain or going for the lesser deferred prosecution agreement or DPA – a financial payment, no criminal charges brought, provided HSBC promised to clean up its act. As exasperating as it was for those who were involved in the thousands of hours of tracking and collecting of data to inform the prosecution, the scale of the investigation, ironically, had now become so big that it was no longer simply a case of prosecuting a bank because of its behaviours. Things, in other words, had just got difficult. The decision about how to prosecute wasn't a simple choice; they had to consider the chances of securing a conviction if there was no negotiation – in other words, if HSBC refused to stomach a plea. In that event, there would be an undoubtedly lengthy litigation, ending possibly in a drawn-out trial with no guarantee of victory. They would have to prove beyond reasonable doubt, which would be expensive and time-consuming, and ranged against the US government would be some of the finest (and most costly) legal minds. Already in HSBC's corner were Sullivan & Cromwell, one of New York's leading corporate law firms who would undoubtedly be joined by a roster of stellar courtroom talent.

Sitting heavily on the minds of Eric Holder, the Attorney General, and Lanny Breuer, the Assistant Attorney General and head of the Justice Department's criminal division, were their personal reputations as well as those of their departments. It was not difficult to forget that not a single bank or senior banker had ever been prosecuted over the 2008 financial crisis, and while taking on HSBC represented a chance to right that widely perceived wrong, it came with its own risk of failure and humiliation. Compared with 2008, which involved mortgage-backed securities and complex financial dealings, this was a much more easily understood and accessible case. One of the biggest banks in the world would be accused of enabling drug traffickers led by one of the most wanted men on the planet to launder billions of dollars of their ill-gotten gains so they could carry on buying more narcotics and weapons and shattering American lives and communities. Against that was one of the principal reasons why no bank, and no senior banker, had been prosecuted over 2008: the fear that the charges could precipitate economic collapse, that the bank in question would be mortally wounded and the resulting contagion would bring down the entire system; in other words, would the wounds inflicted on the huge bank be potentially so big as to cause widespread chaos and irreparable damage? However, those involved in the investigation had been fully aware of the perceived injustices of the 2008 fallout and they thought the case against HSBC was different. By 2012 the world had moved on, the markets had recovered and were no longer so fragile, and many of the bank's most senior personnel who were likely responsible for the crisis had left or been moved on so the impact on the bank and the markets would not be so pronounced. In their view, the markets had proved that they could stomach a successful criminal prosecution against HSBC. Breuer acted cautious and took a sounding. Perhaps not surprisingly, the professional experts he consulted, in the City of London and on Wall Street, claimed there would be widescale market fallout. He carried on deliberating. Said a US Treasury note: 'The timing of completion of the HSBC matter now seems dependent on which way DOJ goes. If DOJ seeks only a deferred prosecution agreement, the matter may be resolved in about two weeks. If DOJ seeks a guilty plea, the agencies think closure will be closer to the end of September. So far, these developments have remained with the agencies and have not made it to the news media . . .' Some of Breuer's colleagues in the Justice Department, in the anti-money laundering section, however, had seen enough and had made up their minds: they wanted to charge HSBC. But that decision wasn't theirs to make; pressing the button on a prosecution of HSBC was down to their departmental bosses – to Breuer and to Holder.

A date was set, 11 September 2012, when the other agencies would be informed of the Justice Department's decision. A Treasury official email said: 'We should learn whether AFMLS's internal recommendation to ask the bank [to] plead guilty to criminal charges was approved by senior DOJ officials'. Treasury officials sarcastically noted the UK watchdog's sudden awakening and concern. 'Yes . . . and they were on the [4 September] call. That's why [Jen Shasky's] announcement was such a bombshell . . . Edna [Young, Strategy Specialist for the FSA's Financial Crime and Intelligence Department], and others were quite taken aback both by the implications of a criminal plea and by the sheer amount of the proposed fines and forfeitures. It seemed as if it were the first time they had taken out their calculator.' Then, out of the blue, the pressure on Breuer and Holder was severely raised. In the UK, the panic at the FSA that Britain's biggest bank, Europe's largest lender, HSBC, was under the US legal cosh, moved up several levels, to about as high up the ladder as it can reach (only the Prime Minister and Queen lie above). The watchdog's reporting line was to the UK Treasury.

The day before HSBC's own 9/11, when the call was due, when the Justice Department would say if its leaders were following the recommendation to prosecute the bank, George Osborne, the Chancellor of the Exchequer, head of the UK Treasury, who when he was in opposition publicly commended HSBC for its performance during the banking crisis and avoiding a government bailout, intervened. On the eve of possibly the biggest financial prosecution in a generation Osborne sent a private two-page letter to US Federal Reserve Chairman Ben Bernanke (cc US Treasury Secretary Tim Geithner). In it, Osborne pointed out to the two men that the New York Financial Services Department's attack on Standard Chartered sparked a 30 per cent drop in that bank's share price. While the shares had since recovered, said Osborne, 'it gives us an opportunity to reflect more generally on how we might collectively ensure that regulatory and enforcement action does not lead to unintended consequences.' The Chancellor requested that more early warning was given, 'to help us manage some of the potential market and stability risks and consider what (if anything) we should collectively do to manage them.' He cautioned that prosecuting such a 'systemically important financial institution' as HSBC 'could lead to [financial] contagion.' The mooted settlement figure he'd heard, $1.9 billion, would be 'three times greater' than any US settlement figure to date for similar breaches. A criminal conviction might require the US to withdraw HSBC's approvals in the US and 'risk destabilising the bank globally, with very serious implications for financial and economic stability, particularly in Europe and Asia.' He suggested that the scale of the action indicated that UK banks were being 'unfairly targeted.' Osborne requested Bernanke and Geithner's 'assistance in demonstrating that the US is even-handed and consistent in its approach.' He ended: 'I would welcome a discussion on these issues when we see each other next.' What was interesting to note was that he omitted to mention that one of the 'unintended consequences' of a criminal prosecution, along with the fall in the share price, would be the awkwardness caused to the UK government by having among its number the person who was HSBC's chief executive, then executive chairman, for the period in question. The claim that British banks were somehow being persecuted deliberately had been made before and in August 2012, according to US Treasury papers, 'an official in the UK government reached out to a US official to complain that US regulators were 'taking aggressive action against UK banks in an effort to make British banks less attractive places to do business.' The accusation even reached the White House when Rory MacFarquhar, the director of the White House's National Security Council, contacted the US Treasury on 13 August to request 'talking points'. Treasury officials told him to reassure the UK that 'there is no truth to the supposition that enforcement actions against British banks are motivated by a desire to undermine London as a premier global financial center.'

The Chancellor's dramatic, personal intervention had its desired effect, and while the interagency call scheduled for 9/11, the following day, still went ahead, there was a sudden, unflagged, alteration in stance, although for many in the meeting it was not immediately obvious why the heat had been taken out of the call. A Treasury official observed: 'Jen Shasky reported that DOJ leadership has not yet made a decision on whether it will seek an indictment or just a deferred prosecution agreement. She indicated that DOJ is very strongly considering a prosecution, but that senior leaders want to better understand the collateral consequences of a conviction/plea before taking such a dramatic step. DOJ is looking particularly for additional input from the Fed, the OCC, and the FSA.' On the same conference call, the OCC said if the bank pleaded guilty or was convicted, they would decide 'whether to hold a hearing to consider revoking the bank's US charter.' That would close down HSBC in the US; it would shut out Britain's biggest bank, Europe's biggest bank,

the one founded on 'sound Scottish principles', that was managed by
a preacher and now UK government minister, from the largest financial market in the world. Listening from their base at London's
Canary Wharf, right by HSBC group headquarters, the FSA team,
led by David Rule, head of large bank supervision, gulped and
'weighed in very strongly that any guilty plea would need to be carefully planned and coordinated.' There would need to be contingencies
in place, said the Brits. They stressed HSBC's systemic importance
and said that 'even the threat of a charter revocation could result in
a global financial disaster [my itals].' This was an extraordinary claim
in the context of both the 2008 crash, which was on a magnitude
many times larger than the isolated case of HSBC, and the previous
examples of banks behaving badly – none of those examples brought
on anything close to global financial disaster. What it smacked of was
hyperbole meant to create a purely emotional rather than logical
response to the findings. In many ways it was a deeply cynical reaction. Moreover, it left more questions unanswered. For example, did
the ruling mean that this kind of ring fencing was only applied to the
very biggest banks, and what about different types of financial services businesses? How had this become UK government policy, who
had decreed it? Where was the official announcement that a bank as
big as HSBC could expect special treatment? None of these questions
were addressed let alone satisfactorily answered, a point that was particularly galling to those who had spent thousands of hours putting
together the cases against HSBC.

For City watchers, these kinds of apocalyptic claims were still
fresh, as similar claims had been made previously, when the FSA's
predecessor, the FCA, was dealing with the 2008 crash. At the time
I had been reporting on the trauma day after day as City Editor for
the London *Evening Standard*. I remember taking a call from one of
those closely involved in the banks' rescue who pleaded with me to
opine that Lloyds must be allowed to merge with the collapsed
HBOS and that the government must pump taxpayers' money into

HBOS. 'If HBOS goes down, the whole system is fucked, we're all fucked,' he said. I asked for his evidence. He replied that he didn't have any, it was common sense, an economic tsunami was bound to be the result. I asked how he could be so sure, where was his evidence? At which point he told me not to be so 'fucking stupid' and rang off.

In the US, while Osborne had come to the rescue, the back and forth between the US agencies and the FSA continued. The US Treasury emailed: 'While the FSA folks did not argue specifically against a prosecution, it was clear they were very concerned about the reverberations such an action could have within the financial system, and they asked for urgent high-level discussions with DOJ on the matter. Jen Shasky offered to arrange a call with Lanny Breuer, for the Criminal Division.' On 11 September, a US Treasury official, Dennis Wood, emailed two colleagues to brief them about the 'dynamic of a possible HSBC criminal plea' after the interagency call: 'Adam and Barbara, it's very important that we brief you, re. the dynamic of a possible HSBC criminal plea as it relates to the UK and global markets. David Rule, the FSA's Prudential Head of Large Complex Banking Groups, is very eloquent about the subject during this morning's interagency call. This is something that definitely should be brought to [Secretary Geithner's] personal attention as soon as possible, if he isn't already aware of it . . .' The following day, there was another email. 'DOJ is very seriously considering seeking a guilty plea or indictment of the bank for the money laundering activities. Based on statements from US and UK regulatory agencies, we understand that a felony plea or conviction could have very serious collateral consequences for the bank, including a possible revocation of its charter authorizing it to do business in the United States. Needless to say, this information is extremely sensitive.' Then, silence. The conference calls and chats about what to with HSBC suddenly ceased. The Justice Department went into purdah and pulled out of the regular multi-bureau discussions while they were making up their minds whether to ignore the pleas of Osborne and the FSA, and to prosecute. Osborne, however, was not done with lobbying. The annual World Bank–International Monetary Fund meeting, the gathering of the world's central bankers, finance ministers, development experts and academics, was due in Tokyo between 9 and 14 October and Osborne arranged to speak to Bernanke and Geithner about HSBC when all three of them were in Tokyo.

On Monday, 8 October 2012, George Osborne delivered his set-piece speech as Chancellor to the annual Conservative Party Conference in Birmingham before being whisked away to the airport and a long flight to Tokyo. In his conference address, received with rapturous applause, Osborne spoke of the need to continue the government's austerity drive, prompted by the banking crash of 2008 and the government rescue, to further reduce the government's budget deficit. His theme was that 'we're all in this together'. In one section of his speech he singled out bankers. Be under no illusion, he said, how hard he would crack down on them. 'We've never allowed uncontrolled capitalism free-rein. It was these Labour politicians, not Conservatives, who let the banks run rampage because they didn't understand that to work for everyone, markets need rules.' Warming to his theme, the pumped-up Osborne pronounced: 'I'm the Chancellor in a government that has done more to reform finance and banking than any before it.' He promised: 'We're reforming banking, so it serves our economy and supports families and businesses. That is part of our enterprise strategy.' He referenced the public aspect of the Tokyo trip. 'It tells you something about just how big it was that the deficit is still higher today than when a British government went begging to the IMF in the 1970s. This Wednesday, I'm also going to a meeting of the IMF. Don't worry. Because of the resolve of the British people, I go representing a country that is seen as part of the solution, not part of the problem! That is only because of the credibility our plans have earned.' What he did not tell the conference was that he would be pushing hard in private in Tokyo for HSBC to avoid criminal prosecution for becoming the bank of choice to the world's most dangerous drugs cartel.

While Osborne was in Birmingham, Treasury officials in Washington were preparing a briefing for Geithner for the private meeting between him and Bernanke. Said the memo to Geithner: 'Chancellor Osborne requested this meeting with you and Chairman Bernanke to discuss his letter dated September 10, 2012, regarding his concerns over pending enforcement matters.' The note went on to explain that the impending action against HSBC, 'seemed to Osborne to entail significantly tougher measures than recent major enforcement actions against other foreign banks, raising unwanted questions about potential US hostility to London as a financial center. While acknowledging the importance of regulatory enforcement, Osborne sought Bernanke's assistance to ensure that future actions involving British banks would be conveyed in advance and be fair.' Officials told Geithner the FSA in London was being 'particularly problematic on enforcement and adopting a light touch approach at industry's request . . .' There was attached a 'background' briefing for the US Treasury Secretary, which left no leeway as far as the US government was concerned, who saw a litany of criminal offending. Geithner was told there was a case pending in the US. It was due to be brought by the end of October or beginning of November and would cover 'pervasive and systemic' failures in money-laundering controls, 'inadequate' risk ratings for countries, customers and products; failures to monitor large volumes of high-risk transactions, clearance of large numbers of alerts without any review; and failures to perform customer due diligence. This conduct was 'exacerbated by the stove-piping of information' across the HSBC network. All told, this resulted 'in $60 trillion in wire transactions through the United States being excluded from monitoring each year, $15 billion in bulk US currency entering the United States from abroad being excluded from monitoring over a three-year period' and the non-filing of thousands of suspicious activity reports. They had hard evidence of

$881 million in drug proceeds going through the bank but they were certain it was much, much more.

The three men, the British Chancellor, the US Treasury Secretary and the head of the Federal Reserve, journeyed to Tokyo and their discussions held on 'the margins' of the conference concerning HSBC remain confidential to this day. Geithner relayed what he'd been told by his officials; Osborne emphasized HSBC's importance and size, how this would be viewed as some sort of anti-British act and the danger of provoking global Armageddon. Back in the US, at Justice, Breuer was continuing to consult those with long knowledge of the banking industry. One of those to whom he reached out was 'Rodge' Cohen, and Wall Street lawyers do not come bigger than Henry Rodgin Cohen. Born in 1944, and educated at Harvard, Cohen is canny, regularly referred to as Wall Street's pre-eminent banking lawyer. The *New York Times* hailed Cohen as 'the trauma surgeon of Wall Street', and he's Senior Chair of Sullivan & Cromwell where he has been for fifty years. A top banking partner, one of his clients was HSBC. In seeking advice on how to proceed with the case against HSBC Breuer turned to HSBC's own lawyer. In a meeting, Breuer took Cohen aside and floated a rhetorical question: 'Is any bank too big to indict?' Cohen's answer was a classic chess outmanoeuvre. 'That cannot be the rule,' replied the sage veteran. So no bank could be too big to jail. Cohen followed that somewhat surprising assertion from him of all people with some advice. What he would do, he said, would be to ask whether the bank in question was aware of the problem and had promised to fix it? And were the senior managers responsible still there? The answer to the first question, in relation to HSBC, was 'yes'. Likewise, the answer to the second was 'no.' Cohen planted in Breuer's mind the thought that there was nothing but trouble to be gained from going after HSBC in the criminal court – it had said sorry, it could reform its ways, why drag it through the mud and risk a financial meltdown? Still, Breuer ended the meeting by saying that he believed the era at the Justice Department of banks and bankers no longer getting prosecuted was over.

A brooding Cohen returned to his office and his next move was straight out of a chess Grand Master tactics book. He looked to take Breuer at his word and had his team draw up a press release in the event that HSBC was indicted – in other words, he called Breuer's bluff. The Justice Department was then made aware that HSBC was ready with the release and what it contained. The document was apocalyptic: HSBC would be deserted by other financial institutions, they would no longer do business with the bank; it would have to leave some markets, causing them to weaken and teeter; the global financial markets, as Osborne and the FSA predicted, would go into meltdown. Was this really what Breuer wanted to happen? was the challenge that was being put to him.

In 1933 Franklin D. Roosevelt famously said that 'the only thing we have to fear is fear itself'. In the wake of the 1929 crash his words were meant to calm the market and restore trust in the system. But this kind of public pronouncement could work the other way. A press release like this, into a volatile market, could have done real damage, and what Cohen wanted to show was that while Breuer could proceed with the charges, it could, potentially, come at a huge cost. On 5 November, the Justice Department informed the US Treasury that senior HSBC officials were flying to meet with Justice officials in Washington in two days' time, 'to plead their case about not being forced to go the "guilty" route.' After all the backwards and forwards, all the hundreds of memos, the phone calls, Osborne's letter and the Tokyo meeting, the Cohen discussion, it was down to this: the moment when the Justice Department would confront HSBC and tell them its intentions. This was high-level, genuine staring-into-the-whites-of-their-eyes stuff, worthy of fast-draw cowboys in a movie such as *High Noon*. Attorney General Eric Holder himself turned up to the showdown, with Breuer. The two gunslingers from the US Justice Department went into the meeting and they caved. They agreed to a 'take-it-or-leave-it' deferred prosecution agreement – there would be no criminal charges, no prime-time front-page trial, no dip in the shares, no threat to financial stability, no prospect of a global financial disaster. Osborne's appeals, his lobbying on the other side of the world, his frantic pressing for HSBC to be allowed to avoid criminal prosecution, the FSA's dire predictions, they had all worked. At his desk in London's Whitehall, Osborne's UK high-profile government colleague, the former HSBC boss Baron Green of Hurstpierpoint, could sit easily as there would be no one pursuing him or his former colleagues.

Remarkably, for the second time in HSBC's history, the British government had rallied round, stepping in to benefit the bank and its business.

A follow-up email confirmed to the US Treasury: 'DOJ indicated it would not insist on a guilty plea as part of the settlement, but instead would be willing to resolve all counts through a comprehensive deferred prosecution agreement. As you may recall, a guilty plea or conviction was likely to have serious collateral consequences for the bank, including a hearing to consider whether to revoke the bank's US charter. The current total liability for all criminal and civil fines and forfeiture actions would amount to approximately $2 billion.' At least one part of the US government, the anti-money laundering section of the Justice Department, wanted HSBC prosecuted. So did some of their colleagues elsewhere, and really it was only when Osborne wrote his letter that the tenor changed, and even then it was only part of the letter that had any real impact. Of his two arguments, the first, about trying to do London down, did not carry much weight. The second, about systemic risk coupled with talk from the UK watchdog of precipitating 'a global financial disaster', it turns out, did make US officials sit up. It goes without saying that the UK trade minister, Lord Green, and his former senior HSBC colleagues were extremely fortunate that Osborne had gone into bat the way he had. They had every reason to be grateful to Osborne – if anyone in high office, with influence, pushed the case for HSBC being too big to jail, it was him. Holder accompanied his 'take-it-or-leave-it' offer with the proviso that the deferred prosecution agreement had to be struck by 14 November. As it was, they missed the Attorney General's deadline by nearly a month because HSBC, with the threat of indictment having vanished, now had the bit between its teeth and was in natural, commercial negotiation, deal-striking mode and fighting over every line, every word of the proposed agreement.

The fact the bank was being allowed to negotiate at all was a remarkable turnaround; with charges not going to be brought there had been a marked shift in power. Just one example, relating to bonuses, is enough to show how this balance of power had shifted after the intervention of Osborne. Instead of insisting HSBC claw back bonuses paid to the senior executives responsible, the wording was changed by the HSBC lawyers to 'could' – as in, 'could claw back.' It was a minor but hugely significant change and carried a completely different meaning, and Justice allowed it. Finally, on 11 December, they were all ready to go public. Breuer was flanked by Loretta Lynch, US Attorney for the Eastern District of New York, and John Morton, Director of ICE, to declare that HSBC admitted anti-money laundering violations and it was going to pay a civil sum of $1.92 billion. As part of the deferred prosecution agreement, the bank also committed to boost its anti-money laundering efforts and to make other reforms to prevent a repeat. HSBC, said the Justice Department statement, 'has replaced almost all of its senior manage-ment, "clawed back" deferred compensation bonuses given to its most senior [anti-money laundering] and compliance officers, and has agreed to partially defer bonus compensation for its most senior executives – its group general managers and group managing directors – during the period of the five-year DPA. In addition to these measures, HSBC has made significant changes in its manage-ment structure and [anti-money laundering] compliance functions that increase the accountability of its most senior executives for [anti-money laundering] compliance failures.' This sounded tough and convincing, and indicated that HSBC had executed a management clear-out. But of the most senior hierarchy, Green was due to retire anyway, and Geoghegan went because he did not get the top post, although HSBC may have decided enough was enough in his case, and he was not thought to get on with regulators as well as his other internal rival, Doug Flint. Flockhart, who had run Mexico from 2002 to 2007 and later oversaw the whole of South America, had quit the bank six months previously. With the bank for almost forty years, a main board director and once thought of as a potential chairman, Flockhart left on 31 July, barely a fortnight after publication of the Senate subcommittee report. He alone was cited twenty-five times in the report, and it was Flockhart who was quoted as having been very much aware that compliance in Bital was poor to non-existent. If there was going to be a fall-guy, Flockhart was clearly it. Colleagues, however, said Flockhart was going because he was suffering from cancer, although he was subsequently well enough to team up with Sir Peter Burt, the former chief executive of Bank of Scotland, in Promethean Investments, the private equity group. A few years later Flockhart was made chairman of B and C, or Bank and Clients, a British deposit-taker, a bank born out of the purchase of Church House Trust from Virgin Money by Ocean Capital, a corporate lender. Welcoming him aboard, Edouard Bridel, a major shareholder of Ocean and then B and C, and chief of strategy, emphasized that Flockhart, 'was not indicted or accused of anything.'

At the time of writing, Flockhart's successor, Thurston, is still with HSBC, albeit in a different post on the other side of the world from Mexico. Michael Gallagher, who also gave evidence, has gone, as has another PSI witness, Christopher Lok, the former head of Global Banknotes. Others, who weren't called, have also left. Similarly, if senior HSBC executives were worried about being seriously out of pocket because their bank was washing the Sinaloa's dirty money, they need not have been. Clawbacks were a much-touted response from banks to scandals surrounding their pay awards – the impression being allowed to arise that they were withdrawing chunky sums from bonus payments and the bankers would really suffer where it hurt them most. At HSBC, it was never specified how much the clawbacks were for each individual and it became a matter of discretion. But in 2012, HSBC clawed back just $700,000 out of $608 million of deferred pay still outstanding for 314 senior staff, which equated to 0.1 per cent of the deferred amount and was less than the $800,000 the bank clawed back in 2011. That $700,000 covered a variety of deeds, not only Mexico. The bulk of the clawback was over the mis-selling of insurance and savings products in the UK, and the poor management of a unit advising the elderly on their finances. Still, on the day, the US government talked a good game where claiming to be hammering HSBC was concerned. The US Treasury stated: 'The bank's breakdowns in anti-money laundering (AML) compliance were particularly egregious because these failures allowed hundreds of millions of dollars from Mexican drug-trafficking organizations to flow through accounts in the United States. Despite HSBC's extensive global operations and the substantial resource it had available to manage transnational risk, it failed to help secure the United States financial borders and left dangerous gaps that international drug dealers and other criminals readily abused.' Declared Breuer, 'The record of dysfunction that prevailed at HSBC for many years was astonishing.'

Continued Breuer: 'Today, HSBC is paying a heavy price for its conduct, and, under the terms of today's agreement, if the bank fails to comply with the agreement in any way, we reserve the right to fully prosecute it.' Lynch chimed in: 'Today's historic agreement . . . makes it clear that all corporate citizens, no matter how large, must be held accountable for their actions.' The Justice Department said it wished to thank William Ihlenfeld II, US Attorney for the Northern District of West Virginia. Stern, who had been out of work since leaving

HSBC, travelled to New York especially for the announcement and he sat expectantly in a hotel, waiting for reporters to call once the news had broken of HSBC's indictment. Instead, on hearing it was a DPA and not criminal charges, he was crushed. 'I thought, "All that for nothing?" I couldn't believe it.' What might have alleviated Stern's disappointment was the document accompanying Breuer's news of the DPA called the Statement of Facts, which, at thirty pages, is a searing read. Everything in it is true – HSBC admits so. The bank says that if there was a trial, the Justice Department would 'prove beyond a reasonable doubt' what it had done. HSBC had 'ignored the money laundering risks' allowing 'at least $881 million in drug trafficking cash to be washed'. It didn't carry out due diligence, it failed to monitor more than $200 trillion in wire transfers and billions of dollars in purchases of physical US dollar bills between July 2006 and July 2009. The bank failed to provide the staff and resources for effective anti-money laundering. They blew the lid on the Cayman operation and admitted 'HSBC Mexico accounts were based in the Cayman Islands, but were essentially offshore in name only, because HSBC Mexico had no physical presence in the Cayman Islands and provided the front and back-office services for these accounts at its branches in Mexico. Customers holding these accounts did all of their banking, including depositing physical US dollars, at branches in Mexico.' Some of the money that went down this route, agreed HSBC, was used to buy aircraft to ferry narcotics. Accounts that should have been closed, simply were not. 'Even when HSBC Mexico determined a relationship should be terminated, it often took years for the account to actually be closed.' In December 2008, there were 675 accounts marked for closure based on suspicions of money laundering. Closure had been approved for sixteen of these accounts in 2005, 130 in 2006, 172 in 2007, and 309 in 2008. All 675 of these accounts remained open and active well into 2009.

HSBC accepted that it was 'told that Mexican law enforcement possessed a recording of a Mexican drug lord saying that HSBC

Mexico was the place to launder money.' Between 2004 and 2007, the bank agreed, HSBC Mexico exported over $3 billion per year to the United States in dollar bills. It acknowledged being warned by the Banco de Mexico that its US dollar exports to the US were far, far larger than its market share. The bank agreed that a small number of Mexican customers accounted for a very large percentage of physical US dollar deposits. 'For example, in January 2008, 312 customers accounted for approximately 32 per cent of total physical US dollar deposits.' From 2006 to 2008, HSBC Mexico exported over $1.1 billion in US dollar notes from Sinaloa state to HSBC in the US. HSBC admitted that 'drug traffickers were depositing hundreds of thousands of dollars in bulk each day into HSBC Mexico accounts. In order to efficiently move this volume of cash through the teller windows at HSBC Mexico branches, drug traffickers designed specially shaped boxes that fit the precise dimensions of the teller windows. The drug traffickers would send numerous boxes filled with cash through the teller windows for deposit into HSBC Mexico accounts.' Part of the Statement of Facts related to bypassing US sanctions. This amounted to six years' worth of sanctions-busting, totalling $660 million, covering embargoes against Burma, Iran, Sudan, Cuba and Libya. This was also bad, but at least here HSBC was not out on its own, as other banks were caught in the same international dragnet, including ABN-Amro, Barclays, ING, Credit Suisse, Standard Chartered, JP Morgan Chase, Wachovia and Citigroup. On Mexico, on being the bank of choice for the Sinaloa, for Chapo, HSBC is alone. On high, the bank reiterated its sorrow, while the UK Department for Business, Innovation and Skills, where Green was now a government minister, said: 'The report by the US Senate subcommittee sets out in detail the evidence submitted to it and the action taken by HSBC to ensure compliance with US regulations at the time that Lord Green was group chairman. At the time of the report's publication, HSBC expressed its regret that there were failures of implementation and Lord Green has said that he shares that regret.'

That was it. No explanation was offered as to how his corporation landed in this mess, how it came to within a whisker of being prosecuted, how it's received the biggest fine in US history. There was no deep sorrow, definitely no apology, only regret. He regretted what is described, deliberately vaguely and blandly, as 'failures of implementation.' There is no mention either of how he could remain a UK government minister. As to Osborne's fear that HSBC's share price might crash, in the most accurate indication as to what investors believed – whether HSBC really had been clobbered by the DPA, as Holder, Breuer and the rest all claimed, or had got off lightly – the market gave its verdict: the bank's shares went up.

THIRTEEN

Drawing a line

In the days after the press conference, officials from the Justice Department tried to put a brave face on the climbdown. It had not been clear-cut; the assistance to the Sinaloa had been going on for so long that it was impossible to point to a single person at the bank to indict – there were layers of management from the teller in a branch in Mexico all the way up, so where could the buck stop? This was a line of defence that made little sense because it suggested that no one could be charged simply because the crime had been going on for so long. As for the layers of management argument, instead of cementing responsibility as they're meant to, here they had had the opposite effect, of acting like a filter, of dissipating the toxicity at the bottom so in the end no one at the top was to blame. However valiant, or preposterous depending on your point of view, these attempts at reasoning, there is no doubt why the US government had behaved in this fashion, why it had chosen not to charge HSBC and why no banker faced the likelihood of jail. Days before the agreement was declared, Breuer gave an interview hinting at the outcome and the rationale, saying, 'if I bring a case against institution A, and as a result of bringing that case there's some huge economic effect, it affects the economy so that employees who had nothing to do with the wrong-doing of the company . . . If it creates a ripple effect so that suddenly counterparties and other financial institutions or other companies that had nothing to do with this are affected badly, it's a factor we need to know and understand.'

In March 2013, Attorney General Holder said as much again, tell-ing the Senate Judiciary Committee: 'I am concerned that the size of some of these [financial] institutions becomes so large that it does become difficult for us to prosecute them when we are hit with indi-cations that if you do prosecute, if you do bring a criminal charge, it will have a negative impact on the national economy, perhaps even the world economy. And I think that is a function of the fact that some of these institutions have become too large . . . I think it has an inhibiting influence—[an] impact on our ability to bring resolutions that I think would be more appropriate.'

It's official. HSBC and other big banks were too big to jail, the Attorney General said so. Then, Holder got the heebie-jeebies. He made a screeching handbrake turn.

The day after Holder appeared before the Senate Judiciary Com-mittee, on 7 March 2013, Elizabeth Warren let rip. She had been a member of the Senate only since the beginning of January but Warren was already proving to be an outspoken scourge of big banks. Origin-ally a Republican in outlook, she switched because the GOP was too much in hock with the giant corporations and financial powerhouses and not enough on the side of ordinary Americans. As a law professor, she campaigned for the rights of consumers in the face of tough bank-ruptcy laws. She chaired the Congressional Oversight Panel assessing the effectiveness of the government bank bailouts in the 2008 crisis. Warren was the driving force behind the creation of the Consumer Financial Protection Bureau and was in the running to be its first chair until her candidacy was blocked by Republicans and Wall Street. When she won the Democrat nomination for the Senate for

Massachusetts in 2012, the *New York Times* commented that 'it was possible to run against the big banks without Wall Street money and still win.' Once elected, as the first woman senator from the state, she wasted no time in going on the attack. Warren joined the Senate Banking Committee and at her first hearing in February 2013, pushed bank regulators to say when they had last taken a major bank to trial, saying, 'I'm really concerned that "too big to fail" has become "too big for trial".' The following month, on the same committee, Warren lambasted Treasury officials. 'How many billions of dollars do you have to launder for drug lords and how many economic sanctions do you have to violate before someone will consider shutting down a financial institution like this?' Her question was directed to David Cohen, the Treasury Department's undersecretary for terrorism and financial intelligence, and he repeatedly refused to answer, hiding meekly behind the excuse that his department had no authority to shut down a bank unless the Justice Department – not present – convicted the bank of a crime. He said the Treasury had come down as hard as possible on HSBC, but despite repeated questioning he still wouldn't answer Warren's question about when a bank deserves to be shut down. 'You sit in Treasury and you try to enforce these laws,' she raged, 'and I've read all of your testimony and you tell me how vigorously you want to enforce these laws, but you have no opinion on when it is that a bank should be shut down for money laundering? Not even an opinion?' Another regulator, Jerome Powell from the Federal Reserve, agreed that closing a bank is appropriate when that bank has been convicted of a crime. But he stressed that only the Justice Department has the authority to prosecute a bank for a crime. Warren snapped: 'If you're caught with an ounce of cocaine, the chances are good you're gonna go to jail. If it happens repeatedly, you may go to jail for the rest of your life. But evidently if you launder nearly a billion dollars for drug cartels . . . your company pays a fine and you go home and sleep in your bed at night – every single individual associated with this. And I think that's fundamentally wrong.' Cue an attempted

U-turn from Holder. Two months later, in May 2013, he was given the opportunity to restate his case. He was asked by Congressman John Conyers: 'Have we an economic system in which we have banks that are too big to prosecute? I mean, the Department of Justice has got to look at this very carefully.' Replied Holder: 'Let me make something real clear right away. I made a statement in a Senate hearing that I think has been misconstrued. I said it was difficult at times to bring cases against large financial institutions because of the potential consequences that they would have on the financial system . . . Now there are a number of factors that we have to take into consideration as we decide who we're going to prosecute. Innocent people can be impacted by a prosecution brought of a financial institution or any corporation.' He stressed: 'But let me be very, very, very clear. Banks are not too big to jail. If we find a bank or a financial institution that has done something wrong, if we can prove it beyond a reasonable doubt, those cases will be brought.'

Holder could not have been clearer the first time. Now, here he was saying that, yes, they were worried about the fallout, the impact on innocent people, and they had to weigh up the prospect of securing a conviction, beyond a reasonable doubt. In relation to HSBC, this last point was not an issue since the Treasury documents showed that the anti-money laundering section of the Justice Department was adamant that they should prosecute and HSBC themselves had admitted breaking the law. Everything was proceeding towards criminal indictment until Osborne weighed in and the FSA talked of causing 'global financial disaster'. To this day, Republicans are demanding the Justice Department come clean. Said the Republican caucus on the House Treasury Committee: 'A nation governed by the rule of law cannot have a two-tiered system of justice – one for the largest banks, and another for everyone else. Accordingly, inasmuch as DOJ continues to believe that certain financial institutions are too large to effectively prosecute, it is imperative that DOJ promptly inform the Congress of this fact, so that Congress can seek to address the problem of "too big to jail" through its legislative function. The American people and their representatives in Congress deserve to know the truth about any difficulties that might exist in prosecuting large financial institutions and their employees who have engaged in serious criminal conduct, so that these difficulties can be properly addressed.' That HSBC shares actually went up after the penalty and DPA were announced masked an underlying truth: as far as the same markets that Osborne and the FSA were so worried about – HSBC 'got off'. It may have been the largest fine in American history, the bank may have admitted to all sorts of crimes that it agreed would be proven beyond reasonable doubt in a court of law, but the investment community did not care. All that mattered to them, as Green himself once said, was the P and L, the numbers. In their eyes, as substantial as $1.92 billion was, they'd done the maths: it amounted to only five weeks of profits.

An awkward episode in HSBC's history had been dealt with; the authorities were satisfied, and save for some changes in procedure the corporation had promised to make, the chapter was now closed. The messaging from the bank was positive, upbeat and forward-viewing. Just like Cohen's reply to Breuer, the line taken was 'we're sorry, it won't happen again, we've changed', and constituted the text-book corporate, organizational, government reaction to a screw-up. Show contrition, blather on about learning the lessons, and quickly move on. So, HSBC's US spokesman Rob Sherman reassured inves-tors that the bank had 'taken extensive actions to put in place the highest standards to protect against current and emerging threats from financial crime.' The bank would continue to expand and keep costs down, but from now on, said Gulliver, they would pay more attention to exercising more control. 'We will continue to implement our Global Standards programme which we believe will increase the quality of the Group's earnings. We have made substantial investment in risk and compliance capabilities across all businesses and regions to strengthen our response to the ongoing threat of financial crime and will continue to do so. This is the right thing to do, in line with our values, and we believe that it will also become a source of competitive advantage.' As a lesson in the feint, the sleight of hand that made for what is regarded as good public relations, this was masterly. The tactic was to deflect, to speak in general, unspecific, bland terms, to direct the listener and reader forwards, not to invite them to look back. The bank introduced something called Global Standards: not only was the corporation going to raise its game against financial crime but in doing so it would become 'a source of competitive advantage', the phrase beloved of the bank's management and camp followers. The bank was very much still in the game of Risk and it was now turning its appalling behaviour into an opportunity. Not everyone was so taken in and one of those who had been at the Justice Department – although not working directly on the HSBC case – and had paid close attention to what was unfolding, was Richard Elias. Like Bill Ihlenfeld, he had studied and worked in journalism – in Elias's case at University of Missouri-Columbia and at KOMU, an affiliate of NBC – before turning lawyer and public prosecutor. 'Rich' Elias attended Missouri Law and won a clutch of honours, including Order of the Coif, Order of the Barristers and the International Association of Trial Lawyers Award for Distinguished Advocacy and he was also Note and Comment Editor of the *Missouri Law Review*.

He began his professional life by defending companies, but 'after seeing first-hand how corporations often use their money, power, and influence to intimidate and thwart smaller plaintiffs' he moved to pursuing corporate misconduct, which meant leaving the comfort and security of a partnership in a large firm to move to Fresno to become an Assistant United States Attorney for the Eastern District of California. As a federal prosecutor, Rich worked closely with whistleblowers in stopping corporate fraud and following the 2008 financial crisis, he hooked up with one of the most celebrated of all. Alayne Fleischmann was the key witness in Elias's successful investigation into JP Morgan for rolling up subprime mortgages, the lowest of the low of mortgages, into investment packages and putting them out onto the market even though the bank knew they were rubbish. His interest in JP Morgan's role in the subprime market started when he was going through some papers while looking after his baby son in 2012 and he noticed an email from Fleischmann warning her bosses they should not be reselling such poor loans. Fleischmann, a securities lawyer, was told to keep her mouth shut, and she later left JP Morgan and was working at a law firm in Calgary, back in her home country of Canada, when Rich tracked her down. She was prepared to tell all if asked but had also got used to the bank lawyers giving the run-around to those from the public service. But that was all before Elias and a colleague came knocking. Elias, she said, was different from public lawyers hitherto. 'He sounded like he had been a securities lawyer for ten years. This actually looked like his idea of fun – like he couldn't wait to run with this case.' Together, they forced JP Morgan into a hefty settlement.

Aside from going after JP Morgan, Elias also prosecuted utility and logging companies for wrongfully starting wildfires that destroyed tens of thousands of acres of National Forest land. His forest fire prosecutions led to nearly $200 million in recoveries for the public, including $122.5 million from timber giant Sierra Pacific Industries. At Justice, same as at school, he garnered prizes: the 2014 Attorney General's Award for Distinguished Service, the 2013 Director's Award, 2012 Attorney of the Year. The *Wall Street Journal* put him on its front page for the JP Morgan takedown. In 2014, he left the department to head his own five-strong eponymous firm in St Louis, Missouri. 'A tight team,' as they describe it, and Elias LLC's speciality is whistleblower cases. 'We are also smart, fearless, and relentless in litigating and trying cases against corporate giants. We beat them and their legal teams with aggressive, targeted case strategies, which has resulted in tens of millions of dollars in recoveries for our clients.' Said Elias: 'I was in the Department of Justice when the HSBC DPA was entered into. It was a very unpopular agreement within the department. I was not working on it but I was aware of it. I was outraged by HSBC's conduct and how that was symptomatic of larger problems with the banks. It had always stuck with me.' Elias moved into private practice, 'with the mission to bring cases of important public interest.' This fitted the bill. His view of the HSBC case was that of a cartel in Mexico committing 'very gruesome acts of violence' and HSBC, the bank that had laundered their money, receiving only 'a relatively light penalty – that's what made it so unpopular in the Department of Justice.' Said Elias: 'It was beyond dispute that HSBC constantly allowed billions of dollars to be laundered through its branches. It was egregious what they'd done – accepting large amounts of US dollars in cash, $200,000 a time, receiving specially packaged boxes filled with cash that were the same size as the cashiers' windows. It was unmistakable what was happening.' The US Anti-Terrorism Act 'imposes liability on those who commit a terrorist act and those who provide support knowingly or recklessly to those who commit the terrorist act.' The more Elias analysed it, the more it was his belief that, 'by laundering their money, HSBC materially supported the cartel and gruesome acts of terror.' Where a bank and a drugs cartel were concerned it is, though, largely an untested law. Nevertheless, Elias decided to give it a go and in February 2016 he announced he was suing HSBC under the Anti-Terrorism Act.

From the point of view of the British legal system it is easy to accuse America of many things, but I wish we had a system that produced so many proactive, brave inquisitors as they have, on their side of the public, working in the service of the public. I look at our bodies, legal and politic, and I lament. We don't have enough, not of the sort who are prepared to take on the very biggest, untouchable targets, who will stick at it, who won't climb down. Where are our Bill Ihlenfelds, Richard Eliases and Carl Levins? Like them I studied law, but not one of my college cohort went into the criminal bar, from day one, as our tutor repeatedly told us, we were heading to where the money was, at the commercial bar or a corporate firm. Elias and his colleagues returned to the records, including the DPA and the Statement of Facts, the Permanent Subcommittee report, and they scoured for US victims of Sinaloa violence during the timeframe covered by those documents, because if the case was going to have any success, Elias needed to have a victim who was a US citizen for the statute to apply.

One of those killed by the Sinaloa was called Rafael Morales Jr. In 2010, Morales Jr and his family were celebrating his wedding ceremony at El Señor de la Misericordia Catholic Church in Ciudad Juárez, the city where his bride had been raised. As the congregation exited the church, approximately sixteen assassins from the Sinaloa, all bearing assault rifles, were waiting for them in the church courtyard. In the distance, barricading the road to the church, were corrupt Mexican federal police officers working for the cartel. Chapo's sicarios were there under orders to kidnap Guadalupe Morales, but people at the wedding tried to dissuade the orchestrator of the attack, Chapo lieutenant Irvin Enriquez, saying that they were innocent people. Enriquez ignored their pleas. They ordered everyone, including small children, to lie face down in the dirt. In a panic, one man attempted to flee but was shot in the back and killed and Chapo's men, enraged, began beating Guadalupe in front of the congregation. Rafael Jr's brother and best man, Jaime, screamed for the men to stop, at which point they grabbed him, his brother and his uncle, forcing them into two separate vehicles, and left. The corrupt Mexican police then closed the courtyard gate and locked it, trapping the horrified wedding guests inside. The Morales men were then transported to two separate 'safe houses' where they were tortured. Later that evening, Enriquez was in a meeting in Sunland Park, New Mexico. He'd been bragging about the wedding abductions, when he received a radio call from one of the Sinaloa cartel killers by two-way radio. He had the three Morales men identify themselves over the radio. People in the meeting again encouraged Enriquez to release the men, telling him over and over again that they were innocent and were not the people they were looking for. Enriquez nevertheless ordered them to be killed. In the pantheon of gruesome murders committed in Mexico, this was right at the top, as the innocent wedding guests were murdered by having their heads wrapped round and round in duct tape leading to death by asphyxiation. The bodies were found discarded in the back of a truck in a residential neighbourhood in Juárez, their heads still bound in the tape.

Various Sinaloa members were indicted for the murder of Morales Jr in the US District Court for the Western District of Texas, including Enriquez, José Antonio Torres Marrufo, a senior enforcer for the cartel, as well as Chapo himself. The FBI said the deaths arose from a misunderstanding, that the victims were members of the rival La Linea cartel and that Guadalupe Morales worked for the person responsible for the death of Enriquez's father, and the brutal murder was an act of revenge. In a minor victory of the FBI, Enriquez and an associate were subsequently caught and pleaded guilty to conspiring in the US – in Texas and New Mexico – to murdering Morales Jr, Jaime Morales and Guadalupe Morales in a foreign country. At the time of his death, Morales Jr was a US citizen who lived in La Mesa, New Mexico, with his parents, sister and nephews. Having read the story of the murder and trial, Elias encouraged Morales's parents, who loved their son very much, to join an action. Their daughter, Moraima, also signed up, as did Juan Cruz, a US citizen, her son and nephew of Morales Jr.

The Morales family was just one grieving set of relatives who Elias managed to convince to join an action, and in all there were five lots of plaintiffs for five murdered US citizens. 'We sat down with them and talked to them – it wasn't easy because they'd been through so much,' he said. 'We were proposing holding HSBC accountable in a way it had not been held accountable before. It was easy for the unengaged to say that was a pretty hefty fine. But they'd still reported $17 billion worth of profits and $22 billion the year before. The fines were not deterring conduct. There were ways for us to play our part – the Anti-Terrorism Act opened the doors of the US courts to victims of international terrorism and those providing material support to terrorists. It also contained a punitive element of triple damages.'

After 9/11, the 1996 Anti-Terrorist Act was amended to allow victims to receive compensation from organizations that provide material support to groups that commit terror acts and it was this act that Elias wanted to use to go after HSBC. Said Elias: 'The evidence is very compelling that there were individuals in the bank who were more than just negligent. There were members of the bank who knew full well the amounts of illicit dollars that were being laundered and in several instances there were employees of the bank who were complicit and were working on the money-laundering schemes, none of whom has been held accountable.' Following the fine and DPA, 'The only tool we have left is damages for the victims. I would like to see criminal prosecutions – individuals need to be held accountable – there is a culture within the Justice Department of not holding individuals accountable in financial institutions who commit significant crimes.' Echoing Elizabeth Warren, he said: 'If you sell a gram of cocaine on the street, you're going to jail. If you're complicit in laundering billions of dollars, your organization pays a fine, and you, the executive who oversaw, and was potentially complicit, you're not individually investigated and you don't even have to give back the bonuses you received during the years it was going on.'

In 2016, Elias brought the civil claim in the Southern Texas Federal District Court in Brownsville, close to the Mexican border. He chose Brownsville deliberately because there they knew what the cartels were, people were all too aware of their barbarity and cruel methods, rather than, say, in New York. Although, at the time, other violent drug-trafficking organizations, such as the Revolutionary Armed Forces of Colombia (FARC), had been designated terrorists by the State Department, a drugs cartel so far had not, and it was far from clear-cut as to whether the action would be successful, but Elias

and the families were determined to press ahead. 'It was unprecedented,' said Elias. 'But the definition is "anyone who commits acts
that are dangerous to human life that are intended to coerce, intimidate the civilian population and the government."' In one of those
nice coincidences that life sometimes presents you with, it just so
happened that the daughter of the judge taking the case was a law
student and she was working on a paper arguing for just that, for a
drugs cartel to be classed as a terrorist organization. The claim,
Zapata v HSBC Holdings Inc, argued that as a result of the bank's
'material support' for the drug traffickers, 'numerous lives, including
those of the plaintiffs, have been destroyed . . . Without the ability to
place, layer and integrate their illicit proceeds into the global financial markets, the cartel's ability to corrupt law enforcement officials,
and acquire personnel, weapons and ammunition, vehicles, planes,
communications devices, raw materials for drug production and all
other instrumentalities essential to their operations would be sub-
stantially impeded. Thus, by facilitating the laundering of billions of
dollars of drug cartel proceeds through its banks, HSBC materially
supported . . . terrorist acts.' As you might expect, HSBC vowed to
fight the action every inch of the way, and they earned themselves an
unexpected early victory when, despite his daughter's essay, the judge
dismissed parts of the action for lack of jurisdiction. Elias promptly
voluntarily stopped the suit and said he would refile in the court of
the Eastern District of New York. Ranged against him, for HSBC,
was a team from Mayer Brown, one of the biggest law firms in the
world, with at least 200 lawyers in each of the financial centres of
New York, London and Hong Kong. Headquartered in Chicago, it
served a high proportion of the globe's largest, best-known corporations and more than half the major banks, and their enlistment by
HSBC was a clear sign of how hard the bank was going to fight this
action. It chose Mayer Brown because the firm had a speciality, in
helping banks defend suits brought against them for aiding the
financing of terrorism. Mayer Brown's favoured ploy was trying to get

cases thrown out early on, because the court lacked jurisdiction or because the claim was not properly made. If that failed, they would frequently settle, but there again, they liked to boast, they played hardball. What also appealed to the image-conscious HSBC was that for a law firm Mayer Brown maintained one eye on the PR fallout, and would do its utmost to ensure adverse publicity was kept to a minimum.

On his side, for extra firepower, Elias turned to New York's Cohen Milstein, described by *Inside Counsel* magazine as, 'The most effective law firm in the United States for lawsuits with a strong social and political component.' Cohen Milstein dynamo, Michael Eisenkraft, joined with Elias. Eisenkraft's specialism is 'innovative cases' – code for he likes to climb a legal cliff-face. He is cited by Law360 as 'one of six attorneys under the age of forty in the field of securities whose professional accomplishments belie their age', and by Legal 500 as a 'Next Generation Lawyer'. But for all their collective strength, Elias and Eisenkraft lost first time round in New York and in 2020, they had to head to appeal. For HSBC, the Mayer Brown field partner was Andrew Pincus. Ex-Yale, and a visiting lecturer at Yale, 'Andy' Pincus is a true legal, out-of-the-park hitter, a high average slugger, just the kind of person you'd want on your team. He's argued thirty cases in the US Supreme Court and been named 'Appellate MVP' twice by Law360. According to Chambers USA, he is 'one of the finest appellate partners in the United States' and 'a master of oral argument, a superb strategist and a super writer'. Pincus is in the Legal 500 'Hall of Fame'. The media often use him for expert comment on Supreme Court cases. Based in Washington, Pincus was previously general counsel for the US Commerce Department. He was the main lawyer on new legislation, including the Digital Millennium Copyright Act and the Electronic Signatures in Global and National Commerce Act, and helped formulate policy on intellectual property, privacy, domain names, taxation of e-commerce, export controls, international trade and consumer protection.

At the Second Circuit Appeal Court in the Courthouse, in Foley Square in Lower Manhattan, the lawyers for the plaintiffs argued the lower court was wrong to dismiss the case because they failed to show 'terroristic intent' and 'proximate causation'. They claimed the fact that HSBC provided 'billions of dollars of money-laundering services 'created a plausible inference', meaning that the bank acted with intent. The money laundering helped the Sinaloa carry out their terrorist activities and that showed sufficient support for what they were doing, enough for proximate cause. They maintained that Congress intended the Anti-Terrorism Act to catch, not just the actual killers and perpetrators of violence, but those in the 'casual chain of terrorism' so as to 'interrupt or at least imperil the flow of money'. Collecting damages against a terrorist organization is recognized as 'well-nigh impossible' but, they said, successful suits 'against financiers of terrorism can cut the terrorists' lifeline.' Much could be made, they asserted, of HSBC 'not intending' to help the drug traffickers or terrorists but the 'plaintiffs do not allege that HSBC discreetly provided routine banking services. Rather, that [the Sinaloa] routinely walked into the local community HSBC branches with bundles of their blood money (sometimes in the millions of dollars) and HSBC openly accepted their deposits without question. In numerous instances, HSBC managers conspired with narco-terrorists to launder money . . .' It wasn't just that the bank supplied money-laundering services but that they knew the Sinaloa were committing atrocities. The plaintiffs' lawyers quoted the HSBC senior compliance official warning about what was going on and saying he did not want his sources fired or killed and him making the comparison with Afghanistan and Iraq. Said Elias and Eisenkraft: 'It was not merely foreseeable that a substantial portion of the laundered proceeds would be used to execute their acts of terrorism – it was certain.' In the lower court, the plaintiffs' lawyers alleged that HSBC was motivated by greed, which was taken by the judge to mean that because they were chasing profits they did not share 'terrorist intent' – it was money they were after. Elias and Eisenkraft disagreed, saying, 'While the HSBC defendants may have been subjectively motivated by greed, the issue is not their subjective intent'. It is a matter of 'external appearance rather than subjective intent.' So, 'the open and flagrant manner' in which HSBC aided the Sinaloa, 'creates a plausible inference that the external appearance of their conduct appears to be intended to intimidate a civilian population or influence a government.'

The duo made it plain they were not alleging that they could trace laundered money to each brutal murder. They said that because of the scale of the laundromat operation, singling out individual tranches of cash and linking them to a particular killing was impossible. Their insistence was that cleaned-up drug proceeds is the 'lifeblood' of the cartels, enabling them to buy equipment, vehicles and guns, and to pay people, including corrupt officials. It was thanks to HSBC, they said, that the Sinaloa was able to move from being a mere criminal gang to a paramilitary force. They cited the US President's Commission on Organized Crime and its report, 'The Cash Connection: Organized Crime, Financial Institutions and Money Laundering'. The 'existence of modern, sophisticated, often international services of financial institutions has contributed to the frightening financial successes of organized crime in recent years, particularly in the narcotics trade.' Says the report, without 'the means to launder money, thereby making cash generated by a criminal enterprise appear from a legitimate source, organized crime could not flourish as it does now.' The plaintiffs' side insisted that they had shown that money laundering was an 'essential component' of the Sinaloa's tyrannical hold, and that but for money laundering, they would not be the barbaric force that they are today, indiscriminately committing terrorist attacks like the one on Morales Jr. Further, they argued, HSBC was the Sinaloa's principal money-laundering vehicle, earning it the title of Chapo's financial institution of choice. Pincus struck back immediately, arguing that Elias and his team had failed to show HSBC had itself committed an act of 'international terrorism' that caused the plaintiffs' injuries. They alleged only that the bank provided 'arm's-length commercial banking services' to the drug traffickers. 'Those acts are neither violent nor dangerous to human life, as the District Court held. And they do not objectively manifest the intent by the defendants to achieve a terroristic end.' In other words, as bad as HSBC's behaviour was, it could have been much worse and accusations levelled at HSBC related to acts of terrorism were a bridge too far in the case against his client. He drew on an earlier case involving Deutsche Bank, where it was claimed that Deutsche committed acts of international terrorism by handling payments to and from Iranian banks and organizations that were subject to US sanctions. In that case, the US court decreed: 'Deutsche Bank's actions . . . do not appear intended to intimidate or coerce any civilian population or government. To the objective observer, its interactions with Iranian entities were motivated by economics, not by a desire to "intimidate or coerce".' The plaintiffs alleged, said Pincus, that on the one hand, HSBC facilitated the laundering of billions of dollars of drug-trafficking proceeds, and on the other, they contended that the Sinaloa carried out the violence. Missing, said Pincus, was any direct connection, a bridge, between the two, between HSBC and the actual acts of murder.

For Pincus, a drugs cartel was not the same as FARC, in Colombia, which used money from the sale of drugs to further its political ends. Chapo just wanted to get rich. Interestingly, in saying as much Pincus, intentionally or otherwise, drew a parallel between HSBC and Chapo that had not been made before. Pincus was admitting HSBC and Chapo were completely aligned in their pursuit of money, that they were united by greed. The plaintiffs had themselves alleged that HSBC Mexico was 'incentivised to, and did, implement inadequate controls for . . . [US dollar] denominated accounts' because those accounts were, 'according to senior HSBC Mexico executives, a 'cheap' source of revenue for HSBC Mexico.' They cited HSBC Mexico's 'culture [of] pursuing profit and targets at all costs' and characterized HSBC Mexico as consistently prioritizing business concerns over [anti-money laundering] issues, that HSBC US earned 'billions in cheap revenue' as a result of its deficient anti-money laundering policies and reduced its policing resources, 'in order to cut costs and increase its profits'. Pincus said that, 'to an objective observer, HSBC's conduct appeared to be motivated by economics, not by a desire to intimidate or coerce.' Elias and Eisenkraft could 'not reconcile their many allegations of profit-motivated behaviour with the conclusion that [HSBC] appeared to act with a terroristic intent.' It seemed that in making his defence against the far more serious crime of terroristic intent, Pincus was willing to concede a closer proximity in principles between his client and the fugitive drug baron.

The senior appeal court judge presiding was Barrington Parker. In 1994, Barrington Daniels Parker was appointed judge by President Bill Clinton, and now, at seventy-six, he was set to decide the fate of the case against HSBC. A Democrat president had elevated him to judge; a Republican, George W. Bush, promoted him to the appeal court in 2001. The American Bar Association rated Parker 'Unanimously Well Qualified' for the nomination and Parker's appointment was confirmed by a unanimous 100–0 vote of the Senate. Parker was highly regarded, viewed as fair and balanced, politically neutral – he was, in 2019, the senior judge on the panel that determined 'a president who governed by Tweet could not block his critics on Twitter'. Parker and his colleagues reasoned that as Donald Trump used his Twitter feed for making government announcements, it was only right that the First Amendment protected those attacking his Tweets.

On 16 October 2020, the appeal court ruled on Zapata v HSBC Holdings Inc. The world was in the grip of coronavirus, which was tearing through the US, two new studies found that the cash from the US government's relief programme to help reduce the effects of the pandemic was running out and the nation's poverty numbers were soaring; on the campaign trail Donald Trump and Joe Biden traded blows with Trump refusing to disavow the QAnon extreme conspiracy theorists and Biden raising public health concerns and arguing for higher corporate tax rates. Little noticed was that Elias, Eisenkraft, the Morales family and the other plaintiff families were slapped down. Parker and his fellow judges ruled that the plaintiffs were accusing the bank of 'materially supporting terrorism' in violation of the Anti-Terrorism Act. In their view, providing 'material support' does not equate to an act of international terrorism. They agreed with the District Court. David had taken on Goliath and Goliath had won.

In truth, it was always a difficult case for Elias. The cartels committed acts similar to those of terrorists but they were not officially terrorists; he had to show they were. Then, joining the laundering with separate atrocities was problematic. HSBC knew this; from day one their lawyers were confident. Reputationally, the case had the potential to cause damage but the virus did its worst and swamped everything. Nevertheless, it brought into relief the lack of government impetus to close the gap, to apply safeguards that would prevent banks from washing money that would then be used to fuel further criminal and terrorist activities. Cleansing dollar bills was vital to Chapo's success. Yet again, HSBC was in the clear.

FOURTEEN

'Ya tenemos el blanco!'

On 22 February 2014, after a string of false leads and bungled attempts, not to mention a considerable degree of organization and cunning exhibited by the drug baron himself, Chapo was finally cornered. The same authorities who had let him slip before had narrowed down his location to one of five safe houses in his favourite Culiacán. In the early hours of the morning of 17 February 2014, the US DEA and Mexican marines raided them one by one, to find that they were connected by tunnels and that linked surveillance cameras were covering the front and rear entrances to each house. Chapo, as ever, was nowhere to be found. Soon after, they hit a Mercedes dealership in Culiacán, having been told that one of Chapo's sons had pulled up outside. Chapo managed to flee, but closer inspection of the cars on the lot revealed fourteen armour-plated vehicles plus a further six luxury cars and a Ducati motorbike, all registered to Sinaloa associates. The fleet was worth millions of dollars.

The Mercedes raid confirmed to Chapo that the authorities had seized control of his beloved Culiacán, and with his wheels and city impounded, he left the area quietly. But this time Chapo's luck ran out, and the turning point came two days later when they grabbed Picudo, his long-time bodyguard, and Chapo's security detail. After the failed raids, Picudo and the guards remained behind, in another house in Culiacán, before hooking up with Chapo, unaware that they were being tracked. The marines took them by storm, battering down the front door at 2 a.m., rushing in and reaching them before they got their hands on the automatic weapons lying on the kitchen table. When they searched Picudo's belongings, to their horror, they found a manual detailing the inner operations of the DEA and its activities inside Mexico. The discovery is true to one of Chapo's arch-principles: know thine enemy. Under interrogation, Picudo told them that he rescued Chapo from the recent raids via a drain leading back to a sewer and then to the network of tunnels at the safe houses, and he subsequently drove Chapo down the Pacific coast and dropped him off at the exit for the beaches and hotels of Mazatlán. Good intelligence as this was, the Mexican military and Attorney General's office became increasingly impatient, not least because they had been down this road before and it was a cul-de-sac – they would score some hits, nab a senior Chapo operative or two, gain a steer, then by the time they got there Chapo had vanished, which was the familiar pattern.

Public money and time were running out and they wanted to fill in the tunnels and turn over the safe houses for sale, to raise some revenue, as they had done with the auction for the Ye Gon mansion. While the raids were going down, a team in Texas was seeking permission to step up their electronic intercepts, which had just come through, and the timing was, for once, perfect. In the words of Andrew Hogan, the DEA special agent who led the operation to arrest Chapo, 'the roving wire finally hit pay dirt'. They had identified a BlackBerry as being used by someone very close to Chapo, possibly by Chapo himself. Culiacán numbers began with the prefix 667, this was 669, from Mazatlán, and when they zoomed in on its location it was being used from inside the Hotel Miramar in Mazatlán. They wanted to mount an urgent operation, exactly like the US Navy Seals' raid on Bin Laden, but given everything that had gone before, it was not a surprise that their bosses demanded firm evidence it really was Chapo. This time Hogan was able to point to the phone being used for text messages by two people. One had good spelling, the other didn't. Given everything that they knew about Chapo at this point, they were confident that the latter was Chapo doing the typing. While they were monitoring the phone the alert sounded: someone was sending a message on that phone: '*Sy pero no tyene pura kosyna mannan en la mana le pone mynysply.*' Hogan translated: 'Yes, but it doesn't have a full kitchen. Tomorrow morning he'll put in a mini . . . supply? Mini-something – who the hell knows what he's typing there?' It was someone talking about a house they were planning on moving to. It was the way kitchen was spelled – *kosyna* not *cocina*, which was phonetic, and how, they had learned, the poorly educated Chapo wrote his words.

They had hit the jackpot, as it was Chapo himself who was using that phone. At 5 a.m. the following day, the operation having been signed off, the DEA launched the raid while one of the agents stood in the darkness by the hotel swimming pool with a scanner pointing at the hotel rooms. As the raid closed in he picked up a strong signal for the phone they had identified as Chapo's coming from the fourth floor at the far end. Room 401. The marines swarmed into the lobby and up the stairs and all the exits were blocked. Even then they took no chances and didn't put it past Chapo to have built one of his trademark tunnels somewhere or have an escape route mapped out and ready. Room 401 had a two-bedroom suite and in the first rooms were Chapo's cook, Lucia, and his children's nanny, Vero, with Chapo's two-year-old twin daughters (the narco family man, keeping his children close). In the second was Emma, Chapo's wife, but still no Chapo. It turned out that he was in the bathroom holding an assault rifle, which was nothing compared to the weaponry ranged against him. He surrendered and the words crackled across the static of the radio: '*Ya tenemos el blanco!*' The target was finally, after more than thirteen years on the run, in custody. Before anything could go wrong, Chapo was put immediately on a military Black Hawk and flown to Mazatlán airport, and onto a Lear jet, guarded by soldiers, to Mexico City. On the same day, Hogan returned separately to Mexico City to be reunited with his wife and sons, and on the following morning, a Sunday, he went for a bike ride with his family. Like many locals they ended up on Paseo de la Reforma, a road closed to vehicles on a Sunday and teeming with skateboarders, cyclists, joggers, people out for a stroll. While his family cycled ahead he stopped to buy a paper from a local kiosk and on every newspaper stand, on every front page, Chapo's face stared out: *Capturan A El Chapo! Cayo! Cae El Chapo!* He bought all of them – *Reforma, El Universal, Milenio* – the lot.

After weeks embedded with the marines, it was 'like living in another life . . . No one snatching up copies of the newspapers could have suspected that the blond-bearded cyclist in a V-neck cotton shirt, shorts and chanclas had been at the heart of the hunt, that only hours earlier I was the agent who led the capture of the most wanted criminal in the world.' On the road in front of the grand HSBC Torre building the DEA special agent stood, reading about the arrest of the man, leader of the organization that the bank and its people on the floors above had done so much to assist.

AS PART OF its agreement with the Department of Justice, HSBC agreed to reform its ways or face criminal charges. The 'to do' list included: HSBC US immediately raising its spending on anti-money laundering, and the costs in that area of the business shot up ninefold from the previous year; HSBC Group 'simplifying its control structure'; adopting 'a more consistent global risk appetite' and promising to introduce standards that were based on the best anti-money laundering practice available in any location where HSBC operates.

Gulliver wrote to all staff: 'We are driving a change in culture so that our conduct matches our values. We have integrated our values into performance management, judging leaders on what they achieve and how they achieve it, because both matter to our reputation and share price.'

This all seemed rather tortuous and discordant, and there was no mention of the simple 'we're doing what is right'. As for the reference to the share price, this was superfluous and struck a bum note, inadvertently or not, echoing George Osborne's obsession during his lobbying push. Gulliver ended by saying: 'while we cannot undo past mistakes, we will be judged on how we respond to this issue and demonstrate that we have learnt from it.' Under the deal, HSBC agreed to a court-appointed monitor to check whether it really was improving. The person chosen was Mike Cherkasky, sixty-three, well-known in Wall Street as a public prosecutor of financial crime turned entrepreneur. Born and raised in the Bronx, Cherkasky went to Fieldston, the leading progressive private school, founded by the son of a rabbi in 1878 to promote social justice, racial equality and intellectual freedom. His career ranged across the legal, business professional gamut: fifteen years a prosecuting attorney in Manhattan; unsuccessfully trying to bring down Gambino mobster boss John Gotti for ordering the shooting of a union leader. It is still believed that Cherkasky failed to send Gotti to jail because the jury were heavily swayed by the mafia leader. Like detective DiGregorio, he was involved in breaking organized crime's hold on the city's waste industry; ridding the bad apples from the top of the Teamsters; he was one of those who brought down the corrupt, money-laundering Bank of Commerce and Credit International; in the private sector, working for Kroll, the corporate intelligence firm; responsible for helping tighten the security of the World Trade Center after it was first hit by terrorists in 1993. He ran Kroll, then worked for Marsh McLennan, the large insurer, after it bought Kroll. Then he joined Altegrity, which bought Kroll. By his own admission, the teetotal non-smoker is 'boring' and 'intense'. Cherkasky lives in Westchester County with his childhood sweetheart wife Betsy – they met when they were at school, aged twelve, and married at twenty. Mike stood unsuccessfully on the Democrat ticket to be Westchester County District Attorney – and after he failed to win, he joined Kroll. In 2003, Cherkasky co-authored *Forewarned: Why the Government is Failing to Protect Us and What We Must Do to Protect Ourselves*, which served as a stark warning: brace yourselves, get ready, there will be more 9/11s unless the US overhauls its national security apparatus and introduces new measures, including a new, more flexible Domestic Intelligence Bureau to fight terrorists instead of the no longer fit-for-purpose FBI, and a 'US ID card' for all citizens even from as young as six years old. 'Mike is a straight arrow,' said Westchester resident Ron Goldstock, former head of the New York Organized Crime Task Force, who has known Cherkasky since their time in law enforcement and as a neighbour.

Cherkasky started monitoring HSBC's clean up in July 2013 and he had two masters – the Justice Department in the US and the FCA in the UK – which precluded him from speaking about the details of his involvement with HSBC, but it was clear from the first day that this was not a job for one person, and before long he had an entire team based in a building overlooking Bryant Park in Manhattan working for him – among them Lisa Osofsky, who later went on to head Britain's Serious Fraud Office. For once HSBC were going to take their responsibilities seriously and provide the necessary resources to get the job done properly. He also turned the assignment to his long-term commercial advantage, forming his own consulting firm, Exiger, to help, for a fee, companies stay out of legal and regulatory trouble. There he was, working with a bank that was in deep trouble, having been hired by the authorities and, in parallel, advising other businesses on how to avoid getting into the same mess as that bank. A cynic might suppose Cherkasky's recruitment was pure window-dressing, that having someone with his history supposedly crawling over the bank's compliance procedures was merely designed to make HSBC look good. They are the ones, after all, who had chosen him – the bank gave three names to Justice and the department picked him. But if that is what some at HSBC had hoped, this is certainly not how it turned out. Cherkasky proved to be no pushover. He didn't, though, have any real powers – his role was to observe and report back. In private. Because, despite his appointment serving a public purpose, coming as a result of a mammoth taxpayer-funded investigation, involving numerous government agencies, in the US and UK, the detail of his work was ordered to stay confidential, and HSBC fought hard to keep it that way, wanting to put their energy into rebuilding their damaged reputation. In response to a Freedom of Information Act request from Buzzfeed reporter Jason Leopold in July 2020, Benjamin Naftalis from Latham & Watkins, another heavy-duty firm of lawyers acting for HSBC, filed a five-page letter with the Justice Department objecting to the release of Cherkasky's 1,000-page Final Report. Said Naftalis: 'The Report was prepared on behalf of and for the use of government entities, including those that supervise the Bank, both in the United States and abroad . . . It is long and detailed, and its disclosure is likely to (i) cause substantial competitive harm to HSBC and other third parties and (ii) impair the government from obtaining such information in the future.' The Latham & Watkins New York partner claimed: 'The 1,000-page Report documents the Monitor's extensive findings in relation to HSBC's anti-money laundering and sanctions compliance around the world. Among other things, the Report contains the Monitor's analysis of confidential client information.' All of which is straightforward, although frustrating. However, the following does require a double take: 'Strong public policy considerations also miligate against the release of the Report. For example, the Report's contents could potentially provide a roadmap for criminals to exploit vulnerabilities in HSBC's compliance program and potentially those of other financial institutions.' It is difficult not to feel cynical about this kind of logic since, in essence, the reason why the material cannot be shared is because their client has been so badly behaved that if we tell you how bad, that could be used as a 'roadmap for criminals'. At least he was being honest – that really was how bad HSBC had become. As contrived as Latham & Watkins' pleading was, it succeeded: Cherkasky's Final Report must stay under lock and key.

The frustrations, however, were not the preserve of curious journalists alone. There were hints, though, during his near five-year stint, that Cherkasky was far from satisfied with what he and his staff were witnessing, that HSBC's progress was slow and unconvincing. Every quarter, Cherkasky and his team were required to update the Justice Department on what they'd seen, what they'd been doing, on HSBC's progress to date. At the end of each year they submitted a report, a summary of which was put into court. In 2015, after his first year, Cherkasky was said to reckon that senior managers of HSBC US had obstructed a 2014 review by HSBC auditors and compliance officials of its 'know your customer' practices. 'The senior managers resisted the review in a manner that caused the final audit report to be more favourable to the business than it would otherwise have been,' the summary report stated. 'Interactions with both internal audit and [compliance] were marked by combativeness, overblown complaints about factual inaccuracy, and a basic lack of cooperativeness.' Cherkasky was said to have concluded that 'the [global banking and markets] business in the United States demonstrated a deficient culture that had not fully accepted the role and legitimacy of the internal audit and control functions.' Yet again, the bank that so liked to tell the world about its culture was found to have one that was 'deficient'.

A year later, in 2016, the Justice Department filed its annual letter about Cherkasky's work during the previous twelve months in the federal court in Brooklyn. The monitor 'remains unable to certify that the bank's compliance program is reasonably designed and implemented to detect and prevent violations of [anti-money laundering] and sanctions laws,' wrote US Attorney Robert Capers. 'Although HSBC made significant progress last year, the monitor believes that the bank continues to face significant challenges,' Capers added. Cherkasky found that HSBC in 2015 made 'commendable progress' towards improving oversight, spending more than $680 million and adding 2,584 compliance personnel, and, significantly, there had been a change in 'tone at the top.' But the monitor also determined that HSBC's monitoring and testing capabilities suffered from 'immaturity,' and affiliates in some countries struggled to obtain information about customers when opening accounts or updating account profiles. Cherkasky also believed 'a great deal of work remains to be done' in improving technology.

In 2017, Cherkasky caused the UK watchdog to get involved, forcing Gulliver to publicly admit that the Financial Conduct Authority was investigating its 'compliance with UK money-laundering regulations and financial crime systems and controls requirements'. The reason for the scrutiny, he maintained, without any irony, was because Cherkasky was crawling all over the bank. As a result, the bank was unearthing more regulatory problems due to higher-quality internal policing, adding that the business has 'been able to identify more bad actors in our 37-million customer-base'. In agreeing to the additional monitoring as part of the terms of settlement, HSBC had welcomed into their midst a group of people who were hell-bent on turning over every stone to find irregularities. It was a classic case of being careful what you agree to when you let someone in to put your house in order. Said the HSBC CEO: 'Our monitor has raised certain concerns, but we have continued to progress and our commitment remains unwavering. By the end of this year, we are on track to have our anti-money laundering and sanctions policy framework in place and to have introduced major compliance IT systems across the group.'

The bank's inadequate computer systems was a recurring theme for Cherkasky, because they simply weren't up to the task of screening the 690 million transactions going across the bank's screens every month. Despite the hugely impressive interactive screens that Geoghegan showed me, it was clear to Cherkasky that some of those flickering numbers and letters might be laundering the proceeds of crime, but the point was that no one could know. To make it harder, it transpired that the IT that HSBC used was set up to clear a transaction in one country, then flag it as suspicious in another, which could only lead to a lack of consistency and reliability. To satisfy these uncomfortable home truths consultants were brought in to help upgrade the software. Thousands of them arrived, and some in London were on rates of £1,000 a day. In an echo of New Castle, Delaware, the outsiders weren't especially loyal or committed to the bank, and one whistleblower even complained that they preferred partying. They loved partying so much they came up with their own diary slang: 'Mad Mondays' and 'Whacky Wednesdays'. Some liked to call at Majingos, the lap-dancing bar near Canary Wharf, between the City and Docklands, in what used to be the old White Swan pub. They would happily splash out 'thousands of pounds a night on a regular basis,' said the whistleblower. One team member was so hungover after a particularly hard night that he crashed out in a toilet cubicle in the office while another nodded off while on a phone call.

Meanwhile, Cherkasky was noticing and highlighting HSBC's slow pace of change and his criticism that the bank was dragging its feet caused waves right to the top of the company, damaging, as it did, the CEO Gulliver's pay package that was assessed in part according to compliance with financial crime. The bank's compliance in 2016 received a 65 per cent rating from the HSBC board's remuneration committee, compared with 75 per cent a year earlier. This translates to a 2.5 per cent cut. Sam Laidlaw, the non-executive director who chaired the committee, said it had been reduced because of 'feedback received from the monitor, matters arising from risk and compliance incidents, and a number of unsatisfactory internal audits covering anti-money laundering and sanctions-related issues'. Not that Gulliver missed it much – his overall pay actually rose from £7.3 million to £7.7 million. At the same time, entreaties from on high to bank staffers to give Cherkasy and his fellow monitors a warm welcome and to cooperate fully, fell on some deaf ears. In Switzerland, not exactly known for its openness on financial matters, the local HSBC managers told Cherkasky's team that they couldn't 'dig around' in customer accounts and eventually, Cherkasky had to ask the FCA in the UK to have 'a word' with HSBC about the Swiss attitude. In another country, an HSBC employee simply told the overseers he couldn't talk because he'd been told he would be killed if he did, without producing a shred of evidence. In yet another, the monitors had to promise that they would avoid looking at the accounts of local politicians, and they struggled to get visas even when they had agreed to look the other way. In China, one of the members of the monitor's team was asleep in his Beijing hotel room when he was awoken by a knock at the door. Outside were two law enforcement officials who won't give their names and they interrogated him about the purpose of his trip and what he would be doing, with no interest in the answer since the point of the call was simply to spook him into backing off. There were also the scheduled interviews with HSBC staffers that were cancelled at the last minute because the interviewees had suddenly been inexplicably called away. One person who went to Hong Kong to check over HSBC's Hong Kong anti-money laundering programmes, was made to wait for an hour before being taken through to the office. The staff suggested his time would be better spent in the city, shopping. 'They basically told me to fuck off and go shopping.'

Meanwhile, files at the US Treasury's Financial Crime Enforcement Network, or FinCEN, showed that reports were filed indicating more than $2 billion in transactions through HSBC Hong Kong, which smacked of possible criminal activity. In July 2021, it emerged that HSBC was aware of an 'established money-laundering network' being run through its Hong Kong branch. Investigators in 2016 were looking into the flow of funds from the South African leading Gupta business family as part of an inquiry into their dealings with the South African government. Three companies with accounts at HSBC Hong Kong were flagged as being linked to the Guptas. The investigation turned up an extensive money-washing operation that had nothing to do with them, involving payments totalling $4.2 billion over four years via ninety-two accounts. An internal bank report was shared with the Zondo Commission in South Africa, examining high-level corruption in that country. The redacted document, released in July 2021, downplayed the Guptas' direct involvement but spoke of an 'established money-laundering network'. It was not clear if Cherkasky's team were informed about this network. The bank refused to comment and reiterated that discussions with him remained confidential. This occurred during the period of monitoring, but the Justice Department chose to do nothing. The mindset is that this was the preserve of Cherkasky, the problems and difficulties were his; at Justice, where the entreaties of some officials was to indict and seek convictions, it was no longer their concern. The monitor is paid by the bank, not the government. Cherkasky had no powers, he couldn't require the bank to do anything, and the bank employees knew this. Nor could he push law enforcers to intervene. 'I thought imposing a big fine, appointing a monitor, and giving the bank a chance to change might work,' said Bean. 'But when the Justice Department, backed by the courts, became very secretive about what the monitor was finding at HSBC, that was the death knell. Secret oversight and secret reports don't produce meaningful change.'

Then there was the Xu case. Based in Temple City, California, 'Dr Phil' Ming Xu went from coast to coast across the US and to Hong Kong pushing his investment membership venture called WCM777 (World Cloud Media and 777, the number of the Holy Trinity as opposed to 666 for the Beast). He targeted, in particular, the church-going Asian and African communities. Charismatic and messianic, 'Dr Phil' liked to dress in an all-white linen suit and white shirt when he addressed would-be investor gatherings and quote from the Bible. He was fond of Proverbs 29:18: 'where there is no vision, the people perish'. In 2013, he was selling computer cloud services for start-ups in video and music production and investors were promised a mouth-watering 100 per cent return in the first 100 days. They were awarded 'points' in return for their money or for bringing in more investors, which they could turn into equity in the outfits WCM777 was backing. He added another, less tangible carrot: they would get 'to glorify God'. Investors queued up to give him their money, but as is usually the case with these kind of promises, it was too good to be true and instead of investing in cloud services, the funds went on buying two golf courses, a luxury home, a chunky diamond plus diamond mining rights in Sierra Leone. It was an old-fashioned pyramid-seller scam, a Ponzi scheme, and all the money poured into his bank account, held at HSBC. In all, between 2013 and 2014, $80 million flowed through the HSBC books, and what was worse was that the FinCEN files revealed that HSBC was aware of what Xu might be up to, and completed Suspicious Activity Reports or SARs, and sent them to FinCEN, and yet the government received the reports and did nothing.

Meanwhile, HSBC continued to profit from Xu ripping off his investors. In 2013, California subpoenaed HSBC about Xu's company and the bank's legal department replied that it was 'unable to locate any accounts with the information stated on the subpoena.' It took four weeks before HSBC filed the first SAR about Xu and WCM777, hardly the kind of speed expected of a bank that was under the spotlight and had promised to reform its ways. They said that the company was suspected of being involved in 'Ponzi activity' and that it was dealing in 'large round dollar amounts for no known legitimate business or economic purpose.' In three months, WCM777 had sent or received 799 wire transfers totalling $6 million. Then Massachusetts regulators said publicly in November 2013 they intended to shut down WCM777 in their state. In January 2014, California and

Colorado did the same, but in Hong Kong, HSBC carried on regardless, and continued receiving and moving the company's money even though exactly the same red flags that had been put in place post-Mexico were being raised. In the US, the bank's staff filed another SAR about WCM777, this time concerning $15.4 million. Still HSBC did not do anything and continued to provide banking services as normal. After investors' grievances mounted and other states moved to ban the firm, however, life got rougher for Xu and WCM777. In late March 2014, the US Securities and Exchange Commission stepped in, shutting down the company, freezing the assets and appointing a receiver. Still, HSBC did not drop him! After the SEC filing, HSBC in Hong Kong let WCM777 withdraw all of the money in its account, more than $7 million. Xu was pilloried by angry investors and he tried to claim it was the fault of other people in WCM777 and that the SEC had overreacted. He subsequently ended up in China where he launched a similar scheme where the authorities were less indulgent and quickly jailed him for three years.

Xu was not the only villain in the eyes of the out-of-pocket investors, because they also blamed HSBC for keeping the scam going, and for not closing his accounts. Julio Ramos, a California lawyer, began a class action on behalf of the investors. The suit alleged that HSBC Hong Kong 'knew that WCM777 was engaging in fraud'. Accused Ramos: 'The Ponzi scheme survived for over a year because defendants HSBC Hong Kong and HSBC USA knowingly delivered, organized, converted and laundered proceeds from an illegal Ponzi scheme.' The court-appointed receiver trying to recover the victims' money sent a subpoena to HSBC Hong Kong, but the bank argued that HSBC Hong Kong was outside the jurisdiction of US courts and did not have to respond. The receiver reported to the court in February 2015 that 'the cost of tracing these funds overseas will be very expensive' because HSBC was refusing to cooperate, but they were intent on making good their promise of recovering the money. WCM777 was a 'worldwide pyramid scheme', said the SEC, and it had ripped off at least $80 million from thousands of investors, and potentially even more if cash payments could have been properly verified and included.

Ramos's class action lawsuit against HSBC Hong Kong failed, however, because a federal court concluded with HSBC that the US lacked jurisdiction over HSBC's Hong Kong businesses. The get-out-of-jail card of HSBC was that it could show that regardless of its other failings, the bank had filed warnings about Xu, and the US government had failed to act. Subsequently, the bank could claim it did what it had been required to do, and it was up to others to react. Nevertheless, it felt like the bank was going through the motions, and doing the bare minimum that the new, cleaner HSBC was obliged to do and was not taking it seriously enough. The bank did not close Xu's accounts and carried on assisting someone it was busy warning others about. Then, when they were asked to help the investors he had deceived, they refused – hardly smart PR for a bank that claimed to be in the business of looking after its everyday, run-of-the-mill customers, and it was not exactly in the spirit of promising to make a fresh start. There was a horrific end piece to the WCM777 affair, as one investor was so furious at being duped by Xu that she took the law into her own hands. Angela Martinez Arias, who owned Botanica Ile Oshun Elegua, a store selling religious items in Rohnert Park, in Sonoma, California, invested $2,000 in WCM777 having been encouraged to do so by one of Xu's followers, Reynaldo Pacheco. In March 2014 she trapped Pacheco into meeting her and drove him to an isolated spot where three men beat him, taped his mouth shut, and bound his wrists and ankles with his shoelaces. They then took him to a deserted canyon in Northern California, where one of them stoned him to death.

In New York throughout 2016 and 2017 Cherkasky repeatedly warned that the bank was struggling to detect and block suspicious activity. Towards the end of his contracted period, he said his work was far from complete and he asked that his contract be extended so that he could be allowed to continue. However, his 2017 report would prove to be his final analysis of HSBC's progress against its own targets of financial transparency. On 11 December 2017, the Justice Department rejected his request and announced that HSBC had met its obligations and would no longer be subject to monitoring. According to the Justice Department, Cherkasky's job was done; the DPA was lifted. HSBC had, apparently, reformed. Two months later, in February 2018, HSBC published its annual report to shareholders. There was mention of Cherkasky, saying the bank had made progress, but nonetheless he 'noted deficiencies in HSBC's financial crime compliance controls and areas of HSBC's programme that require further work, and highlighted potential instances of financial crime and certain areas in which he believes that HSBC is not yet adequately managing financial crime risk.' After nearly five years of Cherkasky sticking to his task, more than five years after the DPA had been struck and Gulliver had said 'sorry' and had written to staff promising reform, not least because of the potential damage to reputation and the share price, and even longer after the Sinaloa money laundering was first brought to the bank's attention, HSBC was telling shareholders it was 'not yet adequately managing financial crime risk.' But it didn't matter – the DPA had been lifted, neither HSBC nor any of its bankers would be facing criminal charges.

It wasn't entirely the end of the DPAs, however, as HSBC entered into two more. One was in 2018, relating to 'front-running' by its foreign exchange trading desk in New York between 2010 and 2011. It was discovered that some traders were using confidential information from two clients to make a personal profit for themselves and for the bank via their 'proprietary' accounts. They were being instructed confidentially to execute trades in sterling, and the traders dealt in advance, knowing what the clients were planning, for their own gain – like insider trading, except it was their own clients they were defrauding. 'HSBC traders then caused the large transactions to be executed in a manner designed to drive the price of the Pound

Sterling in a direction that benefited HSBC, and harmed their clients,' the bank admitted. HSBC settled with the Justice Department to pay $101.5 million and agreed 'to enhance its compliance programme'. In December 2019, there was another issue. At fault this time was HSBC Switzerland, the very people who were so reluctant to cooperate with Cherkasky. According to court documents, the bank's Swiss operation admitted to conspiring with clients to commit US tax fraud, tax evasion and filing false tax returns. How much was being kept from the US tax authorities? 'HSBC Switzerland held approximately $1.26 billion in undeclared assets for US clients.'

According to the court filings, HSBC claimed Swiss bank secrecy when asked to cooperate by the US authorities, it gave accounts' code-names and numbers rather than identifiable names and used nominees in British Virgin Islands, Liechtenstein and Panama to conceal their true ownership.

The HSBC Swiss bankers flew to the US to drum up tax-evasion business – 'at least four HSBC Switzerland bankers travelled to the United States to meet at least twenty-five different clients. One banker also attended Design Miami, a major annual arts and design event in Miami, Florida, in an effort to recruit new US clients to open undeclared accounts with HSBC Switzerland.' The DPA with the Justice Department saw HSBC pay a penalty of $192.35 million and HSBC Switzerland was given three years to demonstrate good conduct. It was as though the sorry episode of HSBC's time in Mexico had been completely forgotten.

Elation and relief in Mexico and the US at Chapo's capture did not last long. In 2014, Chapo was in the high-security surroundings of Altiplano jail, still in Mexico, under twenty-four-hour surveillance, and for him it was business as usual. Records show that he was able to meet his lawyers on a regular basis – in seventeen months he saw them 272 times, added to which he had eighteen family visits and forty-six conjugal visits. One of his closest associates, Manuel Alejandro Aponte Gómez, or 'Bravo', was discovered killed in 2014, along with two others. Bravo, it turned out, was tortured and shot several times and word is that Bravo was meant to ensure Chapo's safety at the Miramar, and he paid the price for his arrest. On 11 July 2015 at 8.52 p.m., Chapo sat on the edge of the bed in his cell, changed his shoes, and entered the shower in the corner of the small room. Five, ten, then fifteen minutes passed and he still hadn't re-emerged and none of the CCTV was any use since the shower was off-limits to the watching cameras. He had gone. Again. In the public recriminations that went on afterwards it transpired that there was a serious flaw with the security because the cameras that were trained on him only observed what was going on above the ground; underground, beneath his cell, someone, most likely a whole team of people, had been busy for months excavating a tunnel measuring almost a mile in length. When the guards searched the cell and found the tunnel, what they found was not like something out of *The Great Escape*. Instead, it came complete with electric lighting, air-conditioning and rail tracks allowing a small vehicle to carry someone, Chapo, speedily away. At one end was an opening cut into the floor of his cell, at the other is a hole in a house in nearby Santa Juana. Needless to say, by the time the authorities charged down the tunnel and reached the house, he had gone. The humiliation of the Mexican government was total, and difficult questions were asked about the complicity of the guards and why he was allowed special treatment. But, as ever, not everyone was distraught, and some even chose to celebrate, and sure enough, *narcocorridos* are written and sung. This is 'El Chapo: Otra Fuga Mas or El Chapo: Another Escape'. It contains the line: 'Well-groomed and through the bathroom, the man came out again'. And on his engineering prowess: 'A well-thought-out tunnel can go any-where'. His return is duly celebrated. There is music in the air and 'his people are waiting for him, through ravines and mountains'.

For the remainder of 2015 Chapo duly returned to being the world's most wanted escapee. He was 'seen' at a café in Costa Rica, in a sweet shop in Argentina. He was somewhere in the high Andes . . .

the rumours kept swirling. The truth was more prosaic: as the song suggests, he was in the valleys and hills of Sinaloa and he had returned to the land he knew best, where he could count on being sheltered and could use brutal methods to ensure that he stayed safe. But some habits die hard, because, again, while he could take steps to ensure silence of the locals, he was too cavalier with his telecoms, as though assuming that the Mexican authorities would leave him in peace rather than suffer the humiliation of another capture and escape. The same marines and techniques that captured him before were deployed again almost immediately, tracking the mobiles of his known associates and picking up their BlackBerry PINs and identifying their locations. In October 2015 they were close to seizing him in a mountain village at Tamazula and came under heavy gunfire. Chapo raced to the coast, just like before, this time at Los Mochis.

On 8 January 2016, the Mexican marines launched Operation Black Swan, and they targeted a white, two-storey house in Los Mochis following the telecoms intercepts provided by the US. Military helicopters circled overhead while a hit squad charged the house. A firefight erupted, resulting in five dead Chapo guards and six injured, and one wounded marine, but like the plot of a bad novel, Chapo had already departed. In a bedroom, a switch opened a trap-door behind the mirror where there was an escape ladder and a tunnel leading into the sewers, and he was back on the run with a close associate, Cholo Iván. They hijacked a white Volkswagen Jetta and when that broke down they carjacked a red Ford Focus. The police were all over the area and stopped the Focus near the town of Che Rios, when Ivan made a run for it, while Chapo, rotund and unfit from months of incarceration, could not get out in time and was found, crouched on the back seat. His first reaction was typical, because he knew the drill, and he offered the police homes and businesses in Mexico and the US and promised they could 'forget about working for the rest of their lives', if they released him.

Iván was also arrested shortly afterwards, and the pair were flown to Mexico City, to Altiplano jail, although this time they took no chances with Chapo: they boosted the security system with more cameras and motion sensors that could detect movement above and below ground, and they reinforced the floors. Added to which he was moved constantly to different cells, and as an extra precaution, they even trained sniffer dogs to sense Chapo's smell. Chapo was duly extradited, on 19 January 2017, to face a US federal seventeen-count indictment that as the leader of the Sinaloa drug cartel he managed 'a criminal enterprise responsible for importing into the United States and distributing massive amounts of illegal narcotics and for conspiring to murder people who posed a threat to the narcotics enterprise.' His appearance in the Brooklyn court coincided with Donald Trump's inauguration day. It also marked the final day in office of the US Attorney General, Loretta Lynch. She had form where Chapo and HSBC were concerned. As a US Attorney, Lynch had personally signed the original indictment against Chapo. She described the Sinaloa as 'the largest drug trafficking organization in the world', responsible for the vast majority of drugs imported into the US. Then, later, Lynch was the lead Justice Department negotiator with HSBC, the bank that enabled Chapo to launder the proceeds from that drug trafficking she so condemned. In November 2014, she was nominated by President Obama to be US Attorney General. Securing Senate approval for her appointment turned out to be fraught, taking a marathon 166 days. Republicans objected to her support for Obama's immigration reforms but also to her role in settling with HSBC. Senator David Vitter accused her of negotiating 'a slap-on-the-wrist' agreement with HSBC. Vitter said it raised 'troubling questions about whether pertinent information of public concern regarding HSBC was 'swept under the rug', if justice was served, and why HSBC was given special treatment that allowed it to walk away from such serious offences unscathed.' Answering Senate Judiciary Committee Chairman, Chuck Grassley, Lynch says she asked about the likelihood of a global financial meltdown. She was told that world banking would crash, the financial markets would collapse, but that was all it was, talk. She admitted to not being provided with 'any substantive evidence'. She went ahead anyway and negotiated HSBC's get out of jail because to prosecute would cause economic meltdown, even though she had no basis for that belief. From government, Lynch joined Paul, Weiss in New York, a law firm that represents major banks and corporations, as a litigation partner. In December 2020, she received the prestigious Women's White Collar Defense Association (WWCDA) 'Champion' Award. She went from pursuing banks and big corporations on behalf of the government to defending them. The awards were sponsored by her employer, Paul, Weiss.

FIFTEEN

Overlapping circles

On 17 July 2019, Chapo was sentenced by a federal court judge in Brooklyn to life plus thirty years in prison and ordered to forfeit $12.6 billion. The judge, Brian Cogan, said the 'overwhelming evil' of the sixty-two-year-old's crimes was readily apparent. Chapo was wearing a baggy grey suit, plain shirt with his tie askew and had grown back his moustache. Reading from a prepared statement, he complained about being held in solitary confinement, claiming he'd suffered 'psychological, emotional and mental torture twenty-four hours a day.' Since being held in 10 South, the maximum-security wing of the Manhattan federal jail, following his extradition in 2017, he claimed he'd been forced to drink 'unsanitary water' and wear earplugs made from toilet paper to drown out the din of the ventilation system. In response, Gina Parlovecchio, a federal prosecutor, said it was ironic that Guzmán was complaining about inhumane treatment in jail given that he had showed no respect to his countless victims, not just those he killed or hunted down, but to the thousands who were harmed by the drugs he 'pumped onto the streets,' earning him a vast fortune in 'blood money.'

His trial in February lasted three months and ended with the jury finding him guilty on all ten counts. The court heard how the Sinaloa leader sent countless tonnes of narcotics to the US from Mexico and caused the deaths of anyone suspected of crossing him. Compelling evidence was presented about his lavish lifestyle, his spending and his management of the criminal organization, from wire intercepts and from fourteen witnesses from inside the cartel, from key lieutenants and drug suppliers and distributors. Chapo moaned that he'd not received justice and that he was going to be sent 'to a prison where my name will never be heard again.' After the sentencing, he was led away and blew a kiss to his wife, Emma. Raymond P. Donovan, the agent in charge of the New York office of the Drug Enforcement Administration, which twice worked with the Mexicans to capture him, declared: 'It's justice, not only for the Mexican government, but for all of Guzmán's victims in Mexico.'

Two days later, Chapo arrived at Administrative Maximum US Penitentiary, or ADX, in Florence, Colorado. It's on 600 acres of open land, out towards the mountains, hence its nickname 'the Rockies' Alcatraz'. ADX is a complex of intimidating fences topped with razor-wire, twelve-gun watchtowers and grey, squat blocks housing 7-by-12-foot reinforced-concrete cells. Robert Hood, a former Supermax warden, said the facility 'is not built for humanity. I think that being there, day by day, it's worse than death.' Among Chapo's 400-plus fellow prisoners would be Unabomber Ted Kaczynski, Oklahoma City bombing conspirator Terry Nichols and 1993 World Trade Center bomber Ramzi Yousef, not that he would ever likely to get to know them since inmates are locked in their cells twenty-three hours a day. Those in Range 13, a prison within a prison, have hardly any human contact at all. Amnesty International reported that the ADX cells have an interior barred door as well as a solid outer door, compounding the sense of isolation. Prisoners eat all meals in their cells, and most cells have a shower and a toilet, so they don't need to leave. Their furniture comprises a small desk, stool and bed, all made from concrete. They're allowed a radio and a black and white TV with limited programming. The beds have thin mattresses. Each cell has a window 42 inches tall and 4 inches wide. Exercise is in cages. Even Chapo would find it impossible to escape from this one.

Meanwhile, in New York, HSBC's fine was being put to good use. In Queens, in New York, the lack of resources was so bad that when lawyers with the District Attorney's office needed to get documents to court, they loaded up wire carts and pushed them across the six bustling lanes of Queens Boulevard. When the office was put in line for $116 million, that all changed. The cash was the prosecutor's share of the HSBC financial settlement, and the NYC Detective Investigators' Association proudly noted: 'The agency, which hopes to use the money for new office space, was quietly awarded the funds because one of its investigators – a former beat cop called Frankie D by his friends – first noticed the suspicious money flows in the bank's accounts.'

In all, twenty-one law-enforcement agencies involved in the HSBC investigation received US Treasury Department handouts, including the Fort Lee, New Jersey police department which got $1.9 million and the Port Authority of New York and New Jersey which received $13.1 million. The Queens award was more than twice the office's annual budget and they hope to spend the money in part on converting into an office the 467-bed Queens House of Detention, next to the borough's criminal courthouse. The jail is largely empty and is often used as a set for movies and television shows, including *Orange Is the New Black*. For District Attorney Richard Brown it was a dream come true. 'Every night when I go home from this office, I pass by the Queens House and see seven or eight floors totally dark, I just say to myself, "What a perfect spot this is for our needs"', he said. The prosecutor's office had outgrown its original quarters in the criminal courthouse, adding two satellite offices, and officials said that all three spaces were extremely overcrowded and in need of new equipment. The office received its award because its staffers, including Frankie DiGregorio, spent more than 5,000 hours on the case, according to Treasury Department documents, and as well as a new building, $49 million was earmarked for a cybercrime lab, new telephone system and other upgrades. Frankie D – Frankie DiGregorio – pronounced it 'very satisfying', adding, 'for me, I don't get 50 cents out of that money.' To DiGregorio, HSBC's $1.92 billion settlement was a huge amount of money, as was the Queens' take of $116 million, but to HSBC it was not. A civil penalty paid by the corporation, indirectly by the shareholders, was nothing like the bank and its senior executives being tried and found guilty, and embarrassing and undermining as it might be, imposing a fine does not cause the bank to suffer. For HSBC, it is simply an additional cost that needs to be subsumed like any other ongoing expense of running such a huge enterprise. It's the sum the bank has paid to avoid justice, an option that is not available to an ordinary citizen.

CARL LEVIN DIED on 29 July 2021; he was eighty-seven and had been suffering from lung cancer. The *New York Times* said: 'With his longish silver hair, affable smile and glasses perched low on the nose, he looked more like a kindly Old-World shoemaker than the terror of the Senate.' But he confronted titans and other corporate giants 'like a barbarian at the gates'. President Joe Biden said: 'Brilliant, humble, and principled, Carl earned the trust of his constituents and colleagues by doing the work. He studied the issues in detail.' Biden added that 'on holding corporate America accountable for abuse and greed, and so much more – Carl always looked out for the people.' Levin, said the President, 'embodied the best of who we are as Americans. May God bless a great American, a dear friend, and a good man.'

Levin was too poorly to revisit for me his inquiry into HSBC, but according to Bean, who remained close to him, the senator's view never swayed. The financial settlement was nowhere near sufficient.

'Carl thought they should have yanked their charter and knocked them out of the US.' Laura Stuber, who worked on Senator Levin's Senate Subcommittee inquiry, said: 'When I found out how big the fine was I was excited – it was a very large amount of dollars.' Then, the more she thought about it, 'It didn't do much. We contributed a huge amount, it took us ages, but all it was for HSBC was five weeks of their profits. That's not much of a penalty, is it?' Others agree. Lord Prem Sikka, Professor of Accounting at Sheffield University and Emeritus Professor of Accounting at Essex University, whose specialist subject is what he calls 'the dark side of capitalism,' says that fining HSBC is meaningless. 'Banks have little, if any, economic incentive to behave honourably. Profits from illicit practices boost share price, dividends and executive pay. Fines become part of business costs and are passed on to customers in higher charges. Directors rarely bear any personal cost.' John Coffee, the Adolf A. Berle Professor of Law at Columbia Law School, was equally forceful: they should have indicted HSBC and its bankers. Professor Coffee viewed HSBC as a standout case. The bank 'worked hand in glove' with the Sinaloa, the Justice Department's decision not to bring charges was 'weak-kneed, overly deferential and even cowardly.'

In 2002, James Comey was appointed the US Attorney for the Southern District of Manhattan. This was a big move among US public prosecutors: Comey was a rising star who had not been afraid of tackling the Gambino crime family while working previously in the Southern District; he'd prosecuted terrorists; he was regarded as a bootstrapper; now in charge, he was going to kick the bad guys. He was aided by his physique, too – Comey is 6 feet 8 inches in his socks and he also has a reputation for speaking straight, exactly as he finds it. The Southern District saw themselves as a powerhouse, a prosecuting special forces unit, not scared of anyone, of any corporation, any individual. Comey had been there a few months, finding out how they worked and gathering his impressions. Then, by Jesse Eisinger's account, they all came together to hear the new boss. 'We have a saying round here. We do the right things for the right reasons in the right ways.' Then he asked: 'Who here has never had an acquittal or a hung jury? Please raise your hand.' These were people who never lost. Hands shot up. 'Me and my friends have a name for you guys. You are members of what we like to call the Chickenshit Club.' The hands quickly dropped down and their shocked owners look sheepish. The reason they weren't notching up defeats, Comey said, is that they weren't playing – they were only going on the pitch if they were absolutely certain of winning. That meant only going after soft targets. They were scared of losing, of being judged as having failed, rather than bringing the case at all. That fear was skewing their decision-making and justice; serious crimes were going unpunished.

But by the time the Justice Department searchlight was shining on HSBC, when senior officials were being tasked with deciding to stick or twist regarding the bringing of charges, Comey had long gone. He was with the Southern District for just shy of two years, leaving to become US Deputy Attorney General. In 2005 he was off again, to Lockheed Martin as general counsel. Then came Bridgewater Associates, followed by Fellow on National Security Law at Columbia Law. At the very end of January 2013, after the settlement had been announced, HSBC made an addition to its group board. James Comey would soon be joining as a non-executive director. The same person who had called out those 'chickenshits' was about to become a director of a corporation that in the eyes of many learned people was benefiting from the Justice Department being chickenshit. HSBC Chairman Doug Flint said: 'We are delighted to welcome Jim as a non-executive Director and a member of our new Financial System Vulnerabilities Committee. His experience and expertise gained from both public and private sector roles at the highest level will add a further dimension to the governance capabilities of the Board.' Flint said that, 'Comey's appointment will be for an initial three-year term which, subject to re-election by shareholders, will expire at the conclusion of the 2016 Annual General Meeting.' As it turned out, Comey was only with HSBC for six months before leaving in July 2013 to become President Obama's new Director of the FBI.

Alongside Comey on this new body were fellow HSBC directors Rona Fairhead and Sir Simon Robertson. As well as Flint and Gulliver, senior executives were to join them in meetings, including the bank's chief risk officer, heads of compliance and the chief legal officer. The committee was advised, among others, by Dave Hartnett, the former head of the UK Inland Revenue; Nick Fishwick, former head of intelligence focusing on international counter-narcotics from HM Customs; and Bill Hughes, ex-chief of the UK Serious Organised Crime Agency. Gulliver said: 'The new committee, which will benefit from the experience of the expert advisers, will provide invaluable guidance and advice as we strengthen our capabilities and enforce the highest standards in particular in relation to combating financial crime. The calibre, status and experience of the individuals reinforce once more just how seriously we are taking this.' The group's remit was to provide 'governance, oversight and policy guidance' on a broad range of subjects, including anti-money laundering, tax transparency and compliance, 'prevention of association with illegal drugs activities', stopping terrorist financing, enforcing financial sanctions, intelligence on all of this and 'effective relationships with law and enforcement agencies'. Later, in 2013, Sir Jonathan Evans, ex-head of the MI5 security service, also became an HSBC director and joined the heavyweight committee, subsequently becoming its chairman. Evans, by now Lord Evans, resigned in 2018 after criticism that his role at HSBC, for which he was paid more than £200,000 a year, clashed with his new job as chairman of the Committee of Standards in Public Life.

Despite Gulliver's words and the presence of luminaries such as Comey, Hartnett, Hughes and Evans, HSBC was fined by the UK Financial Conduct Authority in December 2021 for 'serious weaknesses' in its money laundering procedures. These related to the period between 2010 and 2018, the last five years of which, at least, the committee was meant to be on top of things. The bank had not taken into account indicators of money laundering when it was processing transactions and had not monitored the accuracy of its data. 'HSBC's transaction monitoring systems were not effective for a prolonged period despite the issue being highlighted on a number of occasions,' said the watchdog's enforcement director Mark Steward. The failings were 'unacceptable and exposed the bank and community to avoidable risks.'

The FCA provided two examples of what it was talking about. Customer A was director of a UK construction company with a gross annual income of £40,000, an expected net monthly income of £1,500 and monthly outgoings of £500. An HMRC investigation found that between 2009 and 2011, Customer A had a leading role in a criminal gang involved in an attempt to steal several million pounds by setting up fake construction companies; in May 2014, he pleaded guilty to VAT fraud and received a custodial sentence. On one day, sixteen payments totalling £120,000 were made into his account. This was 'clearly outside of the expected activity for Customer A's account, given his declared income and outgoings.' What is more, the sixteen were rounded numbers – eight of £10,000 and eight of £5,000. HSBC did not do anything. Customer B opened a savings account with HSBC and declared a gross annual income of £81,851. On one day, there were five separate payments made from Customer B's account, 'all in the sum of £9,830.32 – a total of £49,151 in a single day. Given his gross annual income, this activity was outside the expected activity for this customer.' No alert was triggered. It later turned out that Customer B was smuggling cigarettes to avoid duty and he went to jail. His account remained open for a further five years, however – and, notes the FCA, there was 'a sustained period of unusual activity of both incoming and outgoing transactions outside of that expected on the account.'

HSBC was actually fined £91.3m, reduced by 30 per cent for prompt payment, which presumably was not difficult for a major bank with loads of cash to hand. The bank said it had 'initiated a large-scale remediation of its financial crime control capabilities' in 2012. 'More recently, as the FCA recognised, HSBC has made significant investments in new and market-leading technologies that go beyond the traditional approach to transaction monitoring. HSBC is deeply committed to combating financial crime and protecting the integrity of the global financial system.'

As for the much-heralded Financial System Vulnerabilities Committee, it lasted as long as the DPA and was then quietly disbanded.

THE JUSTICE DEPARTMENT could have indicted HSBC and their staff or ex-staffers under the US Bank Secrecy Act, International Emergency Economic Powers Act and Trading with the Enemy Act but chose not to. As Comey highlighted, fear played a part in that decision, the fear of losing, of not being able to prove a case, of securing convictions. Here as well, though, was another fear, the fear of winning. Junior US law enforcers on the case were repeatedly taunted by US HSBC staff with references to Buffalo, home to the bank's US headquarters and several thousand back-office and support staff and support workers. The choice of location was a hangover from HSBC's purchase of Marine Midland, which was based in Buffalo. In Western New York state, in the Rust Belt, Buffalo was hit hard by factory closures. In a similar vein to bankers in London, who leaned out of office windows and set fire to £50 notes as anti-capitalist protestors marched past, the US officials pursuing HSBC were warned to go easy 'in case anything were to happen to Buffalo'. In other words, do not do anything that could jeopardize our business and mean we have to sack people in an unemployment black spot.

The Justice Department believed that if they brought criminal charges, the whole edifice of global finance could collapse. HSBC, declared Professor Coffee, is an 'illustration that political influence works.' Osborne, aided by the British watchdog, the FSA, did their finest and got inside the minds of the leaders of US Treasury and Justice. They took Osborne and the FSA at their word. Coffee sees no problem in seeking convictions. HSBC was not 'a United States-based bank whose collapse would hurt US citizens and possibly jeopardise other US banks or elicit a wave of falling dominoes.' It was a British bank, operating mainly in Asia. 'Its connections with the United States revolved around the need of its clients to convert their ill-gotten funds into dollars – the only international currency that was accepted everywhere.' Professor Coffee did not see how charges would prompt a global financial disaster. 'Why could an indictment have had this effect? A credible explanation was never seriously attempted.' Elliot Spitzer, the former New York Governor and Attorney General, says: 'HSBC committed multiple chapters of impropriety but it got off very lightly. How bad has the wrongdoing got to be before you say, "you're down"?' Says Spitzer: 'HSBC and money laundering was rampant – it was worse than rampant. And it went to the very top. So, wait, you cut a deal to specifically exculpate the top people and the bank? How does that work?'

One influence, never admitted, is that human nature plays a part and the officials, lawyers and advisers found it hard to press for convictions against people who were so like themselves. Hitting a bank with a financial penalty is one thing; bringing criminal charges against people just like us, who hail from similar backgrounds and circles, sending them to jail, ruining them and their families, that is quite another. Lynch's predecessor as US Attorney General, her boss when she was negotiating the agreement with HSBC, the person who ultimately rejected the idea of seeking convictions, was Eric Holder. The ties at the highest levels were close. On leaving government, like Lynch, he headed to a leading private practice, returning to the partnership of Covington & Burling, Washington's Number One-ranked corporate law firm that defends banks and big business. He was joined there by Lanny Breuer, the Assistant Attorney General, above Lynch and below Holder, who agonized over indicting HSBC and consulted Rodge Cohen, the bank's lawyer at Sullivan & Cromwell and was tactically played. When he quit public service he headed for Covington & Burling. Like Holder, he was with Covington & Burling previously, when he ran its 'white-collar defense group' – that was prior to joining the Justice Department and helping Holder in deciding HSBC should not be charged. Breuer became the firm's Vice-Chair.

In the UK, the revolving door also spun. Osborne, who in public said he would crack down on banks as UK Chancellor and promised as much to the Tory Conference, but in private was lobbying hard for HSBC to avoid prosecution, ceased being Chancellor in 2016. He remained an MP until 2017, standing down at that year's general election. In that period, between leaving government but still being an MP, he enjoyed close relations with HSBC. The 'Register of Members' Financial Interests for 2016–2017' shows Osborne made two speeches for HSBC: on 18 January 2017, for which he was paid £51,829 plus travel and accommodation and on 6 April 2017, which earned him £68,225. The first was at the World Economic Forum in Davos, where Osborne spoke at a private dinner attended by twenty HSBC clients. The second was at the bank's offices. Subsequently, Osborne has become a banker himself. In 2021, he was made a full-time partner at Robey Warshaw, the investment banking firm in London. Osborne is an old friend of Sir Simon Robey, chair of the Royal Opera House and the firm's co-founder. Robey is known as 'the trillion-dollar man' due to the size of the deals he's worked on. Osborne was also made chair of an august national body, the British Museum.

If violence is involved, it's a no-brainer: the act is enough to condemn, to make a clear distinction and brand the accused a criminal, even if they're from the same social and work milieu. Non-violence makes it blurry. Professor Anthony Sabino from The Peter J. Tobin College of Business at St John's University in New York, says the authorities view non-violent criminals in a different light from violent criminals, which is wrong. They do not regard them as, well, so criminal. 'Does a banker kill? No, therefore incarceration is said not to be appropriate. But who does more damage: a little punk who knocks an old lady over the head and steals her $200 social security cheque or a banker who, by their actions, ruins thousands of lives? Who is the bigger criminal? It's a difficult question because a balance has to be struck. You can say white-collar crime is non-violent but you can also say white-collar crime can facilitate violent crime, which is what happened here.' A DPA, says Sabino, in one sense provides closure in that the offence is admitted and has been dealt with. 'But you have to ask, does this punishment fit the crime? Is it five weeks' profit or six months'? Since it's a deferred prosecution agreement, it's an agreement, it has to be agreed by both sides, it's a bargaining process.' What's forgotten, he says, is this: 'It should ultimately come down to a question of morality. You can do as much cost-benefit analysis as you want, but the bottom line is morality.'

The bank's strategy of Managing for Value formally came to an end on 31 December 2003. That's when the five years covered by the management paper were up. Anyone investing $100 in HSBC shares at the beginning of that period would have received a total return of $211 compared with $126 from putting the same amount into the bank's peer group. That, apparently, was insufficient – senior management, investors, the City, Wall Street, they all wanted more. Managing for Value was succeeded by Stephen Green's Managing for Growth. HSBC was already big. It was to get much, much bigger. In June 2005, analyst Robert Law of Lehman gave a presentation to the HSBC board. 'It's a super-tanker; just not sure of the speed,' said the man from the bank that was to crash spectacularly three years later, creating the biggest bankruptcy in US history and giving rise to the 'too big to fail' doctrine. The listening HSBC chiefs went along with his assessment. In January 2006, Green told a management offsite meeting that despite 'good top-line growth' and the shares at 930p it was going to require a major drive 'to satisfy investors and get the share price to £12.' The corporation did not reach its vastness slowly and incrementally – in only six years, the total number of employees doubled, to 330,000. Its subsidiary businesses rose five times, to more than 2,200. The bank that gave an innocuous takeover of an obscure Mexican bank the OTT codename of High Noon went all out at the game of Risk. This wasn't creeping gain; this was binge eating – and never mind the health effects. It was irresponsible and reckless, yet it was precisely that irresponsibility and recklessness, that surge for size, that saved the bank and its bankers from the full might of the criminal law.

The US evidence about HSBC, says Sikka, 'should have prompted UK regulators to mount an inquiry, but they did not.' In fact, the reverse occurred: Osborne and the UK regulators begged the US authorities not to prosecute. Asks Sikka: 'What about protection of the people? If, in the pursuit of crime a bank or a major arm of a bank has to be shut down, so be it.' By arguing not to prosecute they were saying 'the system was above the people.' There was no inquiry in the UK into what the country's biggest bank had been up to, into what the Americans had uncovered and the management had admitted to. When he was Governor of the Bank of England, Mervyn King warned that the support handed out by governments in the 2008 crisis, 'created possibly the biggest moral hazard in history'. Why would a bank behave well if it knew the risk of failure would be borne by someone else? King argued that banks had become 'too big to fail'. He left the Bank of England in 2013 and chose the annual dinner at Mansion House in the City of London to mark his farewell. On 19 June 2013, some eighteen months after HSBC and its bankers were let off the hook, with George Osborne and the Chancellor's then wife, Frances, sitting alongside him, in a packed hall of dignitaries, King said: 'Governments, regulators, prosecutors and non-executive directors have all struggled to come to terms with firms that pose a risk to taxpayers, cannot be prosecuted because of their systemic importance, and are difficult to manage because of their size and complexity.

It is not in our national interest to have banks that are too big to fail, too big to jail, or simply too big.'

I wanted to raise this very point with one of the key protagonists involved in this story. I wanted to ask him what he thought of the bank's behaviour, whether he now felt it appropriate for criminal charges not to have been brought, to explain his role. We went backwards and forwards, and I have to confess that I grew more and more exasperated with my questions being replied to with a dead bat. Finally, I said he owed it to the people, to the public, to assist, to tell us what he thought. He sent a final text message. In it he said that he bought the public argument, he understood that people wanted to know, he said, he really did, but he would not be cooperating, sorry. He would not be helping them; the ordinary person would have to remain none the wiser, and that this was between government and giant bank. I asked him why? He messaged back: 'In the clash of the titans the small fry get crushed.'

Acknowledgements

The idea for this book arose because I met and interviewed Stephen Green and Michael Geoghegan for *Management Today* magazine. The editor who commissioned me then was Matthew Gwyther. He wanted long pieces that roamed much further than merely rehashing the bank's figures and recounting their careers. Thank you, Matthew.

While at the *Evening Standard*, as City Editor, over ten years I was similarly frequently given free rein to write about what I thought was interesting, what I believed the readers would be interested in. Much of that involved an unhealthy obsession with banks, especially in the aftermath of the 2008 crisis. It was during that period that I became alarmed at the worship of 'big'; that some businesses, banks in particular, enjoyed the same global status as sovereign states; that increasingly they appeared beyond anyone's control. My job afforded access to senior bankers, regulators and politicians galore, and in their own way their thoughts and attitudes have contributed to the formulation of this book.

Many people were interviewed, in Mexico, London and New

York, and most did not want to be identified. The reach and power of one of the world's biggest corporations extends far and wide and they simply did not want the hassle. That, I respect, and I am grateful they still agreed to trust me and to speak anyway. They know who they are.

Those that agreed to be named were, in no specific order: Elise Bean, Laura Stuber, Eliot Spitzer, Frankie DiGregorio, Prem Sikka, Anthony Sabino.

Special mention must go to the late Senator Carl Levin, Everett Stern, Bill Ihlenfeld and Richard Elias and your courageous stands on HSBC – each of you serve as an inspiration to others.

Friends came to my assistance: Dominic Mills, for introducing me, via various members of his family, to their experiences of being employees for the bank, to the strange, past culture of HSBC; Simon Hayes and Philip Beresford for agreeing to receive drafts of early chapters and for their suggestions; and Nick Poole, who displayed a rare critical ability and drilled down even further. Nick, your analysis was a turning-point.

When I told my agent, Charlie Viney, what I was thinking of writing about, he was immediately seized and rushed a paragraph into the *London Book Fair*. When that was cancelled, he was undeterred, pressing the publishers he would otherwise have met. His judgement of what they wanted and his cajoling were, and are, spot-on.

Among those who declared an interest was Macmillan. When that turned into something more solid, the firm's Robin Harvie proved to be the best anyone could hope for in an editor/publisher. His belief was infectious; but also, when it came to receiving the first draft, his ideas and thoughts were excellent; after that, he proved himself to be a consummate, careful detail person as well. Robin, wholehearted respect and gratitude.

Before I became a journalist, I was contemplating a career in law. One of those that taught me at university was Professor Barry Rider of Jesus College, Cambridge. It was Barry who shone a light on the murky, still little-known to this day world of white-collar crime. Each year, Barry holds a week-long international symposium on economic crime and fraud in Cambridge in early September. It's attended by police, investigators, enforcement officials and regulators. Barry allowed me as a journalist to go and I am forever grateful. Every year I've been, and I've been visiting since 1987, I've come away not only with valuable contacts but with thoughts and lines that one day I would use – some of them are in this book.

One mentor deserves singling out in this context: the late Stephen Fay, who as editor of *Business* magazine and subsequently a friend, taught a young journalist not to be afraid of any target, no matter how large and powerful, who implored him never to drink the Kool-Aid and to 'tell it how it is'.

Part of the incentive in writing the book derived from the enthusiasm of my children: Harry, Daisy, Barney, Archie and Grace. They were excited at the prospect of their father meeting El Chapo in his Supermax, more-or-less solitary confinement. I did try to see him, but alas, there was nothing doing.

None of this would have been possible without the unstinting, cheerful, positive support of Annabelle. How she stayed sane throughout, listening to my trials and tribulations, is beyond me. She truly is a wonderful rock.

I was hoping my father would have remained alive to read it. He was badgering for a copy but it was not ready. Sadly, he died, aged ninety, just before I wrote this expression of thanks. Without him, and his fascination with politics and its links with money and business, and the often deliberate blurring of lines between the legal and illegal, acceptable and unacceptable, and his abiding view that 'there is one rule for the rich and another for the rest of us', I would never have become a journalist. This book is dedicated to him and to my dear mother, Rose.

Source Notes

I have a loathing of footnotes in some books, believing that in those that are telling a story, they can hold up the flow – the reader's eye is drawn to a number at the end of a line and the pace is lost – so I've taken the liberty of not using them.

The material relied upon for this book came from a mixture of sources: interviews conducted by me, some on-the-record, many off-the-record, in the UK, US and Mexico; articles and books; TV footage, websites, podcasts and blogs; academic papers; company annual reports; legal filings and depositions; US Drug Enforcement Agency briefings and releases; US Permanent Subcommittee on Investigations' reports, evidence, materials and transcripts of hearings; US Treasury briefings and releases; US Department of Justice briefings and releases; report of the US House of Representatives Financial Services Committee.

Below are the sources used for each chapter.

1. 'SCOTTISH BANKING PRINCIPLES'

The life of Thomas Sutherland and the early history of HSBC are from the bank's website and official history. The story of the Opium Wars is well-documented and only summarized here. Accounts of HSBC's moral code and discipline are contained in personal accounts of working at the bank and were added to from an interview with the author. *The Lion Wakes – a modern history of HSBC*, by Richard Roberts & David Kynaston, was excellent on the push for growth at the bank. Stephen Green was interviewed by the author for *Management Today*. Green's two books *Serving God? Serving Mammon?* and *Good Value: Reflections on Money, Morality and an Uncertain World* contain explanations of his personal faith and belief in 'ethical capitalism'. Michael Geoghegan was interviewed by the author for *Management Today*. The culture of the bank and its International Officer class were described in some detail in a February 1997 *Euromoney* feature. Geoghegan's management style is also contained in Roberts & Kynaston as is the round-the-world email.

2. WATERLESS URINALS

There are accounts galore of the assassination of Luis Donaldo Colosio and the subsequent Peso Crisis. Roberts & Kynaston was helpful on the bank's response to the crisis. Project High Noon, the purchase of Bital and the warnings about its lack of compliance checks are documented in the 2012 report of the US Permanent Subcommittee on Investigations. HSBC's delight at buying Bital was well documented at the time in press releases and reports. How HSBC was received and regarded in Mexico, and the bank's sales push, came from interviews by the author with Mexican banking officials from that period. Much of the information on the design and building of the new HSBC Torre was described by HOK, the architects. Iain Martin's *Making it Happen – Fred Goodwin, RBS and the men who blew up the British economy* is excellent on the crisis at RBS and Goodwin's aggrandisement, the opening of the RBS headquarters and the Queen's visit. Emporis really is a mine of detail on tall bank buildings. The Juan O'Gorman fresco is described in detail in a specially commissioned commemorative book, *Credit Transforms Mexico*. The bemused reaction of art critics to the unveiling was reported in Mexican newspapers.

3. THE BLOOD ALLIANCE

Ioan Grillo's *El Narco* stands out as the best account, among many, of the growth of the Mexican illicit drugs trade and the rise of the cartels. Anabel Hernandez's *Narcoland* is an expert invaluable guide to Mexican power, and how 'narco' is endemic in the country's economic and political system. Chapo's methods came from interviews with the author and they are also described in several places, but one I returned to time and again was *Hunting El Chapo* by

Andrew Hogan, the DEA special agent who took him down, and Douglas Century. Also, Richard Marosi's 2011 articles for the *Los Angeles Times*. Sean Penn's bizarre, rare interview with Chapo for *Rolling Stone* throws light on the drug lord's character and supplies some of his musings. 'Hondo' was tracked by Andrew Hogan, when he was in the DEA, who also details the DEA's Chapo intercepts. *Narcocorrido* lyrics are relayed fondly across Mexico. Michael Braun is quoted in *Cartels At War – Mexico's Drug-Fueled Violence and the Threat to US National Security* by Paul Rexton Kan.

4. HSBC'S NEW CLIENTS

Jesus Zambada Garcia's profits breakdown was given in evidence at El Chapo's trial. Details of the Sinaloa cash deposits and the bespoke deposit boxes are contained in the report of the US Permanent Subcommittee on Investigations and in interviews with the author. Similarly, the Casa de Cambio Puebla and Sigue cases. The internal management paper proclaiming Mexico's performance is contained in Roberts & Kynaston. HSBC's growth strategy, the acquisition of Household and HSBC's delight in acquiring it came from interviews with the author, press reports from the time and are also described in Roberts & Kynaston. The Nuevo Laredo turf war is detailed by Ioan Grillo.

5. THE CAYMAN CONNECTION

Cayman Islanders love to talk about themselves, their history and the modern-day services they provide. Oliver Bullough's *Moneyland* is a vital guide to the murky work of offshore finance and tax havens. Nicholas Shaxson also brings much-appreciated clarity in *Treasure Islands: Tax Havens and the Men who Stole the World*. HSBC's role on Grand Cayman, the setting up of accounts for the non-existent 'Cayman Islands Branch of HSBC Mexico' was described in interviews with the author and supported by the US Permanent Subcommittee on Investigations. Carlos's experience is portrayed in 'The Disaster of Privatized Banking in Mexico' by Kurt Hackbarth for *Jacobin*. The development of HSBC's investment banking arm and the recruitment of John Studzinski was covered extensively by the author.

6. WORLD-BEATER

The raid on the Ye Gon mansion was of abiding interest in the Mexican press and elsewhere, once the cash haul was revealed. Narcotecture is the subject of various academic studies and a book, *Narcotecture: Mansions Financed by Drug Money (Kabul, Afghanistan, Mexico, and Bogota, Columbia)* by Jacob Cohen. A leading authority on narco culture is Professor Jose Manuel Valenzuela. Operation Dragon and the Ye Gon case was heavily reported in the Mexico media, details were confirmed in interviews with the author. The US Attorney's Office for the Central District of California detailed the activities of Ye Gon at the Venetian-Palazzo in Las Vegas. The US Senate Permanent Subcommittee on Investigations was attentive to Ye Gon and HSBC's treatment of him. The row about Stephen Green's suitability as executive chairman and the Knight Vinke campaign and HSBC's defence were covered by the author.

7. THE THIRD TABOO

No one has written more bravely and authoritatively about the US–Mexico border and the war on drugs than Ed Vulliamy. His *Amexica – War Along the Borderline* is essential reading. On the apparent success of each of its many individual operations, the US DEA cannot help itself, churning out releases galore and calling press conferences. For the *Los Angeles Times*, the work of Richard Marosi and Tracy Wilkinson on Victor Emilio Cazares cannot be bettered. The warnings HSBC ignored are detailed by the US Senate Permanent Subcommittee on Investigations, HSBC's internal self-congratulation surrounding the growth of its Mexico operation is described in Roberts & Kynaston, the growing frustration of the Mexican authorities came from interviews with the author.

8. HSBC WISES UP, SORT OF

Mexico's growing frustration with HSBC was described in interviews with the author. The Mexican regulatory bodies' investigations were detailed in interviews with the author. They are also referred to in the work of the US Senate Subcommittee on Investigations. Those who heard the 'place to launder money' tape spoke to the author. HSBC's reaction and emails are referenced by the US Subcommittee on Investigations. The account of the meeting between Geoghegan and the Mexican bank supervisors is first-hand. Lesley Midzain's perceived weaknesses and unsuitability are detailed in the US Subcommittee on Investigations report, as are Wyndham Clark's appointment and the email exchanges with him regarding lack of staffing. Reaction from other compliance experts to HSBC's failings was gleaned from interviews with the author. The OCC moves against the bank and the coming together of strands of US enforcement to target HSBC were uncovered by the US Senate Subcommittee on Investigations.

9. THE WHISTLEBLOWER WHO WASN'T A WHISTLEBLOWER

Everett Stern's life and his experience working for HSBC is portrayed by Everett Stern in interviews, blogs, videos, documentaries and promotional material and websites for his Tactical Rabbit firm and for his political candidacy. Matt Taibbi's outstanding work for *Rolling Stone* paints an insightful, personal picture. For *Reuters*, Carrick Mollenkamp and Brett Wolf compiled a compelling insider's guide to the HSBC New Castle anti-money laundering centre and Stern's part in it. Deloitte's run-in with Benjamin Lawsky was reported at the time. The 'sting' operation against Lloyds over the handling of customer PPI complaints was skilfully orchestrated by *The Times*.

10. THE DAM BEGINS TO CRACK

Lieutenant Frankie DiGregorio spoke to the author. He was understandably constrained in what he could say but he was able to point to public records. He also rightly pointed to the work of Carrick Mollenkamp and Brett Wolff at Reuters in describing the Fernando Sanclemente bust that led to Julio Chaparro and to HSBC. DiGregorio revealed the NYPD visit to HSBC headquarters to the author. Bill Ihlenfeld talked about his background and legal career in interviews and in accounts given during his rise in West Virginia politics. The Dr Barton Adams prosecution and indictment was well documented. Ihlenfled's determination to target HSBC following the uncovering of Adams's fraud and laundering, and his anger at being stood down was first described by Mollenkamp and Wolf for Reuters. The Mexican authorities' frustration at HSBC's failure to take its fine seriously and the passing of information to their counterparts in the US was conveyed to the author.

11. EVERYONE'S IDEA OF A PUBLIC SERVANT

The search for Chapo is reconstructed in Hogan and Century. Stephen Green's departure and the non-promotion of Michael Geoghegan was covered by the author and by Roberts & Kynaston. How Stephen Green came to be approached is contained in a *Ministers Reflect* interview he gave for the Institute for Government. The comment about the job not being designed with Green in mind was in the *Evening Standard*. Lord Green's speech in Mexico City was publicized at the time by the British government. Elise Bean helpfully described for the author working for Senator Carl Levin and the Permanent Subcommittee on Investigations. Her own book, *Financial Exposure – Carl Levin's Senate Investigations into Finance and Tax Abuse*, was also useful. Laura Stuber also supplied her perspective. The Permanent Subcommittee's 334-page *US Vulnerabilities to Money Laundering, Drugs and Terrorist Financing: HSBC Case History* is a tour de force. The transcripts of the Subcommmittee sessions quizzing HSBC executives are a line-by-line must.

12. ALL THE WAY TO THE TOP

The US Treasury papers detailing the back and forth between the US departments and the UK Government concerning the investigation into HSBC and whether the bank should be prosecuted were made available to the Financial Services Committee of the US House of Representatives. The report by the

Republican staff of that committee, 'Too Big to Jail: Inside the Obama Justice Department's Decision Not to Hold Wall Street Accountable' was a valuable source, containing the Osborne letter and the behind-the-scenes build-up to the Tokyo IMF meeting. The account of Lanny Breuer's approach to Rodge Cohen is contained in Jesse Eisinger's *The Chickenshit Club – why the Justice Department fails to prosecute executives* and the *New York Times*. The rap sheet that never was against HSBC is laid out over 30 pages in the Justice Department's *Statement of Facts* accompanying the deferred prosecution agreement.

13. DRAWING A LINE

The aftermath of the DPA announcement and the efforts of Lanny Breuer and Eric Holder to explain themselves, and Elizabeth Warren's intervention, are contained in newspaper reports and US Senate records. Rich Elias and the taking down of JP Morgan was reported by the *Wall Street Journal*. He has described his career in the publicity material for his law firm. The papers for *Zapata v HSBC Holdings Inc* cover the claim and the subsequent legal arguments and the different hearings in detail.

14. 'YA TENEMOS EL BLANCO!'

Chapo's arrest was described in newspapers and magazines, but by far the best account is in Hogan & Century. It's there as well that Andrew Hogan recounts the sensation of walking along Paseo de la Reforma and buying a newspaper proclaiming his capture. Hogan, though, does not make the connection with the towering HSBC building above. Gulliver's email to staff is repeated in Roberts & Kynaston. The description of Michael Cherkasky came from interviews with the author. *Buzzfeed* pushed hard for release of Cherkasky's *Final Report*. Its *FinCEN Files Investigation* in collaboration with the International Consortium of Investigative Journalists or ICIJ is where you will find warts and all accounts of the atmosphere and the hard partying inside HSBC's Canary Wharf clean-up effort, and the subsequent money-laundering transgressions. The monitor's annual reports on the progress of the reform programme for HSBC are summarized in US Justice Department letters to the federal court. HSBC's own responses are referenced in the bank's annual reports. The calculation of Stuart Gulliver's pay was disclosed by the bank. The lyrics of *El Chapo: Otra Fuga Mas* or *El Chapo: Another Escape* were penned by Lupillo Rivera.

15. OVERLAPPING CIRCLES

The views on whether HSBC and its executives should have been prosecuted and possibly convicted largely came from interviews with the author. Professor Coffee makes his case in *Corporate Crime and Punishment – The Crisis of*

Underenforcement. Jesse Eisinger's *The Chickenshit Club* describes the Coney staff meeting. The birth and short life of HSBC's *Financial System Vulnerabilities Committee* was revealed by the bank. Robert Law's board presentation is contained in Roberts & Kynaston, as is Green's offsite presentation. Governor King's farewell speech is available on the Bank of England's website.

Index